The Politics of
City Revenue

This volume is sponsored by the
OAKLAND PROJECT
University of California, Berkeley

The Politics of
City Revenue

Arnold J. Meltsner

UNIVERSITY OF CALIFORNIA PRESS
BERKELEY, LOS ANGELES, LONDON 1971

University of California Press
Berkeley and Los Angeles, California
University of California Press, Ltd.
London, England
Copyright © 1971, by
The Regents of the University of California
ISBN: 0-520-01812-5
Library of Congress Catalog Card Number: 71-129610
Printed in the United States of America

For

RUTH, LAURA, CAROLYN, *and* KENNETH

The Oakland Project

At a time when much is said but little is done about the university's relationship to urban problems, it is useful for those who are looking for ways of relating the university to the city to take a brief look at the Oakland Project of the University of California, which combines policy analysis, service to city officials and community groups, action in implementing proposals, training of graduate students, teaching new undergraduate courses, and scholarly studies of urban politics. The "university" is an abstraction, and as such it exists only for direct educational functions, not for the purpose of doing work within cities. Yet there are faculty members and students who are willing to devote large portions of their time and energy to investigating urban problems and to making small contributions toward resolving them. Our cities, however, do not need an invasion of unskilled students and professors. There is no point in hurtling into the urban crisis unless one has some special talent to contribute. After all, there are many people in city government—and even more on street corners—who are less inept than untrained academics. University people must offer the cities the talent and resources which they need and which they could not get otherwise.

Nearly four years ago I assembled a group of graduate students and faculty members at the University of California at Berkeley to become involved in a program of policy research and action in the neighboring city of Oakland. As members of the Oakland Project, we have tried to meet some of the city's most pressing analytical needs and also to make suggestions that can be implemented and, if successful, transferred to other urban areas.

Members of the project have made substantial time commitments (usually about two years) to working in a particular Oakland city agency. Normal working time has been two days a week, although special crisis situations in the city have sometimes necessitated much larger blocks of time. Since project members work with city officials and remain in the city to help implement the suggestions they have made, they avoid the "hit-and-run" stigma that members of city agencies often attach to outsiders. By attempting first to deal with problems as city officials understand them, project members have developed the necessary confidence to be asked to undertake studies with broader implications.

The Oakland Project has become a point of communication for individuals and groups in the city of Oakland and throughout the University of California. Our focus has expanded from a concentration on city budgeting to a wide range of substantive policies and questions of political process; for example, revenue, police, personnel, federal aid, education, libraries, and the institutionalization of political change. We have provided assistance to governmental (mayor, city manager, chief of police, head of civil service, superintendent of schools) and nongovernmental (community group) actors. In order to transmit the knowledge we have gained, Oakland Project members have taught courses—open to both undergraduate and graduate students—dealing with urban problems and policies. Our scholarly objective is to improve policy analysis by providing new ways of understanding decisions and outcomes that affect cities. We have based numerous research essays on our experience in the city. We are hopeful that the books in this series will be another means of transmitting what we have learned to a wider audience.

AARON WILDAVSKY

Preface

Sometimes research is more a product of accident than design. After spending more than a decade in the field of defense economics, where I worried about the costs of jeep trails, helicopters, army divisions, and air force squadrons, I found myself working in the city of Oakland, California, where the total budget was small enough to have been a rounding error in the Department of Defense. I had come from a program-budgeting background in which analysts ran around trying to gather information to improve the quality of critical decisions. In Oakland I found that a critical decision was whether to renovate a park rest room or to buy a new typewriter for a city department.

I had come to Oakland by a circuitous route. I was studying the presidency with Aaron Wildavsky at the University of California, Berkeley; he had told me about a project he was starting in Oakland, which would examine local resource allocation and decision making. Since I was interested in budgeting, I decided to join the Oakland Project, and in the summer of 1966, I went to work as a part-time participant-observer in the office of the city manager of the city of Oakland. The manager, who was trying to be the manager in fact as well as in name, was delighted to get some help. At the time, I naively thought that this would be an opportunity to try out some of my program-budgeting notions for local government. I would learn how local officials allocated their resources and how these resource decisions were reflected in the budgetary process—but I was wrong. Shortly after starting to work, the city manager told me that there was no budgetary problem because there was no money, and that revenue was Oakland's key problem. The economist in me argued that program budgeting and its related techniques under a tight resource constraint would be even more relevant. The political scientist in me argued, however, that the manager might be right. A revenue study might help the city. At the same time, I would have a unique opportunity to observe the behavior of political officials in their attempts to obtain resources from what they believe to be a hostile environment. Thus for academic reasons and because I wanted to help the city, I undertook to analyze Oakland's fiscal capability. This study effort on the part of Oakland's officials and myself led to much of the material used in writing this book.

The tradition of lone-wolf scholarship surely must be a myth. How else could I have finished this book without the help of so many? I want to express my appreciation to them while not attempting to spread the blame for the final product. First let me thank Aaron Wildavsky, friend and colleague, who was more often right than I care to admit, whose energy level and insight are something to admire, and without whose encouragement I would never have finished. Many other members of the academic community contributed useful comment and discussion: Eugene Bardach, Robert Biller, Jesse Burkhead, Malcolm Davisson, Roy Hansen, Todd La Porte, Roscoe Martin, William Niskanen, Joseph Pechman, Earl Rolph, and Ira Sharkansky. I owe a particular debt to the officials of the city of Oakland who taught me much about local finance. Both City Manager Jerry Keithley and Finance Director Robert Odell made me sympathetic to the problems of local officials. My colleagues on the Oakland Project, Judy May, Jeff Pressman, Frank Thompson and David Wentworth, saved me from making many errors. Mary Ellen Anderson, administrative assistant of the project, took a personal interest in my work, helped me with my writing, and conducted many of the interviews used in chapter 6. Stan Naparst gave me computer programming assistance. The secretaries of the Oakland Project typed many drafts.

An earlier version of chapter 7 and some other material used in this book were published in *Financing the Metropolis: Public Policy in Urban Economies,* volume 4, *Urban Affairs Annual Review,* edited by John P. Crecine (Beverly Hills: Sage Publications, Inc., 1970). I also wish to acknowledge the financial assistance of the National Aeronautics and Space Administration (NASA grant NGR 05-003-125) for support during the research phase of my investigation, and the Urban Institute, which supported the writing of this book under a prime contract with the Department of Housing and Urban Development. However, I am solely responsible for the accuracy of the statements and interpretations in the study.

Contents

Introduction

The field of taxation has been a subject of importance to political economists throughout the ages. More recently in the history of social science, this area has been the particular domain of economists and students of public finance, who have tended to concentrate their efforts on the fine tuning of a national economy. Their assumption has been that economic growth can take care of most of our problems. Moreover, public finance theory has also focused on the unitary state. Of course these students recognize the existence of a fiscal federalism; but the important issues, such as stabilization and income redistribution quite correctly are of national concern. Since much of the action is at the federal level, there is no economic theory of local finance to speak of.

As social scientists we want hard evidence to be able to draw inferences. This drive for statistical significance often directs us to aggregative approaches which in turn may mask solutions to local finance problems. Suppose a city needs money and an expert has been called in to help: What good is it for the expert to know that measures of wealth, such as assessed valuation, are related to levels of taxation? How can he use this information to acquire money for the city? Descriptive and explanatory aggregative analyses fall short of providing relevant information for fiscal first aid. For revenue gathering purposes, even less aggregative approaches which examine the economic effects and attributes of different taxes have limited utility. Tax shifting, demand effects, business location impacts, and the income elasticity of taxes are all important topics of investigation. But what these studies tell us is that certain taxes do certain things, not which taxes can be implemented. Implicit assumptions behind such work is that finance officials have many options and that the problem is to choose first- or second-best economic alternatives. In other words, all taxes have an equal probability of implementation and public acceptance. But in fiscal reality not all taxes are politically equal. Moreover, economic principles and desirable norms such as efficiency, neutrality, and vertical and horizontal equity are in plentiful supply; but what is lacking in the literature is the identification of the means to achieve these ends.

The economist, quite rightly, will point out that the implementation problem is a political problem. Given the academic division of labor, he erroneously assumes that political scientists are concerned about it. If the problems of city finance are political problems, then surely political scientists would have something to say. But with the exception of a few case histories and some literature on urban problems, political scientists have not been overly concerned about metropolitan finance. Here we have a central process, taxation, that is an intrinsic part of most public organizations, and yet we know very little about how the process works or how decisions are made or who makes them.

Local finance is a critical problem. The choices for local officials are sometimes harsh and difficult: either find new revenue resources or incur a diminution in services. Often, they must make these decisions without realistic guidelines because nobody knows what is being done currently. Political scientists can make a major contribution toward solving some of the dilemmas of our central cities by concentrating on the question, How should a city get revenue? At the very least, a political study of local finance would show how things work, which could provide a concrete point of departure for improvement.

Besides developing basic knowledge on which revenue decisions could be made, there are theoretical reasons for a political study of local revenue. Taxation is an important link of the citizen to the political system. Although taxes indicate the cost or the negative side of the relation of the citizen to the political system, to some extent the payment of taxes also conveys the citizen's approval and esteem of that system. Taxes are a form of political support. In the black-box model of the political system, support and demands flow in and suitable policy outputs flow out. The black-box concept is a modular definition of the political system. As with other black-box concepts (such as stimulus-response in psychology), one tends to characterize the box as an almost neutral conductor of input to output. Of course, inside the black-box model of the political system are political actors who may convert rather than conduct, but they get lost in the shuffle of support and demands and other abstractions. Support is consistent with the demands and the outputs, otherwise the system would be unstable. Gliding over temporal hurdles, the system finds equilibrium by assuming that people in the environment support the system because their demands are satisfied by that system. One difficulty with this description, at least for me, is that it is vague and abstract.

In the context of our cities' fiscal problems, however, the concept of political support takes on tangible meaning. There is nothing abstract about the payment of taxes for public services. We often stress the importance of voting for political leaders as a confirmation and approval of the political system. Theoretically, the payment of taxes and voting on tax referendums are other important indices of approval of the political system. Indeed, voting on revenue issues is, I believe, a more refined index of political support than voting for leaders. In the election for leaders, the voter usually chooses between similar leaders. He can crudely express rejection of system performance by voting for an ideological extreme candidate who cannot win or by not voting at all. In the tax referendum, the voter can, by voting no, directly reject the particular policy outputs of the political system. He can say by his negative vote: I do not like what they are doing, and I am not going to give them my money to enable them to keep doing it. When the choice between leaders is not much of a choice, referendums are a concrete and specific way of giving or withdrawing support. On a lesser scale, one can observe instances of citizens announcing that they are withholding part of their tax payments because they do not agree with certain policies.

Furthermore, support may be inconsistent with demands. The

black-box model of the political system assumes that at some aggregative level demands will be consistent with support. And at some level, this assumption is valid because individual pluses and minuses probably cancel each other. But beneath this level, there are citizens who have demands and do not want to pay for them or may not be aware that they will pay for them. And it is not unusual to find citizens who pay their taxes and are unhappy with the system's output of goods and services. These citizens may be unhappy with the benefits which they personally receive or they may be unhappy because they have to pay for someone else's benefit, such as welfare. Recently, a friend complained to me that he was paying more in taxes every year and getting nothing for it. He admitted that he sent his children to public schools, that he used the public library, that he walked and drove on city streets, and that he enjoyed band concerts in the park. Nevertheless, he insisted that, considering the cost, he got nothing. Evidently the tax price was not worth the benefits.

The balancing act between support and demands is supposedly achieved on the fulcrum of the electoral process. As political scientists, we hopefully assume that elections ensure consistency; simultaneously, voters determine the demand and tax support for public services. For example, there are cities where politicians run for office on a program to expand services, get elected, and then raise taxes without much trouble. Financing in such cases is a secondary matter because the question of taxpayer support is resolved by the election. But as we know, not all elections are like this. Many elections simply elect public officials; they tell us little about citizen preferences. Nor can politicians always afford to clarify issues of public policy. How many politicians find it feasible to run for office on a program to increase taxes and yet maintain the same level of services? Why seek a mandate for increasing taxes and be defeated? First get elected and then worry about the annual financing requirements of the city budget.

Long ago the payments of taxes to support the king's courtesans was an understandably onerous burden. Paying for the king's pleasure was no fun. Yet the pain of taxation carries over to the modern democratic state where there is a tenuous relationship between what citizens want and what they pay. Ironically, in a sense the monarchial model of taxation fits the revenue behavior of many of our cities' citizens and officials. Not many citizens seek tax increases, and officials, to keep their cities in business, stay up nights devising ways of extricating money from a reluctant public.

The growing inconsistency between political support and demands provides the context for this inquiry into the politics of local revenue. In city government, the politics of taxation is bureaucratic politics. Since citizens believe they pay too much, public officials must devise tactics to obtain the requisite resources to keep our cities functioning. Officials have to manipulate the citizen into paying his tax bill because they cannot just go to the public and ask for more. As a result their revenue behavior may appear hypocritical to an outsider when, in fact, such behavior is a necessary result of their fiscal situation. Officials often believe the constituency for increased taxes does not exist. When there are groups that are concerned about taxes, they agitate to reduce taxes, not increase them. On the other hand, public officials must get the money to meet rising operating costs, wage increases, and changing community demands. As the resource inputs and policy outputs flow in and out of the political system, these forgotten men in the black box obtain the requisite tax support. The tax link of the citizen to the political system is thus indirect, and the nature of that link is heavily influenced by the revenue behavior of public officials. Therefore, in exploring the complex relationship between officials and citizens, I have concentrated on how city officials get sufficient financial resources to maintain the local political system.

In short, my interests as a political scientist, as a student of public administration, and as an investigator who believes that his research should have relevance for policy provided sufficient justification to undertake an exploratory investigation of the politics of city revenue. I hoped to find some basic outlines of bureaucratic fiscal behavior, some important concepts that could be molded into hypotheses for explanatory purposes, and some insights as to the political aspects of taxation.

AN OVERVIEW

In chapter 1, the fiscal context of the study is set forth in an outline of Oakland's financial crisis and a description of its major revenue sources. Oakland is a good example of many central cities in which fiscal resources grow slowly, while social and economic problems increase rapidly. In my view, Oakland has undergone considerable fiscal atrophy; the gap between available revenue and expenditure requirements is large. The erosion of resources has been sufficient to contribute to a certain amount of ostrich-like behavior on the part of city officials. They have decided that the property tax, as a source of additional revenue, is exhausted; so, much effort goes into the search for new revenue sources. Much of this effort, however, is devoted to obtaining only enough resources for maintaining the city system but not for coping with its severe problems.

The city appears to be hemmed in from many directions; its fiscal discretion is quite narrow. To some extent it has to give up its discretion to the state of California in order to achieve favorable revenue outcomes. City officials encourage the transfer of tax responsibility to the state not only to ensure efficient collection but also to maintain stable sources of revenue supply. Such actions tend to have unintended consequences. Once the area of discretion is transferred, the state is in the position to set rates and determine apportionment procedures, which further limit the resources that are available to the city. Moreover, Oakland's officials do not view the federal government as a meaningful alternative because of the vagaries of federal official actions and because federal programs are not designed to aid traditional city functions such as fire protection. Federal programs are fiscal devices designed to take care of extras.

Therefore, local officials are left to their own devices in trying to find revenue, a difficult task because they want to make taxes palatable to the citizens of Oakland. Since political support in the form of taxes is not offered without a struggle, officials try to design revenue sources so that the public's tax consciousness is reduced. Providing property tax relief means getting the same person to pay with less pain.

After this introduction to the basic components of Oakland's complex but, hopefully, painless tax structure, the discussion shifts to the city's key participants in the revenue process. Oakland has a sleepy political system. With a weak city council and a strong city manager, this system chugs along trying to meet the humdrum requirements of municipal administration, from zoning variances to trimming trees. Having an elected auditor does not make the system any more open or any more responsive to changing demands. But the city government is honest and for the most part the streets are clean. Despite the myth of the Knowland hegemony,[1] there are no old and powerful families. Nor are there any political machines. Partisan politics goes on, but not much attention is paid to local affairs. The city's Republican mayor is not much different from his Democratic councilmen. Political resources no doubt exist, but they are hard to find. Emerging in the 1960s from a basically indifferent citizenry is a new set of political actors who attempt to represent the city's increasing minority population; Oakland, however, is very much an administrative city.

In chapter 2, the behavior and orientations of the city manager and his immediate staff, the city council, and department officials are discussed. These three groups constitute the main official actors in the tax arena. Of all of these participants, the city manager plays the crucial role. Finance is one of his major concerns. Hard working, dedicated, and a competent administrator, he is the pivotal actor in the revenue scene. He contributes to making fiscal innovations and also socializes the other participants in the process: he reiterates constantly the no-money premise of Oakland. In a sense he is the fiscal conscience of the council. By attempting to cut costs, by believing in the virtues of efficiency, and by trying to pull together a badly fragmented public organization, the manager continually attempts to take the pressure off the property tax. The property tax rate is embarrassing to city officials because it has been one of the highest in the state for many years.

The Oakland City Council reflects many of the manager's beliefs. Councilmen are products of the reform orientation of local government. Good government in this context is honest government, where the lack of corruption is sometimes more important than the responsiveness of the institution. However,

1. The Knowland family has been active in civic affairs for a number of years. As publisher of the *Oakland Tribune* and a member of the Chamber of Commerce, Senator William Knowland has supported projects which he believes contribute to developing Oakland. There is no evidence, however, that he cares enough or has the resources to run the city.

councilmen are responsive to a rhetorical constituency which they frequently refer to as the taxpayer. Because of the taxpayer, they have to worry about not increasing the property tax rate, and they must guard the city's tax resources from encroachment by other jurisdictions. While councilmen are preserving the revenue status quo, the manager initiates most tax policies.

Whereas the council and city manager are concerned with the revenue side of the city, department officials are concerned with the spending side. The departments' service objectives conflict with the manager's revenue maximization attempts. For example, department officials pay obeisance to a cost recovery norm but seldom design fees with that norm in mind. They cannot be relied on for fiscal innovations; and in the final result they are the spenders, not the providers.

The providers are, of course, the manager and his finance staff. Their behavior is central to an understanding of the effect of the revenue constraint on some basic organizational processes. Therefore, chapter 3 presents a conceptual framework which shows how the revenue constraint affects search, decision making, and the resource inputs to the city organization. The basic feature of this framework is the officials' avoidance of the public in order to bring revenue into the system. The process is described in a series of stages, from search and decision through acceptance and administration. Throughout each stage, the city officials who want to increase revenue resources try to anticipate public conflict and avoid it; they do not relish negotiating with hostile taxpayers.

Public avoidance starts with the officials' search processes. Because the revenue problem is always there and is never considered to be solved, search is recurring and open ended. The choice of which tax to present for public approval is simplified by finding precedents in other cities and by following the leadership of the larger cities in the state. By these tactics, indirect taxes and nominal charges are introduced into the tax structure which reduce the tax consciousness of the payer and result in low-yielding taxes and small, attentive tax publics. Public participation is also made difficult, so as to keep these tax publics small, fragmented, and quiet. Negotiation with the public is usually with friends or with the members of the small tax public. Once the concurrence of the small tax public is achieved, it is assumed that the majority of taxpayers will pay a new tax without much complaint, and low delinquency rates usually verify official premises. The administration of the existing tax structure is also characterized by public avoidance and anticipatory tactics. The property tax rate is never cut to a minimum and revenue is estimated conservatively to create a surplus for meeting future contingencies. The net result of these public avoidance tactics is that the city is able to maintain itself from year to year but does not have sufficient resources for an expansion of services. Additional taxes just cover employee pay raises. The advantage for city officials is that they avoid conflict, and they do not have to negotiate with what they consider to be a hostile or at best an indifferent public. Because Oakland officials feel they do not have many options, they have chosen the low-yield, low-political-cost revenue sources.

In chapter 4, the concepts dealing with the public avoidance process are grounded in the details of a specific case history, the ten-year history of the adoption and administration of the city's sewer service charge. One of the difficulties of working with revenue, as a focal point of the analysis of a public organization, is that there are not many important tax events to observe, so a genetic approach sometimes does have payoffs. An interesting finding, from the case history, was the illustration of the continuity of behavior during the ten-year period. The occupants of the key offices changed, and yet the premises of the past dictated most of the decisions. Starting from the premise that the property tax must be relieved, city officials searched for a painless form of taxation, pushed for it, and, when the tax became difficult to administer, raised the rates, which confirms the maxim: when you have an inefficient tax, raise your rates.

Chapter 5 looks into two revenue aspects which are important to the budgetary process. In Oakland the budget is no longer used to allocate resources but is used as a control device for the city manager and as a communication device for departments. The city bureaucracy is dichotomized into budget spenders (the departments) and budget cutters (the city manager and his immediate financial staff). The adoption, by most of the participants, of a no-money premise in the city and the continuous deprivation of funds have resulted in several disjunctions in the budgetary process. Budget spenders ignore revenue limitations in formulating their budgets so as to communicate the needs of their organizations. At the same time the city manager and his budget staff ignore service and program implications in cutting the budget. Since, by law, the budget must be balanced—expenditures must equal available resources—the manager and his staff have to consider budgeting as a form of revenue behavior. They are the same people who have to find additional funds if they allow spending increases. The more they can hold down spending, the less they have to search for new sources of revenue. Thus, cutting the budget is a form of revenue behavior.

Because officials, in their revenue behavior, are heavily influenced by their perceptions of the public, I wanted to find out for myself how hostile or supportive the public is. In chapter 6, the results of some exploratory interviews conducted with Oakland's citizen-leaders are discussed. Oakland's leaders generally understand taxes, see the connection between taxes and services, and believe everyone should pay a fair share to meet the city's tax burden. Whether they would support tax increases turned out to be difficult to determine.

I was looking for a way to identify support for tax increases in general, and it may be that tax support can only be defined in terms of specific referendums and issues. I assumed that those leaders who understood taxes and at the same time saw the need for improving services would be the potential support nucleus for increases. Leaders generally evaluated the city's performance as inefficient, inadequate, and inferior when compared to its neighbors in the San Francisco Bay Area. But unhappiness with City Hall was not necessarily linked to an awareness of the city's major problems. One of the findings of the survey was that only about a third of the group of leaders was aware of the financial, social, and economic problems which the city faces. Although the leaders' tax comprehension and negative performance evaluations are important conditions for tax support, they are not sufficient. Unhappiness with Oakland's major financial, social, and economic problems probably would be the central motivation for leader support. To the extent that Oakland's elites are not aware or are not sufficiently concerned with these problems, then the expectation for widespread support for major tax increases is considerably reduced. Officials will have to continue to pursue their nickel-and-dime tactics.

As part of the survey, the leaders' tax preferences were obtained. Their first preference, the sales tax, and other forms of excises are the very sources which local officials have depended on over the years. Their least preferred source of revenue is the municipal income or a payroll-type tax, which many experts have suggested cities adopt. As of now, no California city is using the tax, and in Oakland there is resistance against it.

In the final chapter the policy options that are open to the nation's local officials are discussed. Although taking the viewpoint of the local official who is searching for additional revenue resources, I argue with his conception of fiscal reality. The local finance problem is seen as a political problem, and local officials are urged to question the assumption of taxpayer hostility and to take sufficient action to build coalitions for increased levels of taxation and public expenditure. Although the federal government may provide relief to our cities, this relief may be a long time in coming. Therefore, it is imperative that local officials no longer sit and wait while things get worse. They must take a multiple approach. Officials should try to get outside funds. They should also try to avoid public conflict and work with small tax publics for small tax increases. And at the same time they must seek the support of the larger community for significant revenue increases. They must use a variety of public avoidance and public contact tactics. Above all, city officials must provide the political leadership to their community so that an adequate resource base can be established to deal with mounting problems. The fiscal crisis is in reality a crisis of political leadership. Officials have to walk a thin line between a threatened taxpayer's revolt and a poor people's riot. The resources, though, are there. What is needed are political officials who will assume a certain measure of risk and at the same time seek to ensure that local institutions are responsive to the needs of its citizens.

1

Revenue Sources

Most of Oakland's officials are pessimistic about their city's fiscal condition. As in other organizations, officials face a budget constraint; but in Oakland they do not face it with equanimity. There is a fiscal crisis or a revenue-expenditure gap. The property tax base grows slowly, but this slow growth in assessed valuation is perceived as no growth at all and talk of tax base erosion is commonplace. Thus the fiscal glass is always half empty rather than half full. We will probably never be able to isolate the antecedents of this fiscal pessimism. How much of it is due to objective social and economic conditions or how much is due to the officials themselves is difficult to discern. The net result, however, is clear: Oakland's officials perceive only a few of the possible financial policy options open to them.

It is within the context of this restricted policy space that an exploration of the fiscal behavior of Oakland's officials can begin. In order to understand their pessimism and its consequences for the city's tax structure, some aspects of Oakland's *perceived* fiscal crisis will be examined and, after briefly noting Oakland's social and economic problems, its revenue-expenditure gap and some major revenue trends will be discussed. Then there will be a discussion of some specific aspects of its tax structure. Using descriptions of Oakland's major sources of revenue, I will show that it has limited its capacity to raise revenue, that it is the willing fiscal creature of the state of California, that it makes and loses money, and that much fiscal behavior, as in many forms of human behavior, is characterized by pretense.

THE FISCAL CONTEXT

THE GROWTH IN SOCIAL AND ECONOMIC PROBLEMS

The local Chamber of Commerce usually describes Oakland as the "All-American" city; and in one sense this is not an exaggeration since, indeed, it exemplifies the dilemmas confronting many cities throughout the United States. As a student of one city, my tendency is to view Oakland, with all its complexities, as something special; but this is not the case. One simple way of demonstrating this point is to use census data as a rough indicator of the involved social and economic problems of our cities. Cities which are not growing, are crowded, and have high percentages of undereducated and unemployed citizens are bound to have problems. Thus Table 1 shows that by these criteria Oakland is not very different from Newark or Miami.

The thirteen cities in Table 1 were selected on the basis of their 1960 unemployment rates from the set of 27 cities having populations between 250,000 and 500,000 in 1960. Those selected were in the first and second quartiles (5.1 to 8.2 percent unemployed). Those cities whose unemployment rates were in the third and fourth quartiles were omitted. The table shows which of these selected cities also ranked in the top half on other demographic variables. In 1960, Newark had the highest unemployment (8.2 percent); Oakland ranked second with 7.9 percent. Miami had the oldest population, median age 37.4 years; Oakland ranked third with a median age of 35.7 years. Five of the cities experienced a loss of population during this period. Jersey City lost the most (−7.7 percent); Oakland ranked fourth with a 4.4 percent loss. Jersey City had the most people per square mile (18,285); Oakland, with 7,041 people per square mile, ranked seventh. Newark ranked first in low educational achievement with 12.6 percent of its population over 25 years old having completed less than the fifth grade; Oakland ranked eighth with 7.2 percent not having completed the fifth grade. Miami had the largest percentage of families with incomes below $3,000 (29.7

TABLE 1: Oakland Is Not Unique

	Unemployment 5.1–8.2%	Median Age of Population 30.8–37.4 Yrs.	Population Change 1950–1960 +17% to −7.7%	Density People per Sq. Mi. 5,848–18,285	Education Under 5th Grade 7.2–12.6%	Income Under $3,000 17.3–29.7%	Nonwhite 16.6–39.7%
Oakland	X	X	X	X	X	X	X
Newark	X	X	X	X	X	X	X
Miami	X	X	X	X	X	X	X
Louisville	X	X	X	X	X	X	X
Birmingham	X	—	X	—	X	X	X
Norfolk	X	—	—	X	X	X	X
Jersey City	X	X	X	X	X	—	—
Rochester	X	X	X	X	X	—	—
Toledo	X	X	X	X	X	—	—
Portland	X	X	X	—	—	—	—
Akron	X	X	—	—	—	—	—
Long Beach	X	—	—	—	—	—	—
Columbus	X	—	—	—	—	—	—

SOURCE: U.S. Bureau of the Census, 1960.

percent); Oakland with 17.3 percent ranked seventh. Birmingham had the largest proportion of nonwhite inhabitants (39.7 percent); Oakland and Norfolk shared fourth place with 26.4 percent.

Behind the demographic picture of Oakland lies the misery of the poor. The elements of the urban crisis are all there: racial conflict, a high unemployment rate, substandard housing, poor educational achievement, and low family income. According to Oakland's Model Cities application, the city is a "port of entry" for low-income households. Although the total population has been declining to around 360,000, the mix within this total has changed quite dramatically. In 1950 the black population in Oakland was 47,562. By the 1960 census this population was 83,618, an increase of 76 percent, and it is estimated that the 1966 black population was 110,000. Similarly there has been an increase in the number of Spanish-speaking (Mexican-American) people in the city, from 16,500 in 1950 to 23,700 in 1960. But between 1950 and 1960 there was a decrease of 18 percent in the white population. With this change in population and the reduction in defense and other industries within the city, the unemployment rate in 1966 was about 6 percent for males and 10 percent for females. The Model Cities application also reports that in the poverty target areas the percentage is much higher—around 11 percent for men and 16 percent for women. Among black teenagers, unemployment runs as high as 20 to 30 percent. Fifteen percent of all housing units in Oakland are considered substandard. In addition, educational achievement is lower than in other central cities in California: 70 percent of Oakland's nonwhites over 25 years of age have not completed high school. Considering the lack of education and job opportunity, it is not difficult to understand why Oakland's family income is lower than that in the rest of the East Bay metropolitan area. In 1960 family income for one-fourth of the city's families was under $4,000. In a single year, 1964, the number of welfare cases increased 13 percent.[1]

City officials, with a few exceptions, have not enlisted in the

1. Population and other demographic data were taken from Oakland, *Application for Planning Grant Model Cities Program*, April 3, 1967, pp. 1–3, 26–37.

war on poverty. They make contingency plans to defend against possible riots, but the "war" takes place on other sites, in a maelstrom of quasi-private and independent public agencies. Welfare and health are run by Alameda County. Education, redevelopment, public housing, manpower, and community action programs are all in the domain of separate districts, autonomous agencies and authorities.

THE RECURRING CRISIS:

FISCAL ATROPHY AND THE REVENUE-EXPENDITURE GAP

In the excitement of current poverty programs, however, let us not forget the importance of the traditional functions of a municipality. City officials, with their concerns for fire protection and street repair, for example, have much to do which can improve the quality of life for Oakland's citizens. In 1966 officials estimated the city's "capital improvement needs" and came up with a modest five-year capital program of $45 million.[2] A minor part of this amount will support Oakland's recent booster projects such as the coliseum complex and the museum. But most of the needs are less dramatic and visible: mercury vapor lights, traffic signals and signs, storm drains, recreational equipment for tot lots, and picnic tables for the parks. Yet many of these needs will not be met. There is just not enough money in the city budget to pay for them. Undoubtedly, the city's Library Department will continue to regard the purchase of books as a residual budgetary category.

Incorporated around the time when California became a state, Oakland is an old city with an old physical plant. Yet only $6–$7 million is spent annually for capital improvements, and most of this small sum is from earmarked funds, such as street construction under the state gasoline tax program. Without an aggressive bonding program, city officials defer capital improvements and complain about increased maintenance and operating costs. Repair rather than replace has been the prevailing motto. This deferral syndrome exacerbates the general fiscal problem, because many of the facilities were built between 50 and 60 years ago and are now wearing out. All the city has to show for its pay-as-you-go policy is an excellent bond rating: the low total indebtedness,

2. Oakland, *Capital Improvement Program, 1965–1970*, May 1966.

$18.9 million, is only 17 percent of the legal limit.[3] The less Oakland does to meet its problems, the more bonding capacity it has left. Because school district and city improvement issues have been turned down in the past, officials generally are afraid to turn to the voters for approval of bonds. At the same time, citizen needs are changing and few resources currently exist to meet these needs.

The main problem officials try to solve every year is simply to find sufficient revenue to maintain their current payroll. Their problem is that the city's budget increases at a faster rate than the tax base. Fiscal atrophy is a chronic malady. For local officials there is as much romance in the revenue-expenditure gap as there is for national defense officials in the missile gap.[4] The city manager put it this way to the council in a report on the fiscal potential of Oakland: "Simply stated, the disquieting fact is that under existing policies and within the constraints of the financial structure, the City of Oakland's expenditure requirements will soon exceed its income."[5] The manager based his projection on the fact that in the 1956–1966 decade the budget had risen 86 percent, while the property tax assessed valuation had gone up only 36 percent. The atrophy of Oakland's tax resources has resulted in the city's making efforts to maintain itself rather than trying to cope with the larger social problems it confronts.

Oakland's tax problems are compounded by its land usage and by the business and population that have migrated to surrounding communities. The city has no more land to annex; it is boxed in within its 53 square miles of land. One cause of tax-base erosion is that not all property within Oakland's 53 square miles is included on the tax rolls. Much of the excluded real property is occupied by governmental utilities, public institutions, streets, and freeways or is merely vacant. The city's finance director has

---

3. Oakland, *Seventy-eighth Auditor-Controller's Annual Report, Fiscal Year 1966/67*, p. 138.

4. See Malcolm M. Davisson, *Financing Local Government in the San Francisco Bay Area* (Berkeley: Institute of Governmental Studies, University of California, 1963), p. 1. For the Oakland statement of the revenue-expenditure gap, see Oakland, *Financial Capability Study*, Part 1 (no date), pp. 5–7.

5. Oakland, "Analysis of the Fiscal Potential of the City of Oakland," attachment to 1967/68 budget (May 1967), pp. 1–2.

estimated that over 40 percent of real property is tax exempt. City officials lament not only the loss of taxable property but also the flight of heavy industry and citizens who pay taxes instead of consume services.

Fiscal atrophy started after World War II when Oakland reached its population peak, and since then the population has been gradually decreasing. According to census figures, the total population fell from 384,575 in 1950 to 367,548 in 1960. The decrease has slowed somewhat (an estimate of the 1970 population is 361,561), but unlike the rest of California, Oakland is not growing in population.

Previous studies of California finance have indicated that the rise in city budgets has been due to increases in population and prices.[6] We know that Oakland's population has not been growing, but one might conjecture that Oakland's budget increase is due to changes in the mix of population. I call this conjecture the blame-the-poor-blacks hypothesis. In my estimation, however, Oakland could have remained all white and still would face the same fiscal problems today. The budget has expanded to meet the increased costs of operation, not to meet the needs of Oakland's deprived population. The budget is an operating budget: 70 percent of the total budget is for personnel-related costs. Oakland is not a case of expanding bureaucracy; it is a thrifty, almost frugal city. In 1960 there were 3,014 budgeted full-time personnel positions; by 1968 this number had increased to 3,254, an increase of roughly 1 percent per year.[7] While the number of personnel has not increased appreciably, the costs of personnel have gone up every year, with wage adjustments to keep pace with other cities, built-in merit raises, and rising expenditures for retirement plans. Thus, it is easy to see that with the possibility of a 2 to 3 percent price increase for nonpersonnel costs, with

6. See John P. Shelton, "How to Keep Local Expenditures Under Control," in California Local Finance, ed. John A. Vieg et al. (Stanford, California: Stanford University Press, 1960), p. 92. For the fact that the per capital local government burden has increased, see California, Legislature, Assembly, Interim Committee on Revenue and Taxation, Financing Local Government in California, prepared by Wilma Mayers, December 1964, pp. 13–14.

7. Oakland, Tentative Budget Fiscal Year 1968/69, May 1968, p. D–1.

standard salary increases of 4 to 5 percent, with slight increases in number of personnel, and with no increase in productivity, Oakland could have an 8 percent growth rate in expenditures each year without a marked increase in the level of service.

TRENDS IN CITY REVENUE

Oakland is the fiscal creature of the state. Talk about independent home rule is rhetoric. As a charter city, Oakland has extensive legal financial discretion, but in practice the area of financial discretion is quite circumscribed. For our purposes, revenue is any financial resource that flows into the city over which the city has some expenditure control. Generally speaking, the larger the source of revenue in dollars, the smaller the discretion. For example, the city has a great deal of influence over fees and licenses but has very little discretion over the extent of subventions and grants which come to it. Over a 20-year period subventions and grants have gradually increased, but as Table 2 shows, subventions and grants have varied on a percentage basis. The percentage decline of subventions and grants in 1960/61 and the increase in 1965/66 were typical for the whole state. Table 2 also shows the heavy reliance on the property tax, starting from over 75 percent at the end of World War II and leveling out at roughly half of the total revenues of the city.

TABLE 2: Trends in City of Oakland Revenue

Source	Fiscal Year (in percent)				
	1945/46	1950/51	1955/56	1960/61	1965/66
Property tax	76.6	50.5	47.4	50.9	47.1
Subventions and grants	7.4	17.3	17.0	13.0	17.0
Sales tax	—	12.1	18.7	19.5	17.1
Other revenue	16.0	20.1	16.9	16.6	18.8
	100.0	100.0	100.0	100.0	100.0
Total revenue in millions of dollars:	9	18	26	37	48

SOURCE: Oakland, Auditor-Controller.

The property tax traditionally has been the main source of financial support for local governments. The sales tax is the second most important single source of financing. Originally, this tax had been reserved for the state; but in 1943 the state of California was in an excellent fiscal position due to limited wartime expenditures and increased revenues, and decided to reduce its sales tax levy. Shortly thereafter, cities started adopting sales tax ordinances, and Oakland began collecting sales tax in 1946. In that year the sales tax brought in almost one million dollars, and it has continued to play an important role in Oakland finance ever since. Cities resorted to the sales tax in the mid-1940s because they perceived that the property tax had about reached its limit. This same perception exists now, and once again there is a tendency to search for nonproperty-tax revenue.

The trend toward nonproperty-tax revenue is more apparent in Table 3, which presents a comparison between Oakland and all the California cities during 1958/59 and 1966/67. For Oakland and the other cities there are increases in nonproperty taxes, service charges, and use of money. However, Oakland relies on the property tax more than other California cities. The differential reliance on the property tax by Oakland ranges from 44 percent to 47 percent, whereas for all California cities the range is 34 percent to 37 percent.

During the eight years that are represented in Table 3, revenues for all California cities have increased 92.3 percent, or have nearly doubled. This is an annual increase of about 11.5 percent. However, Oakland's revenue has not grown as fast, increasing only 65.9 percent, or an average of 8.2 percent per year for the same period. Since the city must balance expenditures with revenue, this slower growth rate in revenue illustrates that Oakland has not been expanding services, but rather has been in the box of maintaining itself.

The city of Oakland has almost a no-slack financial system. The budget does not have much fat in it. What are the revenue resources on which the city relies? Where does it get the money to survive? How much discretion do officials have in raising revenue? The remainder of this chapter will outline the city's financial discretion, show that the city can make and lose money, and show that tax behavior is deceptive.

TABLE 3: City Revenue Comparison of Oakland with All California Cities

	Amount of Revenue (in millions of dollars)				Percentage of Revenue			
	All Cities [a]		Oakland		All Cities		Oakland	
	Fiscal Year		Fiscal Year		Fiscal Year		Fiscal Year	
Source	1958/59	1966/67	1958/59	1966/67	1958/59	1966/67	1958/59	1966/67
Property taxes	323.1	573.8	15.0	23.1	37.2	34.3	47.2	43.9
Franchise taxes	9.1	16.8	.5	.3	1.0	1.0	1.5	.7
Sales and use taxes	166.8	292.0	6.6	8.7	19.2	17.5	20.9	16.5
Other nonproperty taxes	.7	32.7	—	1.0	.1	2.0	—	1.9
Licenses and permits	52.9	85.6	1.9	2.4	6.1	5.1	6.0	4.5
Fines and penalties	31.6	54.2	1.4	2.2	3.6	3.2	4.5	4.2
Use of money and property	22.2	71.7	.4	1.4	2.6	4.3	1.3	2.6
From other agencies	135.2	298.7	4.5	9.9	15.6	17.9	14.3	18.9
Current service charges	72.4	155.7	.6	2.3	8.3	9.3	2.0	4.3
Other revenue	55.2	89.5	.8	1.4	6.3	5.4	2.4	2.6
Total [b]	869.0	1,670.7	31.7	52.7	100.0	100.0	100.0	100.0

SOURCE: California, Controller, Annual Report of Financial Transactions Concerning Cities of California, 1958/59 and 1966/67.

[a] The city of San Francisco performs county functions, such as welfare, which slightly distorts these figures.

[b] Totals may not add up due to rounding.

NARROW DISCRETION

Financial discretion is the capacity *to raise* revenue. The area of financial discretion defines the object of city decisions. From Table 4 we can arrive at two conclusions: (1) with the exception of the property tax, the decisions that officials can make concerning revenue are "nuts and bolts" decisions; and (2) a large

TABLE 4: The Narrowing Area of City Financial
Discretion, 1966/67
(in millions of dollars)

Revenue Groups Mainly Within City Discretion:	
Property tax	23.1
Franchise tax	.4
Transient occupancy tax	.2
Parking and street privilege fees	.5
Business licenses	.9
Other licenses and permit fees	.1
Building inspection fees	.4
Concession and facility fees	.7
Sewer service charge	1.1
Other service charges	.2
Interest on bank deposits	.9
Management of city assets—sales and rentals	.5
Subtotal	29.0
Revenue Groups Mainly Outside City Discretion:	
Sales tax	8.7
Cigarette tax	.8
Off-street parking	.9
Court fines	2.1
State gasoline taxes	4.0
In lieu tax payments	2.5
Alcoholic beverage tax	.4
Revenue and grants from other agencies	4.4
Subtotal	23.8
Total revenue	52.8

SOURCES: Oakland, *Seventy-eighth Auditor-Controller's Annual Report, Fiscal Year 1966/67;* and Oakland Budget and Finance Department, "Financial Capability Study, Part 2" (draft, no date).

amount of money, almost half of the annual budget, is outside the area of city discretion.[8]

Within their area of discretion, officials do make many decisions. To the uninitiated, city revenue decision making appears trivial. The social scientist who treats urban revenue in terms of aggregates, such as property tax and "other," will miss most of the action. Local revenue decisions are in the category of "other." Behind many of the revenue groups in Table 4 are hundreds of revenue sources. A future major policy decision is whether to include vending machine operators under the business license or whether Oakland's new museum should charge twenty-five cents for admission. If a frequency count of decisions by dollar amount were computed, there would be only a few million-dollar decisions. In the aggregate, the small dollar decisions, the rounding errors of other studies, allow Oakland to adapt. In Oakland small dollar revenue sources get as much attention and are as significant as large ones.

The state is the locus of decision making for much of the revenue the city uses. The sales tax, cigarette tax, court fines, gasoline taxes, most in lieu tax payments, alcoholic beverage revenue, and grants are controlled by the state. The city can and does influence the state, but generally rates, exemptions, and apportionment formulas are under state control. As I have said, the city is the fiscal creature of the state, and as we shall see, the city is often willing to give up its discretion. Because of pressing expenditure demands, officials find all revenue sources equally attractive and they are not particularly concerned about the future possibility of having to negotiate with the state concerning rates and apportionment procedures. The fact that the state will collect revenue and send the city a check is sufficient incentive to gain the city's concurrence.

The sales tax is one local revenue which is not local. Its yield is equivalent to almost one-third of Oakland's property tax rate, and the sales tax comes to the city with no spending strings attached. Other than moving around within the 1 percent limit

8. Unless otherwise indicated, the data in this chapter come from the study conducted by the author jointly with city officials. The study has not been published but is identified by officials as "Financial Capability Study, Part 2."

reserved for local taxation, Oakland has no control over the rates. In 1967, for example, the state raised the sales tax from 4 percent to 5 percent with no proportionate increase for the city.

Oakland can increase its sales tax yield by improving its business climate so that people will spend more within the boundaries of the city. Revenue from the sales tax has increased about 4 percent a year over the past five years, but this revenue has not actually kept pace with the increase in sales throughout the *total* trading area in which Oakland is located. A study done by the Oakland Planning Department in 1965 indicated that there had been a considerable shift of trading to outlying shopping centers, and the city's share of retail sales had substantially decreased since 1948. Part of the 4 percent growth in sales tax revenue has been due to price increases. The Consumer Price Index for the San Francisco area increased an average of almost 2 percent per year for the 1958–1966 period.[9] Considering Oakland's relatively stable population and the disruption of its downtown area due to the installation of a rapid transit system, city officials use a 3 percent annual growth rate to estimate the yield of the sales tax.

The loss of local rate and base control of the sales tax resulted from the state passage of the Bradley-Burns Uniform Sales and Use Tax Law of 1955. The incentives in this law were structured so that the cities would have trouble with their merchants if they did not join with their respective counties in the uniform program. Maintaining a separate city sales tax meant, in effect, that the cities' merchants would have to collect a higher rate and would be at a competitive disadvantage. Thus, in 1956 Oakland passed an ordinance to participate in the Bradley-Burns Act. At that time, Oakland and Alameda County agreed that the 1 percent reserved for local taxation would be split by having 95 percent of it go to the city and 5 percent to the county. City officials now feel that there is no justification for the county to receive any part of the city-generated sales tax. They argue that in many counties, such as Orange, Los Angeles, and San Diego, all of this tax goes to the cities, and, in any case, Oakland needs the money more than the county.

9. U.S. Department of Commerce, Bureau of Labor Statistics, *Consumer Price Index.*

Two areas remain for the city's discretion. First, it can pressure the county to change the arrangement so that Oakland gets all the local sales tax collected within its area; and second, it can make an effort to increase retail sales within city boundaries. In order to remain under the state uniform program, with its advantages of efficient collection, the city cannot go above the 1 percent legal limitation. For all practical purposes, the city has little discretion with respect to the sales tax. Some taxes, like the sales tax, are outside city discretion because of reality; while others, such as the property tax, are outside city discretion because of a fiction that everyone accepts.

Embarrassed about their reliance on the property tax, Oakland's officials analyze their situation simply. First, they know that the city tax rate is considerably higher than the average rate in the state. For a number of years, Oakland's rate per $100 assessed valuation has been around $3.00 while the state average has been less than $2.00. Indeed, in the sixties the city had one of the highest municipal tax rates in Alameda County and the state. Second, officials worry about Oakland's small rate of growth in assessed valuation. They know that other cities, such as San Diego and San Jose, have really been growing. When they read the state controller's *Annual Reports,* they see that the assessed valuation for all cities has increased by 7 to 8 percent.[10] Nor are they comforted by knowing that some of the other cities' growth may not be real but just related to different assessment procedures. Unfortunately, they know that their own growth rate of 2.6 percent increase in assessed valuation has been fairly reliable in estimating future property tax revenue yields. Ignoring the complex interdependence between tax base and tax rate or between services, tax rate, and market value, Oakland officials have adopted a simple decision rule: the property tax rate cannot be raised, and when possible it should be lowered.[11]

10. Average tax rates and assessed valuation percentages for California cities are available in California, Controller, *Annual Report of Financial Transactions Concerning Cities of California.*

11. Making decisions solely on the basis of comparisons of nominal tax rates may be foolish. A high property tax rate, for example, can indicate a high level of public service or a low tax base, or some combination of both. Moreover, increased tax rates can result in an increased tax base when the additional revenue is used to enhance the value of the property.

Thus, Oakland officials have placed the property tax in quarantine. The tax has reached its limit. Nor is Oakland alone in this perception. By a process of mutual reinforcement throughout the state, officials have convinced themselves that the property tax can no longer be used to meet increased financial requirements. What to do with the property tax is a major concern of reform-minded policy makers within the state, as any casual newspaper reading will document. Plagued with assessment scandals, expensive exemptions, and a plethora of small tax rate jurisdictions, people have a notion that the property tax has reached its limit. As one county official puts it, "The property tax has, of course, not reached a *legal* limit, but we in county government do think that for all practical purposes it has reached a *working* limit." [12] Or, as a League of California Cities executive says, "We are inclined to agree with those who state that the property tax has reached its limit. However, revenue derived from property taxes will continue to be a substantial source of municipal revenue for years to come." [13] Oakland officials have found it convenient, for the moment, to join these prophets of the demise of the property

For an excellent discussion of these matters, see Dick Netzer, *Economics of the Property Tax* (Washington: Brookings Institution, 1966), pp. 34–35, 116–131. A recent survey of 124 cities with populations of 100,000 or more finds that Oakland's effective tax rate (annual tax billing as a percent of sales price) on single-family houses ranked seventy-eighth; Trenton had the highest and Baton Rouge the lowest. (U.S. Bureau of the Census, *Census of Governments*, vol. 2, *Taxable Property Values*, Table 21, 1967.) Although this survey suggests that Oakland's property tax rate is fairly moderate, data from the Census Bureau's *Governmental Finance, 1966/67* shows that Oakland does rely heavily on this tax:

Property Tax as a Percent of Total Revenue

Newark	73.3	Norfolk	29.1
Jersey City	68.1	Birmingham	27.0
Miami	51.9	Louisville	22.8
Rochester	49.4	Long Beach	20.0
Portland	49.0	Toledo	18.5
Oakland	44.5	Columbus	11.5
Akron	36.3		

In the final analysis, it makes little difference whether a rate is objectively high or not, so long as people believe it is high and act accordingly.

12. California, Legislature, *Financing Local Government in California*, p. 79.

13. *Ibid.*, p. 90.

tax, but they could always change their minds. Since they have made similar prohibitions in the past and later ignored them, I consider the property tax to be within the area of city discretion (see Table 4, p. 22). Political limits on taxation can be raised when the fiscal barrel appears empty. Surely it must be a myth that any tax is ever permanently exhausted.

Since city officials have decided not to tinker with the property tax rate, they have tried to increase the tax base in Oakland. Such economic development has not been a smashing success (with the exception of the Port of Oakland, which is not under city control), so officials have taken the logical step of finding other revenue sources. In this process of what is called broadening the tax structure, or charging twice for the same thing, the city has narrowed its own fiscal discretion. In a survey of California city managers and officials in 1962/63, over 60 percent of the respondents felt that the property tax would not be adequate to meet their needs over the next ten years. Over three-fourths of the city managers who foresaw this inadequacy have initiated new tax levies. Over half of these managers were "unreservedly in favor of increasing the importance of the role played by locally levied and state collected taxes. If allowance is made to include those cities which would favor such an increase with varying degrees of safeguards or conditions, the share in favor climbs to 78 percent." [14] In other words, most of these cities do not insist on maintaining complete control over their own fiscal resources and would gladly surrender some discretion in exchange for the efficient collection of revenue by the state. The statewide attitudes apply quite well to Oakland. The city has historically relied heavily on the property tax. But the property tax is "exhausted," so the city is now looking for and has been levying a series of nonproperty-tax revenue sources. Furthermore, Oakland is content to give up its fiscal discretion, as we shall see.

THE CITY GIVES AWAY ITS DISCRETION

City officials deliberately narrow their own fiscal discretion. Officials tie their own hands by establishing autonomous organi-

14. California, Legislature, Senate, Fact Finding Committee on Revenue and Taxation, *Property Taxes and Other Local Revenue Sources*, Part 9, March 1965, pp. 86–88.

zations and funding them out of general purpose revenues such as on-street parking fees. At the state level, city officials are content to join a state program and give up discretion because they can cut administrative costs and also maintain a stable source of revenue supply, or so they believe. Unfortunately, officials are not aware at the time that they are giving anything away. Their successors, however, live with the consequences of a narrower fiscal discretion.

Parking fees are much bigger business than the average person who puts ten cents into a meter realizes. In Oakland on-street parking fees yield about $1 million a year and are designed for control and rationing as well as for revenue. Many on-street parking meters gross over $130 annually, even though they are often placed not to maximize revenue but to maintain turnover in areas where parking demand is high. Administrative costs for repair, collection, and accounting run to approximately 14 percent of meter revenue.

Parking revenues are a significant resource for the downtown merchants who have been able to reserve about half of the city's parking revenue. Because the City Council wanted to encourage the development of the downtown business area, it established an autonomous Off-Street Parking Commission and pledged half of the meter revenue to finance the acquisition and construction of off-street parking lots. Not only did the general fund lose half a million dollars to a special off-street parking fund, but the general fund is also used to support the staff expenses of the commission. The city manager cannot recoup this revenue, but he is attempting to encourage the commission to pay for its own minor expenses.

The history of the cigarette tax in Oakland is an excellent instance of the cities' flight from fiscal independence. In 1959 the state of California passed a statewide cigarette tax of three cents a pack. In 1961 Oakland officials considered the feasibility of adopting their own cigarette tax. At that time, the city manager recommended to the council that Oakland support an arrangement for state administration of a cigarette tax similar to sales tax procedures under the Bradley-Burns Act. Five years later, however, the climate for passing a local tax was appropriate and the need sufficient, so that the City Council passed an ordinance imposing a two-cent tax on each pack of cigarettes. City officials had concluded that the cigarette tax would have stable revenue yields as health hazard pronouncements, such as the Surgeon General's Report, seemed to have little effect on consumption.

In the following year, 1967, the state legislature passed a new law providing for state administration of the cigarette tax. The League of California Cities had been recommending this step, and the city manager and other Oakland officials had supported the proposal, urging in letters to legislators that such a state-administered tax would be "desirable and effective" and would achieve a "uniformity and equity" similar to the sales tax administration. The new tax, which became effective in October 1967, allowed three cents out of a total of ten cents per pack to be returned to local governments. Apportionment to the city and county governments was to be computed on the basis of the percentage of total sales tax revenue received by the local government.

Not only were local officials happy to support the state legislation on grounds of efficiency, but state adoption of the cigarette tax would avoid controversy over suspected cigarette smuggling from other jurisdictions. One council candidate had made cigarette smuggling an issue in his election campaign. With uniform statewide procedures, Oakland could not be charged with encouraging cigarette-tax avoidance or putting its own retailers at a disadvantage. The most advantageous aspect of this state legislation, as the city viewed it, was that Oakland would be getting an additional million dollars in revenue per year due to the increased rate and more efficient means of collection. City revenue estimators expected the tax to yield almost $2 million a year. However, one problem remained: some cities were interested in having the apportionment based on population instead of sales tax revenue which would have put Oakland at a severe disadvantage. Oakland stood to lose $400,000 annually if the apportionment rule was changed to a population basis. Fortunately, the rule was changed so that half of the revenue would be distributed on the basis of population and half on the basis of total sales tax revenue. As a result, Oakland lost only about $100,000 annually. The revenue yield was not as stable as officials had expected. Instead, city officials had to bargain to restrict their losses. The $100,000 is a minor symptom of the loss of discretion which the city embraced.

SHOULD THE CITY TRUST THE STATE?

The usual argument for city home rule and less reliance on state or federal fiscal support is that outsiders will determine how a city spends its money. Concurring in the popular wisdom, local officials worry about state strings. Seldom is it noted that the state can also determine the amount of funds a city will actually receive. The state as the controlling jurisdiction can determine the rules as to who gets what. Nor is the state neutral in making these determinations. The state also needs money and is often another site for tax politics.

Yet city officials seem anxious to trade control of their own revenue sources for the administrative efficiency of state collection or as a preemptive tactic against adverse state action. This trade, however, can backfire, and the alcoholic beverage tax is a good example. This tax, which is more commonly known as a liquor license for the retailing of alcoholic beverages, is a state revenue. The state receives the revenue from the original license fees, which cost about $6,000 each. The annual renewal and transfer fees for this license are about 10 percent of the original cost. In the administration of this revenue source, cities and counties used to receive 90 percent of all annual renewal fees and transfer fees. In the 1967 legislative session the law was amended so that 100 percent of the transfer fees will go to the state and none will go to the cities and counties. For Oakland this change represents roughly a 25 percent reduction in revenue. Whereas in 1966/67 the city received approximately $400,000 in alcoholic beverage tax funds, it expected to receive approximately $300,000 per year by 1970; moreover, the Oakland Police Department enforces the liquor laws for violation of any state law on licensed premises.

One might think that local franchise taxes could be reserved for city use, but even here the state has cut into the fiscal pie. Through the use of franchise taxes, the city sells the right for corporations to conduct certain activities on or below city property. Franchise agreements with utility, railroad, and oil corporations are usually for extended periods of time, ranging from 10 to

50 years, and are based on annual charges, such as 25 cents per track foot. The largest source of franchise revenue comes from utility companies. Originally, the city taxed the Pacific Gas and Electric Company and the Pacific Telephone Company. However, the California Supreme Court ruled that the telephone company state franchise, under the California Public Utilities Code, applies also to the streets of California cities; [15] therefore, the telephone company discontinued annual franchise payments of about $320,000 to the city and currently pays only an annual business license of about $3,000. The Pacific Gas and Electric Company, however, still pays the city a 2 percent rate on their gross annual receipts, which amounts to approximately $340,000 each year.

MAKING MONEY

Although granted that government is not business, sometimes Oakland officials act as if they were running a business. They do not make a profit but wish they did. In the following sections it will be shown that the city has something to sell, that it loses money by not recovering its costs, and that officials are not, although some would like to be, revenue maximizers.

THE CITY HAS SOMETHING TO SELL

The city puts price tags on many of its services and facilities. Taxes do not pay the complete freight of the costs of local government. Charges, licenses, permits, and other fees pick up some of the slack. However, there are other sources of making money which are not as well known.

Revenue is received by the city from the Oakland Scavenger Company for their refuse collection contract. Since the garbage collected by the Scavenger Company is legally the property of the city, Oakland was paid a small fee and was provided with free garbage collection and disposal for city-owned facilities. In 1967/68 the City Council approved the Scavenger Company's request for a rate increase and, at the same time, levied a 5.5 percent tax on Oakland Scavenger's gross receipts. As a result the

15. *Pacific Telephone and Telegraph Co. v. City and County of San Francisco*, 197 Cal. App. 2d 133 (1962).

city expected to receive between $250,000 and $300,000 per year from the Scavenger Company rather than the almost $30,000 paid previously. Of course, the taxpayer pays for this additional revenue indirectly, because his costs for garbage removal have been increased.

Interest paid to the city for fiscal year 1966/67 was $900,000 and it will increase due to the efforts of the finance director. Although the increases are small, they illustrate two points: the importance of the finance director's role in getting more revenue for the city; and when a city is looking for revenue, even the smallest amount will be considered.

Like many households, the city has the problem of determining how much money to leave in its checking account, or what is called the "active noninterest-bearing account," and how much money to invest in order to receive the highest interest rate possible. The problem revolves around the estimation of cash flow requirements. The object is to avoid early redemption of a particular deposit which might result in a loss of interest.

Prior to January 1967, Oakland put its money in banks under a certificate of deposit agreement with the bank. The shortest time period for any one certificate was thirty days. If funds were required before the thirty days, then the city would lose its interest. This characteristic of certificates of deposit required the city to maintain a high cash balance in its active or checking account. In January 1967, however, at the finance director's suggestion, the City Council authorized him to place available funds in other legal instruments, such as U.S. Treasury notes and bills. Such instruments are more flexible and allowed the city to reduce its average cash daily balance from about $1.2 million to a daily balance of $255,000. The amount of cash invested increased from 94 to 99 percent. The net increase in revenue for this more flexible investment policy resulted in a $50,000 increase per year in total interest paid to the city.

Rental and sales of city real estate and equipment accounted for almost a half a million dollars in 1966/67. Most of the money comes from selling surplus city real property. In addition, every year the city holds several bargain day sales of unclaimed stolen bicycles, lost and found items, and surplus automobiles. Each sale yields about $40,000. The city also rents bleachers, utility poles for $1.50 a pole, and an expensive pavement-marking machine for $100 a day. Officials once considered charging rent to the Oakland Municipal Employees' Credit Union for the free space it occupies in the City Hall.

HOW TO LOSE MONEY BY
NOT RECOVERING COSTS

Building, other license and permit fees, and service charges illustrate the dilemma of cost recovery in Oakland. Officials pay obeisance to the norm that the fee should cover and compensate for the extra expense incurred by the regulatory activity or for the benefit received from the service. However, many of Oakland's fees do not even begin to approach a recovery of costs. Depending on the fee, the ratio of costs to revenue can range anywhere from two-to-one to ten-to-one. There are several explanations for violating the cost recovery norm which will be introduced now and analyzed in chapter 2.

Building inspection fees include revenue received for the issuance of permits and inspections for the regulation of plumbing, electrical, and various other construction activities. These fees were expected to follow the city's cost recovery norm. Several years previously, inspection fees brought in well over $500,000. In the late sixties the yield was about $400,000, which covered approximately 60 percent of the city's building inspection costs. The reduction of revenue was partly beyond the city's control, since inspection activities and revenues are linked to the level of construction within Oakland. In the late 1960s there was a slump in construction during which costs remained constant, due to the city practice of not firing employees, while revenue dropped.

The residual area of other license and permit fees involves literally hundreds of minor fees which have been established over the years. Bicycle licenses, blasting permits, city manager permits, and close-out sale permits are some of the fees in this revenue area. Since the city does not have a revenue manual that lists them, no single official is aware of all of them. This is one revenue area in which the city could exercise a great deal of discretion in setting rates and recovering costs. However, officials have limited resources; so they can only review and change a few fees at one time.

Fees are established and become part of an operating routine where they are seldom reviewed. Charges continue to be collected as a matter of habit. For example, the taxi and ambulance driver permits, which allow a person to drive a taxi or ambulance within the city, are administered by the Police Department. In 1938 a fee of $1 was established. A recent review disclosed that it cost approximately $8.50 to process an applicant for this permit.

The conflict between regulation and cost recovery is well illustrated by the case of animal licenses and fees. Revenue is $53,000 and the cost of the animal control function is $120,000. Why is there over a two-to-one difference between revenue and costs? The city operates an animal control section as an exercise of its public health function. The current annual dog license fee is $4. The number of licenses sold since 1957 has decreased by almost half. Officials estimate that the dog population totals somewhere between 35,000 and 40,000, and 75 to 80 percent of these dogs are not licensed. These facts should not be interpreted as mere trivia because they illustrate the dilemma faced in exercising regulatory functions. The city lacks the staff to police this activity and to discourage people from violating the law. The decline in license sales can also be attributed to a stiffening of health laws which require the owner to pay for a valid rabies certificate in order to license a dog. During the period of decline a leash law also went into effect. Both of these regulations, plus the lack of enforcement, tend to discourage people from licensing their dogs; the cost, particularly for poor people, is prohibitive. The more stringent the regulations are, the more they discourage compliance.

The city has to maintain an animal control shelter even if people do not license their dogs. Raising the fee to recover costs would only punish the minority who obey the law and would reinforce the trend not to license. Since there is reluctance to make the investment for enforcement of animal control, officials have a voluntary program which relies on the citizenship of the individual. When regulations get onerous, the citizen finds it easier not to comply; thus revenue goes down and the city pays for the regulatory activity from general funds such as the property tax. Costs for the animal shelter continue regardless of the amount of revenue receipts.

Service charges also carry the expectation that the city should recover its costs. Theoretically, if an individual benefits from a specific service, he should pay the costs of that service. The problem with the administration of charges, however, is that the norm is more a matter of rhetoric than practice. For example, the city recovers less than half of its costs (around $450,000) for issuing publications, recording legal instruments, zoning variances, map reviews, building condition reports, recreation and museum craft programs, library fees, and charges made to Alameda County for prisoner maintenance. Another example is "driveway tipping" where the city paints red no-parking areas adjacent to private driveways for the citizen's convenience; this activity costs twice as much as the amount recovered in revenue. Similarly, the charge for the maintenance of a taxicab zone, which is supposed to cover painting the curb and installing the signs, is half of the cost. Years ago, when contractors and workmen had to park their vehicles on a job where there were meters, the Police Department issued free bags to cover the meter. Now the Police Department charges for these bags, but their charge accounts for only half of the lost meter revenue.

CONFUSION AND CONFLICT—BUSINESS LICENSES

Business licenses yield almost a million dollars a year. However, I believe that Oakland is not maximizing business license revenue. Officials do not want to discourage business in Oakland even though they need the revenue. Businesses are charged but can bargain for adjustments in rates and choice of the measure of tax liability. The net result is a hodgepodge ordinance which costs 10 percent of the collected revenue for administration and which officials are reluctant to revise completely. The last time Oakland changed its business license ordinance was in 1957. Prior to that time, rate schedules had been in effect for periods ranging from ten to thirty years. Rather than taking on all the diverse businesses at the same time, officials make marginal changes and avoid conflict. To confuse matters, city officials do not agree on several important issues: what is the purpose of the license, who should pay, and what should be the basis of the charge or the measure of tax liability.

Originally, municipalities used licenses as an extension of their police power for the protection of public health, safety, and morals. The charge as such was designed to recover the costs of regulation. However, as years passed, the business license became a revenue rather than a regulatory device. By the mid-1960s, a particular business may have required a permit in addition to a business license. For example, garages and auto repair shops, miniature golf courses, service stations, and skating rinks are charged for both a permit and a business license. These permits are supposed to be for regulation, but in fact they are just another revenue device. It is likely that if officials reviewed this area, they would find that some business licenses are being collected for regulatory purposes and permits are being collected for revenue purposes. The only clear operational distinction between a permit and a license is that the permit is issued once, and the license has to be renewed annually.

Not all businesses have to pay the license fee. City officials gradually extend the coverage of the license. In 1957, the city cancelled exemption from the license for 4,000 veteran businessmen. They also extended the provisions of the ordinance to include some amusement vending machines. About ten years later the city contemplated extending the license to cigarette and candy vending machines.

Describing the present measures of tax liability is no easy task, because in many cases they have been tailored to the particular kind of business. Generally one can discern four main categories: wholesale and retail, professional and semiprofessional, apartments and hotels, and manufacturing. These categories differ by measure or rate. For example, the business license for apartments, hotels, and motels is a flat rate of 80 cents per room, while the wholesale-retail category is based on the number of employees, $20 for the first person and then a declining graduated schedule up to over 100 persons at $1.50 each.

Within the Budget and Finance Department, which is responsible for making recommendations on what the rate base should be, there is disagreement over how to charge for business licenses. One analyst has insisted that net income would be the most equitable way of charging. Current rates are mainly based on the number of employees, which is not likely to be equitable.[16]

16. For a discussion of the equity of the business license, see California, Legislature, *Financing Local Government in California*, p. 45.

Equity is difficult to determine because the relationship of profit to the number of employees is not clear. However, the finance director has felt that a net income basis would not be feasible because of the unavailability of state income tax records and the difficulty that would be involved in administration. The finance director would prefer to use a gross receipts basis. He feels that the business license fee should be related to the extent of profit that a business can achieve by operating in Oakland. The director would like to have a gross receipts tax with firms grouped by similar profit margins. He recognizes that a "turnover type tax" might result in pyramiding and double taxation, but a .2 percent gross receipts tax, which might yield $10 million, is an attractive prospect. However, such a change would be a radical departure from present procedures. Instead, the finance director has suggested changing the definition of the number of employees from "average" to "greatest," which would slightly increase the business license yield.

LET'S PRETEND

One of the frustrating but fascinating aspects of studying revenue is that appearances are deceptive. Fiscal reality is such that actors cannot always do what they claim to do; norms are established and have to be ignored; and words do not mean what they usually mean. Local revenue is a world of pretense and make-believe behavior.

LET'S PRETEND THAT REIMBURSEMENTS ARE NOT REVENUE

Recall that I defined revenue as any financial resource that flows into the city over which the city has some expenditure control. The city receives money called reimbursements, which it excludes from the budget and does not consider to be revenue. In one year about $800,000 was reimbursed for services provided for outside agencies, such as the state of California, Alameda County, the Rapid Transit District, the Redevelopment Agency, the Port of Oakland, and even for private utilities and individuals.

Does a reimbursement for a service constitute payment of a service charge, or is it, in accounting parlance, a nonrevenue receipt? The distinction between service charges and reimbursements is murky. Formally, a reimbursement applies to city activity that is beyond the usual scope of city functions. This bit of speciousness means essentially that it is possible to define when a specific service is within the scope of city functions. Many of these reimbursed services have *standard* rates and procedures indicating that for all practical purposes there is no difference between a service charge and a reimbursement. And if there is no difference in the clients, or the service, or the methods of charging, then there is not much reason to maintain the distinction.

The distinction between service charges and reimbursements may at times be only a matter of the auditor-controller's interpretation. Once a revenue is put in one pocket or another, a precedent is established. To take a minor example, Oakland conducts elections for the Board of Education, the Peralta Junior College District, and the Port of Oakland as a service to these agencies and to avoid duplicating elections. Oakland computes the total cost of running the election and then receives reimbursements on the basis of the number of offices reserved on the ballot. For instance, in the nominating municipal election held in April 1965, Peralta Junior College accounted for three of the sixteen offices on the ballot. Therefore, Peralta paid the city three-sixteenths of the total cost of that election.

LET'S PRETEND THAT TAXES ARE NOT TAXES

One of the great arts of the tax game is to design revenue sources so that people will not know that they are paying taxes. Taxes should not be seen nor felt, only paid. There is a contrary school of thought, which I believe to be in the minority, that claims that taxes should be visible and that the taxpayer should know he is paying. However, the revenue behavior of Oakland officials is consistent with the hide-the-tax rule. Furthermore, the state helps in this endeavor by establishing fines and setting procedures for some in lieu taxes.

The municipal courts of Alameda County are a source of revenue to the city of Oakland. Court revenue is collected when bail is forfeited, and for fines relating to vehicle code violations and to misdemeanor arrests for nonvehicle-code violations. The yield from this revenue source has steadily increased over the years. In 1962/63 it was $1.5 million and by 1966/67 it was $2.1 million. Of the $2.1 million total, approximately half a million dollars came from fines and forfeitures for nonvehicle-code violations, while the rest came from vehicle-code violations. The nonvehicle-code court fines become part of the city's general fund, while the vehicle code fines, by state law, are deposited into a special earmarked fund called the Traffic Safety Fund.

The city has no discretion over what these fines will be or what revenue it will receive. The maximum and minimum penalties are set by various state legal codes, and the Alameda municipal court judges determine the fine and bail schedules within these state limits. The only possible area of discretion is related to who actually does the arresting. For example, if an Oakland police officer writes the citation for a vehicle-code violation, then the resulting fine money is split with 22 percent going to the county and 78 percent going to the city. On the other hand, if the individual is cited or arrested by state officers within the city, the city only gets 50 percent of the money and the rest goes into a special county road improvement fund.

The normal procedures for the property tax do not apply to certain kinds of property. The taxes paid on these kinds of property are usually called in lieu taxes because they are paid instead of the locally assessed property tax. For example, motor vehicle license fees provide the city with in lieu taxes amounting to $2.4 million without the pain of collection or taxpayer resistance. Because apportionment and collection procedures are complicated, most Oakland citizens probably do not realize that their motor vehicle license fee includes a 2 percent in lieu tax, based on the market value of the vehicle, part of which goes to the city. Apportionment for the motor vehicle license fee is based on county population within the state. Each county keeps 50 percent of the money it receives and the rest is redistributed to its cities on the basis of their populations. Oakland's per capita amount for 1967/68 was $6.80.

Besides being palatable another feature of in lieu taxes is that "in lieu" often does not mean "instead." The term is misleading, because the city does not receive as much revenue as it would if the property were subject to the usual real property procedures. Consider the in lieu tax on private aircraft. This tax is levied locally by the county assessor at a rate of 1.5 percent of market value, and the collected taxes are distributed evenly between the city, the county, and the school district. If aircraft were treated as real property, the property would be assessed as a percent of market value and then a tax rate for each jurisdiction would be applied. The in lieu procedure, applied to 365 private aircraft (worth about $8 million), yielded the city approximately $35,000. The city would have received about twice this amount if the real property procedures could have been used.

LET'S PRETEND THAT EARMARKED FUNDS ARE NOT EARMARKED

A primary characteristic of an earmarked fund is that the money is set aside for a special use. The primary reaction to such funds by city officials is to broaden the use of the money. By using particular funds for general purposes, officials are able to reduce the impact on their general fund and keep their property tax rate stable. The California Penal Code, for example, specifies items which can be expended out of the "fine" revenue that is in the Traffic Safety Fund. Officials then attempt to cover general fund traffic safety expenditures, such as traffic control devices, with money from this special fund.

The city also establishes its own earmarked funds, usually as a means to justify a new tax. A few years ago it adopted a service charge to be collected from users of the sanitary sewer system and to be used for the replacement of sanitary sewers. Gradually, officials have extended the use of the Sewer Service Charge Fund to cover not just replacement but maintenance, billing, and collection costs and other city overhead expenditures. A detailed case history of this charge is presented in chapter 4.

For all practical purposes, the Transient Occupancy Tax Fund is no longer an earmarked fund. Both the special use of the money and the special interests that were involved have disappeared. When the transient occupancy tax was instituted in 1965, it imposed a 4 percent charge on hotel and motel accommodations rented for periods of less than thirty days. The League of California Cities had urged its adoption in order to avoid state preemption of the tax. The tactic was that if the state levied a similar tax after many cities had adopted it, the cities would then have to be given part of the revenue.

On the home front, Oakland officials got support for the tax by stressing the special purpose for the funds and by including their opponents, the hotel and motel owners, in the decision process. The tax was passed and justified because of the specific requirement to encourage tourism and convention promotion for the city and not as a general revenue device. Since it was a tax which directly affected hotel and motel interests, a special Transient Occupancy Tax Committee was established to make recommendations for the allocation of these funds. The original membership of this Committee included two members from the East-bay Hotel Association, two from the Motel Association, two from the Chamber of Commerce, two from the City Council, and one from the city manager's office. In theory, this committee was to make recommendations on how the money should be spent and these recommendations would then be endorsed by the City Council.

Historically this fund, like other earmarked funds, was operated to broaden the original use of the money and to provide some offset or alleviation to the general fund. As the fund was administered, there was an emphasis on using the money to cover costs that were being paid out of the general fund. One time, officials attempted to use the fund for entertainment and advertising activities and became involved in a set of legal entanglements. The city auditor claimed that a charter restriction on entertainment and advertising appropriations applied to the Transient Occupancy Tax Fund. The charter was then amended by the voters, which freed the fund from the restriction. Officials continue to broaden the use of the money, so that practically any general fund expense for tourism, visitors, entertainment, and advertising is paid out of the Transient Occupancy Tax Fund. In the 1968/69 budget, all expenses for community improvement activities, such as support of the Chamber of Commerce, the Oakland Symphony, and Columbus Day, Fourth of July, and special celebrations were transferred from the general fund to the Transient Occupancy Tax Fund.

The Transient Occupancy Tax Committee has also disappeared. Originally, the city gave the hotel and motel people representation on the committee to gain their concurrence for the tax. Now, allocation decisions and rate increases are made by city officials with some advice from the Chamber of Commerce; but no direct consultation with hotel or motel operators takes place.

The state gasoline taxes are another example of the operation of earmarked funds. Although the average citizen may worry about control of city government by the state, control is not an adequate word to describe the bizarre set of arrangements that result from the establishment of such funds. It is not a simple matter to say to a city, "You will spend this money in only this way." Problems of definition and legality are widespread when earmarking takes place. The League of California Cities, for example, does more than lobby for funds from the state legislature; it also provides an important educational service by informing cities as to what and how they can spend existing state donations.[17]

A great deal of activity in past years has been devoted to trying to "beat the system" legally. The art of city administration of earmarked funds lies in avoidance of the constraints imposed by the authorities who originally established the fund. The idea is to spend the money on what you want to spend it on without losing any in the process. This objective requires a small army of clerks to shift funds from one pocket to another.

Californians pay a tax of seven cents per gallon of gasoline of which the state keeps four cents for highway construction; the rest is sent to the cities and counties. Part of this revenue which the city receives is usually termed the "old gas tax." This tax has a more formal legal description, but I will use the City Hall name. In 1966/67 the old gas tax brought in $1.7 million. State law provides that at least 40 percent of the city's old gas tax receipts must be used for construction of the "Select System of Streets." These streets are determined by the City Council and approved by the state. What this means in practice is that the *major* city streets which serve as arteries for traffic coming from outside city limits, as well as for local traffic, are included in the list of select

17. See League of California Cities, *Limited Expenditure Funds of Cities*, March 1963.

streets. The other 60 percent of old gas tax funds may be used for maintenance or, with the approval of the state Department of Public Works, for construction purposes. What constitutes maintenance, construction, or a select street is subject to negotiation and is defined by administrative fiat and practice.

Another source of revenue is the "new gas tax" established in 1963 that allows 1.04 cents per gallon to be apportioned directly to cities and counties for street construction purposes. In fiscal year 1966/67 new gas tax funds amounted to $1.5 million. When the new gas tax fund was established, it required the city to match the grant with its own money. This requirement was eliminated in 1967. Elimination of matching requirements for the new gas tax alleviates an administrative headache and saves the cities from having to find additional revenue. Until then Oakland officials worried that the city would be unable to find enough money to match on a dollar-to-dollar basis.

The city's final source of gas tax revenue is known as the Alameda County Street Aid Fund. Since 1955 the mayors of Alameda County cities have had an agreement with the Alameda County Board of Supervisors to share a portion of the county's gas tax funds for city street construction. Funds are to be used for streets that have more than local importance. The agreement between the mayors and the county has been renewed every five years and is based on the recognition that, although the cities may receive more gas tax funds in absolute figures, it is the cities which suffer the greatest deficiencies in the Select Street System. It is also recognized that the cities have used a greater percentage of their own local sources of financing for street-related expenditures than have the counties. Revenue from this source was around $800,000 for fiscal year 1966/67. This type of agreement is typical for urban counties, like Alameda County, where the total city street mileage accounts for 78 percent of the total county streets and highways.

The fact that the county gives away some of its revenue is an indication that the state allocation of gas tax revenue is not satisfactory. In addition, there are inequities in present apportionment procedures, which are based on population. Current distribution rates for Oakland are over $3.00 per capita. The apportionment procedure tends to favor the city with a rapidly expanding population. In Oakland's case, that of an old city with a set of deteriorated streets and a stable population, the apportionment procedures are to the city's disadvantage. The money is not being being placed where the need is. Thus, resorting to higher-level government allocations of funds does not necessarily result in a rational distribution.

The administration of gas tax funds is complicated, and the central administrative headache is to find matching funds. Not just any city expenditure on streets qualified for matching. The state wants the city to spend nongas-tax revenue on the Select System of Streets and for only certain street improvements; for example, expenditure for sidewalks did not qualify for matching. In the past the city would use expenditures from its Traffic Safety Fund for its matching requirements because this fund is derived from nongas-tax revenues. However, one year a significant part of the Traffic Safety Fund was scheduled to be used for construction projects which would not qualify as matching expenditures.

Oakland's superintendent of streets had a way out of the dilemma which would allow the city to construct what it wanted and still not lose any state funds. His ingenious suggestion was to get Alameda County Board of Supervisors to agree to a confusing accounting substitution of funds. First, the county would be asked to approve the use of Alameda County Street Aid Funds to help finance some freeway construction. Second, the county would agree to the city transferring funds from the city's Traffic Safety Fund to finance the same freeway construction. Thus the Alameda County Street Aid Funds, which were made available by the transfer, could be used for the originally scheduled non-eligible construction projects. The net result of these machinations would be that the county would get some select system street work accomplished which it wanted, and at the same time the city would be able to show that it had the necessary matching expenditures. By the marvels of accounting the city could meet all state qualifications for matching. The eligible construction projects would be aligned with the eligible funds.

LET'S PRETEND THAT GRANTS ARE
NOT REAL MONEY

I have been discussing recurring revenues which have a fairly stable impact on the city. The area of grants is an important one, but it is unpredictable, involving one-time projects without sufficient continuity for the city to rely on this revenue source.

Cities are not expected to rely on grants to pay for their usual functions. Grant systems are established to take care of extras; grant programs are deliberately designed to prevent recipient cities from relieving their own tax burdens. Unfortunately, cities like Oakland need fiscal aid for the traditional functions of local government as well as money to deal with pressing social and economic problems. Oakland officials search elsewhere to relieve their revenue constraint.

Currently $95 million of federal funds comes into Oakland, and only a relatively small part of these funds is included within the budget for usual functions.[18] To get some perspective on the impact of federal and other agency funds, one only has to consider that the entire budget for Oakland for 1968/69 was $56.7 million. As an example of funds excluded from the budget, it was estimated that a little over $8 million for fiscal 1967/68 would be coming to the city for urban renewal. Such funds are under the jurisdiction of Oakland's Redevelopment Agency, which is a separate agency created by the City Council to administer the federal urban renewal programs within the city.

Some grants, such as the Urban Planning Grant from the U.S. Department of Housing and Urban Development, under Section 701 of the Housing Act of 1954, do go directly to city officials and are in the city budget. This act provided around $600,000 to the city in 1966/67. It is expected that the total planning grant will be approximately $1.5 million. The planning grant is designed to support an extensive city-wide planning study which will attempt to develop a comprehensive plan to deal with all the physical and social problems of the city. The grant is, however, for a one-time planning project. From a variety of local, state, and federal agencies there is a miscellaneous set of grants amounting to about $400,000 per year which supports city activities. This amount includes repayments on the Hall of Justice by the county, state grants for training police officers, and federal funds for civil defense and a library demonstration project. Within the total for grants, the details vary from year to year as to what

18. Oakland, *Digest of Current Federal Programs in the City of Oakland,* prepared by Jeffrey L. Pressman with the assistance of the Redevelopment Agency of the City of Oakland, October 1968.

the money is being spent for and who is actually the contributor. Only about 1 to 2 percent of the annual budget is conceivably supported by federal funds.

LET'S PRETEND THAT TAXES ARE JUST

Equity is an elusive goal which local taxation will never reach. At the local level fiscal cynicism supplants fiscal justice. The question is seldom who should pay but rather who will pay. Local officials emphasize yields and leave the problem of income distribution to the federal government.

The property tax is inequitable because not everybody pays. Certainly it is legitimate to have welfare exemptions, but sometimes reductions in the tax base can be excessive. During past years property has been excluded from assessment due to exemptions, welfare considerations, and illegal or underassessment practices. Oakland budget officials estimate that over $300,000 will be due to the city because of past underassessment. In Oakland and throughout California, exemptions from property tax such as those for veterans, churches, homes for the aged, hospitals, schools, and cemeteries resulted in about a 5 percent reduction in assessed value. Oakland's exemptions reduce its assessed valuation by $35 million. In other words, the city "loses" over a million dollars of tax revenue annually because of exemptions. If, for example, the 17,000 veterans in Oakland had to give up the exemption on their $14 million worth of property, the city would gain over $400,000 and its tax rate could be reduced by about six cents.

Reduction in assessment is also due to the fact that some public property, particularly that controlled by the Port of Oakland, is leased to owners and is appraised only for the occupant's possessory interest in the property. By leasing a person can pay less taxes. The appraisal of possessory interest is made by an estimation based on use and not on the value of the property itself. The port uses such leases for warehouses and office buildings to attract business. These possessory interests had been assessed at 14 percent of value, but with the new assessment procedures of 1967/68 the ratio was to be increased to 25 percent. However, there still remains the difference between the value of use under a possessory interest basis and the actual appraisal of the property as if it were owned rather than leased. Officials would like to have a study of possessory interest practices of the port because the city believes that revenue could be increased if the port would sell property rather than lease it. Unfortunately, one government's benefit is another government's cost.

The property tax is inequitable because old people have different burdens. Old people who live in their own homes must pay property tax, but those who live in homes for the aged do not share a similar burden. Not only are the aged treated unequally because of the exemption for old age homes, but rich old people can escape property taxes by living in "luxury" old age homes. Oakland has eleven old age homes, and several new homes are currently under construction. Some of these, like Lake Park (California-Nevada Methodist Homes), satisfy a California legislative committee criterion for a home that "could be strongly suspected of opulence." [19]

A regressive tax is one where the burden of the tax decreases as one's ability to pay increases. The property tax is inequitable because it is regressive. A recent study for the state concluded, "the relative burden of the property tax on income tends to drop substantially as income increases." [20] For the second important source of Oakland's revenue, the sales tax, the evidence indicates that, with different measures of ability to pay, the California sales tax is roughly proportional. However, in chapter 6 it will be shown that some leaders consider the sales tax to be regressive while businessmen and other leaders, to some extent, deny this. Because of major exemptions of food and prescription drugs, one analyst says, "this regressivity may be more apparent than real in the case of California's type of sales tax." [21] So the property tax remains the necessary evil of local finance, perhaps mitigated by the benefits received. One student describes the property tax:

19. California, Legislature, Assembly, Interim Committee on Revenue and Taxation, *Problems of Property Tax Administration in California*, vol. 4, no. 20, Final Report, Part 1, December 1966, pp. 63–65.

20. California, Legislature, *Property Taxes and Other Local Revenue Sources*, p. 77.

21. California, Legislature, Assembly, Interim Committee on Revenue and Taxation, *The Sales Tax*, prepared by Harold M. Somers, December 1964, p. 31. For another study that indicates proportionality in the sales tax, see State of California, Legislature, Senate, Fact Finding Committee on Revenue and Taxation, *General Fund Consumption Taxes*, Part 2, January 1965, pp. 11–14.

"This tax is shown to have many faults. It cannot be defended on the grounds of the ability-to-pay principle, and its use can only partially be justified on the basis of benefits received by the tax payers. Its regressivity is acknowledged; its incidence is often uncertain; its failure to contribute to economic stability is recognized; and its administration results in frequent and serious injustices." [22]

SUMMARY

Oakland is perceived by its officials as an impoverished city whose revenue resources are not likely to match increasing expenditure requirements. Officials no longer rely on the property tax for new funds because they believe it has reached a limit. Therefore, they are looking for new sources of revenue, which will probably be adequate for maintaining the existing organization but not for meeting the city's growing social and economic problems.

In my description of the numerous sources which comprise the revenue structure, we have seen that the city has a circumscribed capacity to raise revenue. The area of financial discretion continues to narrow because the city is the willing fiscal creature of the state. Federal fiscal first aid does not help because officials are restricted from using grants for traditional functions.

Officials do not always properly manage their own resources. They violate their own cost recovery norm. When they attempt to maximize revenue, they are not always successful. Much of the behavior associated with local taxation is characterized by pretense: taxes have to be designed to be palatable, not equitable.

22. California, Legislature, *Property Taxes and Other Local Revenue Sources*, p. 33, citing C. Ward Macy, "The Property Tax in the Fiscal System," in *Proceedings of the 51st Annual Conference*, National Tax Association (Columbus: National Tax Association, 1958), p. 74.

2

City Officials
and Oakland Finance

In Oakland one has to look hard to find politics. The usual grand drama of political scientists, the electoral battles for office, the conflict of interests and groups, and the disparities between men who seek power and men who have it is muted in a mélange of separate public arenas and private concerns.[1] No single factor can explain Oakland's present political scene, but indifference can go a long way. Ask not who rules, but who cares.

When Oakland Project members interviewed the man on the street as to his attitudes about his city, the city turned out to be San Francisco. Besides Oakland's nice climate, it was a convenient location because of its proximity to the "real" city of San Francisco. Oakland as a city does not exist; it is a collection of neighborhoods without community. Indifferent citizens and indifferent party leaders make a great combination. Party activists spend their time on the state or the national scene, not on municipal elections. Incumbents usually get reelected and appointment politics prevails. Coalitions are hard to assemble because groups do not exist or may not know each other. The savvy political actors on the Oakland scene, the black activists for the

1. Given the division of labor on the Oakland Project, I will not fully describe Oakland's political system. The following brief introductory comments are based on the many discussions which the Oakland Project has had in trying to understand the complexities of a "nonpolitical" political system. Readers who wish an in-depth analysis should see the work of Jeffrey Pressman, particularly "The Non-Politics of Non-Leadership in Oakland," draft manuscript (Berkeley: Oakland Project, University of California, October 1969).

most part, are busy in the federal arena of various poverty programs. As one black activist put it to me, "Why bother with the city? It has nothing to offer." Nor do William Knowland and his *Oakland Tribune* dominate the political scene. I found out more about Oakland from neighborhood papers such as the *Montclarion* than from the *Tribune*. Indeed, a common complaint of Oakland's officials is that business and community leaders should care and be more involved in city affairs. Couple this citizen and leader indifference to the complex set of local institutions and one can easily see the validity of applying Norton Long's ecology of games to Oakland's political system.[2] Accepting the dictum of the turned-on generation, the port, the county, the water district, the several school districts, the regional parks, the rapid transit district, and the city are all doing their thing.

Because the people, activists, and institutions are all doing their own thing, there is no single voice for Oakland. Occasionally, the mayor will attempt to speak for the city. But for the most part city officials pay attention to their own troubles. For example, no one worries about Oakland's financial condition more than its officials. And among city officials, no one worries more than the city manager. Our man on the street hardly knows that he exists, but if anybody runs the city, he does. Oakland is an administrative city.

Officials respond differently to Oakland's revenue constraint. The manager is very concerned about the lack of money and expends great effort getting officials and citizens to be equally concerned. Making the revenue crisis salient and finding new sources of revenue are major components of his missionary role. His administrative belief system or code, with its emphasis on efficiency, and the professional city-manager norm that a low property tax rate is an index of efficiency are crucial behavioral determinants.[3] The City Council and the mayor have been adequately socialized by the manager. The council wants to

2. Norton E. Long, "The Local Community as an Ecology of Games," *American Journal of Sociology* 64 (November 1958): 251–261.

3. There seems to be a combination of beliefs and conduct, a sort of "operational code," which may cut across city managers as a profession; for the concept "operational code," see Alexander L. George, "The 'Operational Code': A Neglected Approach to the Study of Political Leaders and Decision Making," *International Studies Quarterly* 13 (June 1969): 190–

lower the property tax rate. Councilmen defend the tax base, view the taxpayers as their constituents, and have a business orientation. Like the manager, they value efficiency. City department supervisory officials are aware of the revenue constraint but do not do much to alleviate it. Most departments provide services or facilities to the public, and these service objectives conflict with attempts at revenue maximization. Department heads cannot bring in revenue when the charging of fees would interfere with the main purposes of the organization, such as regulation of health and safety or the provision of recreational services. Within the context of conflicting objectives, a few department officials attempt to make a profit while others ignore revenue considerations. No department is self-supporting.

In the discussion that follows, the manager, council, and departments are considered in turn. Administrative departments, like the Budget and Finance Department, are extensions of the manager and are not separately discussed. Similarly, I view the mayor as one member of the council since his financial behavior is not significantly different from other councilmen. The view of all these key officials will be one-sided because of my emphasis on their fiscal behavior.

CITY MANAGER

In the 1968/69 Oakland budget the following statement was made: "The property tax rate was decreased from $3.14 to $3.06 per $100 of assessed valuation, a reduction of 8 cents. This marks the third consecutive year that the Oakland municipal property tax rate has been reduced." [4] More than any other actor on the Oakland scene, the city manager is responsible for the reduction in the property tax rate. In a world of complex interaction, it is

222. However, I do not claim that Oakland's manager is a typical model of his profession, since city managers also exhibit a wide range of behavior; see Gladys M. Kammerer, "Role Diversity of City Managers," *Administrative Science Quarterly* 8 (March 1964): 421–442 and the classic, Harold A. Stone, Don K. Price, and Kathyrn H. Stone, *City Manager Government in the United States: A Review After Twenty-Five Years* (Chicago: Public Administration Service, 1940).

4. Oakland, *Budget Summary, 1968/69*, prepared by Jerome Keithley, Robert M. Odell, Jr., and Thomas E. Heubner.

not often that a single causal agent can be identified. Of course there are other actors who are concerned about Oakland's high tax rate; however, no one is as concerned as the city manager. The local tax association official feels the city is a small fry and spends his time with the big spenders, such as the county. The council says that the property taxpayer needs relief, but then votes salary increases, passes an occasional booster-type project, and engages in such community projects as partial support of the Oakland Symphony. Councilmen believe it is good politics to cut the tax rate; they also do things which put pressure on the rate in the interest of good politics. City department heads are in the business of providing service, of satisfying community needs; tax revenue is not their headache. Thus, the city manager often complains that no one seems to care that Oakland has the highest municipal property tax rate in California. The manager is concerned and expresses his concern by attempting to centralize his control of city government, by emphasizing the importance of efficiency, by searching for new sources of revenue, by socializing city actors to adopt his administrative orientation, and by maintaining his position as the city's key executive.

THE CITY MANAGER IS AN

EFFICIENCY-ORIENTED, PROFESSIONAL ADMINISTRATOR

Being efficient and searching for alternative sources of revenue are functional equivalents to cutting the tax rate. No one directly pressures the manager to do these things. He looks for efficiencies, tries to cut costs and find money, because this is the way he defines his administrative role. The norms of his profession are such that good managers do these things and Oakland's city manager is a good manager.[5] A high tax rate can indicate a

5. It can be disastrous for a city when there is a lack of fiscal expertise and concern. Expenditures have to be controlled to match revenue expectations. Cities just cannot print money to make up for deficits. Richard E. Winnie, in a seminar paper, "The City of Martinez Deficit," describes such a troubled fiscal situation. He found that Martinez, a small Bay Area city, had accumulated a deficit of 39 percent of its annual general fund. To meet general fund obligations such as payroll expenses, city officials had used a variety of short-term and tax anticipation notes and had also improperly transferred special earmarked funds. The state then put a freeze on subventions. The finance officer was demoted, and the city manager resigned.

meager tax base, but it can also be a sign of inefficient administration. When the city manager came to Oakland in the beginning of 1966, he felt that the city was inefficient and it also had few financial resources. In his words, the city had milked the kitty; it was a matter of common sense to perceive the limited growth in its fiscal base. Moreover, the city had not used its limited resources wisely. It was fragmented with many autonomous departments; the manager's office was inadequately staffed, because the previous manager had not been concerned with internal problems of administration. But his successor is different. He wants to make decisions about internal administration; he is an inside administrator.

The manager's problem is to coordinate the fragmented pieces of city government and at the same time protect his own free time. He is an intelligent, almost shy man who is not easy to know. He shuts himself off from people so that subordinates and constituents alike complain about not being able to see him. Coordination without intensive self-involvement is no easy task; therefore, he attempts to coordinate by slowly, cautiously centralizing the decision process. He does not put himself at the center of the communication network, but close to the top.

The manager has a hierarchical view of organizational structure, and he uses the budget process to gain central control (see chapter 5). Because of the resource constraint, he does not view budgeting as significantly affecting the allocation of resources. His feeling is that officials should not spend much time on budgeting. However, he spends a great deal of time on it because with marginal dollar changes he can use the budget as a control mechanism. Furthermore, he uses reorganizations for control: so many department heads report to the manager that few of them see him; thus, he is moving to collapse smaller organizations into larger ones such as the recently established umbrella-type Public Works Department.

Related to his personality and administrative style, the manager's centralization strategy reflects his basic belief that centralization improves the quality of service. He is not just an economizer, but believes that to avoid duplication, to be efficient, to have centralized functions, and to control improves service. Therefore, he is willing to spend money on a central yard facility to achieve economies in equipment, maintenance, and utilization. The manager links centralization to improved service without any definite information on economies of scale. He transfers the logic of achieving economies by centralization to a general cost-cutting strategy: cut overtime, control part-time people, use old equipment, repair and renovate rather than replace. It is a one-sided cost-effectiveness equation where cost reduction is assumed to be equivalent to enhanced effectiveness. Obviously at some level such "efficiencies" can impair service, but this possibility cannot be given much thought because of inadequate information resources. The manager and his immediate assistants in the Budget and Finance Department believe that there is waste and that the fat can be cut out. After all, Ossian Carr, Oakland's first city manager in the 1930s, cut his own salary from $20,000 to $15,000. To cut costs and to centralize is to be efficient. Efficiency, in turn, is equated with the norms of good management, and the net result is some relief to the upward pressure on the tax rate. Regardless of whether the source is federal, state, or local, the city manager does not want to waste money.

THE CITY MANAGER IS THE
CITY'S FISCAL INNOVATOR

Another way to reduce the property tax rate is to find other sources of revenue. It was the manager who suggested that Oakland conduct a comprehensive review of its fiscal capacity and resources. One of his first acts as manager was to write the mayor:

For some time now I have been telling you of my concern for establishing a fiscal plan for the City of Oakland, which would serve as a guide for the future, relative to the financial ability and capability of the Oakland city government. . . . What do I mean by a fiscal plan for the city? Simply, this means reviewing the total sources of revenue for the city, making projections for the future along with programming and planning fiscally for the future operational and capital needs of the city.[6]

He wanted the mayor to appoint a citizens' committee to do the review as was done in San Diego. The mayor was not as con-

6. Letter from Jerome Keithley, city manager, to Mayor John Reading, March 23, 1966.

cerned about the city's revenue constraint as the manager; consequently, the review was conducted by city staff officials under the formal direction of the manager with my part-time participation. The manager's plan, the Financial Capability Study, undertook to review each present source of revenue and to suggest new sources to meet the projected revenue-expenditure gap.

The manager's role in this revenue exercise was not to direct overtly, but rather to stimulate action on the part of other officials. Since he was new to the job and uncertain of his staff, he reduced his administrative risk by keeping the situation ambiguous and allowing the task to be defined by other participants. Department heads were to review their sources of revenue while the finance director was to compile a report which would analyze the potential for bonds, project expenditures and revenues, and suggest new revenue sources and administrative improvements.

Although the manager directed the study by hints rather than commands, much of his administrative style and tax preferences are reflected in its output. For example, the city manager is a detail man. Through the years he has learned about the detailed operations of city government; if he sees a confusing traffic sign or an overturned garbage can, he will call the appropriate department head to fix it. In budgeting, he will pay attention to a fifteen-dollar item. He worries about telephone costs, the council's business cards, and why the Police Department has uniformed personnel running their motor pool. Big and little items often get the same attention, although he warns his subordinates not to get inundated in details as he has done. Thus it was not surprising that he asked the staff to review *all* of the myriad minor fees which the city levies. His detailed interests and style, in this case, were congruent with the city's narrow area of fiscal discretion.

The manager is a somewhat pessimistic fiscal realist. He ranks his tax preferences by what will pass and what would be politically acceptable. Tax equity is not particularly important to him. Once, a downtown merchant complained about the creation of a special assessment district by stating that businessmen paid about one-third of the burden but did not get one-third back. The manager replied, "That's just tough . . . somebody has to pay, as a lot of people don't get back what they put in." The manager does not worry about who *should* pay; his question is who *will* pay.

His tax preferences provided the framework for the Financial Capability Study. He felt that the property tax was exhausted and that the city had better get busy and find nonproperty-tax revenue. Study personnel accepted this perception as an assumption and did not question the exhaustion of the property tax. The manager felt that Oakland would never adopt a municipal income or a payroll tax and certainly would not pioneer it in the courts. There was no chance of getting it. The utility tax was a good idea, but perhaps the city would run into trouble with the utility lobbies. Similarly, the real estate lobby would be against a real property transfer tax. The amusement tax sounded good, but the city would have to soft-pedal it until Oakland got its major league baseball team. No doubt bonds would have to be recommended for certain capital improvements, but the staff should be concerned with selling the bonding program to the voters. It is hard to sell bonds for a corporation yard and sewers. These negative comments do not mean that the manager excluded these revenues from consideration. Indeed, the utility tax was proposed and adopted. But what he was doing was assessing the political feasibility of each source of revenue.

The manager's fiscal realism is also apparent in his attitude toward federal funds. The city needs the money, but sometimes the frustration of dealing with the federal government is not worth it. As he says, "People want sidewalks and the federal government tells you to be innovative." In his view, the government raises expectations and then delivers very little money. And even after a city gets some money, the federal government's auditors and program managers have different ground rules. He is fond of telling the story about two representatives from different parts of the Department of Housing and Urban Development who did not know each other. They flew from Washington on the same plane and, in separate appointments, gave him conflicting instructions on the same problem. In spite of the frustrations, he feels, unlike many Oakland citizens (see chapter 6), that the city is not aggressive in getting federal funds. By the time the city pulls itself together and fills out the paper work, the program is curtailed or cancelled. The city is always late in getting federal funds. Federal funds are not predictable and even though the manager is content to receive them, he looks for more stable sources of revenue to meet Oakland's requirements.

THE CITY MANAGER IS A
FISCAL SOCIALIZATION AGENT

The manager has tried to educate councilmen, city officials, and citizens about the revenue constraint faced by the city. Since he feels no one cares, he uses every opportunity to make them care. If invited to a businessmen's luncheon to speak, he will use the opportunity to develop support for economies in government and to inform the audience that the property tax is in a bad way and that the city must find new sources of revenue. After several lectures by the manager on revenue problems, the finance director evaluates all alternative revenue sources in terms of their possible reduction of the property tax rate. When the mayor tries to make an optimistic speech, the manager is sure to add a pessimistic note that "in a few years our revenue resources will not meet our expenditure requirements."

One of the payoffs for the city manager of the Financial Capability Study was its use as an educational device. By involving the department heads in its preparation, the manager felt that they would come to appreciate the revenue situation and start to cut costs. If community leaders were exposed to the study's pessimistic conclusions, then perhaps there would be community pressure on the council to become fiscally responsible and be more concerned about efficiency. The manager also hoped to develop a consensus among city officials on the importance of efficiency as a guide to good management. The more he is successful and city personnel share his management orientation, the less he has to be concerned about coordinating a fragmented organization and finding additional revenue.

THE CITY MANAGER IMPLEMENTS THE
POLITICS-ADMINISTRATION DICHOTOMY

The manager believes that politics should be separate from administration. He is a vigorous partisan of the city-manager form of local government which adopts this premise of separa-

tion. He believes the city-manager form is capable of being
efficient and honest. His defense of the manager-type political
system is not due to self-interest but represents the operational-
ization of his ideology of efficiency. The problem of honesty and
corruption was dealt with many years ago and the paramount
problem of management today is efficiency. In order to be efficient, the manager believes that elected officials, politicians,
must be kept away from the operating departments; department
heads should be shielded from councilmen; and these administrators should not be allowed to make end runs to politicians.
The belief in the politics-administration dichotomy is an important correlate of the manager's centralization efforts.

Keeping politics out of administration means keeping politicians out. The mayor, according to the charter, is supposed to be
part-time; the manager therefore encourages him to take days
off. In the manager's view, the mayor's role is restricted to ribbon
cutting. When the manager was reviewing a draft of the Financial
Capability Study, he deleted a suggestion that the mayor's job
be full-time. A good city-manager government lessens the burden
on political officials. The mayor has only one vote on the council,
and the council should give part-time advice and not be active
in administration.

On the other hand, the manager understands that administration has a political component. He realizes that he is a policy
maker and that politics are a part of his job. For example, he is
sensitive to the need to build a community constituency, but he
finds it difficult because he does not believe that problems of finance and efficiency are, in his words, sexy. As the city's full-time
chief executive, his office is exposed to all kinds of community ex-
pression. He cannot escape from the public even if he would like
to. He views himself as having good political radar; he knows
what the traffic will bear. He does not present recommendations
to the council unless he is well prepared with supportive data. Although he claims he implements council policy, he makes policy
by his own decisions and by influencing the decisions of the council. In the Oakland world of mutual interaction, it is not entirely
clear who is giving advice to whom. Nevertheless, city officials
complain that the council does not provide policy guidance, but
concerns itself with trivia. An examination of council activities

seems to verify this inference. However, it is doubtful that the manager and his assistants really want guidance when they are pursuing their own policies.

Because the city manager wants to cut needless costs, he assumes the role of the council's fiscal conscience. Councilmen make decisions one at a time and do not think of the cumulative consequences of their decisions.[7] The council commits the city to expensive projects like the coliseum without fully understanding the fiscal consequences of these decisions.

The city manager plays this fiscal conscience role by providing the council with what he considers right information. The Financial Capability Study, for example, was designed to provide information that would make clear the terrible fiscal position of the city. The manager also had to remind the mayor to include in the "State of the City" speech that the tax rate had been cut. When the council discussed whether to help subsidize a helicopter transportation experiment, which the manager considered an extravagance, he quickly pointed out that an impoverished city cannot afford such an expenditure. If the council wants to spend money on something which has not been budgeted, the manager points out that some nonproperty tax will have to be levied to pay for the item. He feels it is his job to make the council aware of the financial consequences of its actions.

The manager has superior tax knowledge. He knows the nuts and bolts of taxes, follows the relevant state legislative activity, and makes an effort to be aware of what other cities are doing about finance. With his penchant for operating detail and his superior tax knowledge, he is quite effective in providing right information. The fact that the manager is knowledgeable allows him to structure the council's decision process so that right information can often determine right policy. However, the manager views the council as softer on fiscal issues than they are; in fact, there is more of a consensus on fiscal policy than the manager realizes. It is a question of degree: the manager is willing to cut costs where the council may not find it politically

7. For the piecemeal nature of council decision making, see W. H. Brown, Jr. and C. E. Gilbert, *Planning Municipal Investment: A Case Study of Philadelphia* (Philadelphia: University of Pennsylvania Press, 1961), pp. 106–111.

expedient to do so. The council is willing to spend money where the manager would not. Both have adopted a hold-the-line imperative and believe they originated this guidance for budgeting. Both are frugal and efficiency oriented. Both are in favor of making small cuts in the tax rate, thus stabilizing the rate. The manager may have to prime councilmen with information, but he does not have to manipulate them completely because they share much the same set of values.

Who pays what is often decided by the manager and his finance people. Tax choices are usually bureaucratic choices, because the decision process is not particularly visible and the attentive public for any single tax decision is small.[8] The city manager's response to the revenue constraint illustrates the importance of an administrative belief system. Emphasis on the efficiency of central control, efficiency, cost-cutting, political expediency in revenue choices, and the importance of information and knowledge are all components of this system. It is this belief system and the related norms of professional city management that orient the manager as he copes with Oakland's revenue problems.

CITY COUNCIL

Council actions usually reinforce the manager's fiscal behavior. Oakland does not have a Wilbur D. Mills on its council. In federal finance, Chairman Mills of the House Ways and Means Committee is a powerful figure who significantly affects tax outcomes. In the politics of Oakland finance, councilmen legitimize the finance policy of the city manager. The council does not initiate, but reacts to citizens' complaints and the city manager's recommendations. The trivia of zoning appeals, approving purchases among competitive bidders, and the passing of perfunctory resolutions and ordinances occupies most of the council's time. Its twice-a-week agenda is characterized by gerunds—approving, awarding, instructing, reapportioning, repealing, amending—but the policy gerund, *steering*, is missing. The council, as gatekeeper, selects among financing alternatives which the manager suggests to it. The council, as watchdog, defends—

8. For attentive publics, see V. O. Key, Jr., *Public Opinion and American Democracy* (New York: Alfred Knopf, 1961), p. 544.

sometimes with rhetoric and sometimes with action—the city's tax base and taxpayer. Councilmen are elected at large and their constituents are the taxpayers.

COUNCILMEN HAVE HIGH TAX COMPREHENSION

Councilmen are not experts in public finance theory, but they do understand the mechanics of municipal finance. They are knowledgeable because they are businessmen or associated with business. In addition, the eight councilmen plus the mayor know about taxes in order to play their roles as defenders of the tax base and taxpayer. Background and official position are directly related to their high tax comprehension.

They know about establishing special ad valorem assessment districts, possessory interest charges, and the relevant state legislative activity and legal codes. One councilman, a retail merchant, who ran on the platform to eliminate the city's cigarette tax, followed state legislative efforts quite closely and was anxious to inform his colleagues: "Mr. Mayor, this memo from me here regarding cigarette tax was a matter strictly for information. However, I am informed that the State Cigarette Tax Assembly Bill 484 and Senate Bill 556 could quite likely be passed by tomorrow night. And actually enacted into law at any time. I am also further advised that at the moment that it is enacted, any city that has a tax will not receive taxes from the State Tax."[9] In this case the councilman was premature in his concern; the state legislature did not pass the tax bill for ten days and it was several months before the new state law affected the city. Even if his timing was off, the councilman knew such details as the legislative bill numbers and the possible impact on the city. As a city merchant, the elimination of the city cigarette tax was important to him because it would help Oakland's business compete with its neighbors.

Because of their role as defenders of the tax base, councilmen are knowledgeable about assessment practices, which is illustrated by the mayor's report on the Alameda County Mayors Conference where the effect of state legislation on assessment practice, known as the Petris Bill, was discussed:

9. Oakland, City Clerk, Council Minutes, July 18, 1967, p. 7.

There was considerable concern about the next assessment procedure as specified on the Petris Bill, which as you are probably all aware moves the assessment bill up to 25% for both personal property and business property. It is now being assessed on 28% for business and 21.8, I believe is the figure, on personal property. There was considerable concern, as I say, as to the possible effect upon the cities to this re-assessment program.[10]

Or a councilman becomes knowledgeable to regain some of the reduction in the tax base due to welfare exemptions:

A few minutes ago I mentioned sales taxes with regard to these [old age] homes. What I had in mind was an amendment to the Revenue and Taxation Code which was passed by the [state] legislature at its last session, in which they charge sales taxes on leases on services and I refer to those sections as Sections 6006, subparagraph g2 and also the Section 6091 which may be applicable here. With your permission I will check that and let you know later. The legislature did pass such an amendment to the Revenue and Taxation Code, and it has to do with furnishing and leasing and furnishing services and that may come under these homes. These homes may come under that section, I don't know for sure. I think it is worth looking at.[11]

Councilmen's tax knowledge is an important factor in the revenue search processes of the city. Elected officials legitimize and provide a supporting climate for city manager revenue actions. Of course, councilmen are not all equally informed; but generally the council, as a body, is not ignorant when it comes to tax matters. When they do not know something, they can cut their information costs by asking the city manager and attorney to prepare special reports. In any case the level of tax knowledge is directly related to the councilman's business orientation and his public role as the defender of the tax base.

COUNCILMEN WANT TO LOWER THE
PROPERTY TAX RATE

Councilmen used to have champagne tastes with beer pocketbooks. In the past they have been accused of being fiscally irresponsible because they have committed the city to expensive

10. *Ibid.*, September 8, 1966, p. 11.
11. *Ibid.*, April 13, 1967, pp. 13–14.

projects that have affected increases in the tax rate. After much prodding and educating by the city manager, they accept the fiscal facts of life, recognize the revenue constraint, and, most of the time, guard the city purse. They are realistic in not expecting the property tax rate to be lowered without some alternative source of revenue. Sometimes their talk of lowering the rate is rhetoric, designed for taxpayer constituents. Councilmen try to keep the rate constant even when there is a slight surplus, so that the funds can be used for future expenses. Where the surplus might be large, they suggest a token cut. Of course they wish that the rate could be slashed, but they let the city manager worry about doing that.

It is important to realize the pervasiveness of the councilmen's tax rate attitude. The feeling that the property tax is too high and that it ought to be cut influences many council actions. For example, this general perception encourages a low rate of indebtedness because councilmen do not want to commit a part of the property tax revenue for debt servicing. They think, talk, and make decisions in terms of the property tax rate. The effect on the rate in most decisions is an important consideration; for example, when the Fire Department wanted to increase its personnel authorizations to provide for vacations, this dialogue took place:

Mayor: That would be at a cost of approximately what, $65,000?

Assistant city manager: My recollection is between $65,000 and $70,000.

Mayor: Which means another penny on the tax rate.

Assistant city manager: Yes, sir.[12]

When Oakland hired a new finance director, the mayor told him, "We welcome you to the city family" and "We expect at least a 10 or 15 cent tax cut next year." [13] The mayor was joking, but the council does take reduction in the tax rate as a sign of efficient management which is to be applauded:

12. *Ibid.*, June 27, 1967, p. 7.
13. *Ibid.*, October 27, 1966, p. 5.

City manager: Mr. Mayor, you have before you an ordinance recommending that the tax rate for the coming fiscal year be established at $3.14 per hundred dollars of assessed valuation. I so recommend.

Mayor: Thank you, Mr. Keithley, any discussion on this? If not, Mr. Maggiora.

Councilman Maggiora: A very good job.

Mayor: I will again comment, Mr. Keithley, I think that you have done a good job on holding it and in fact a two-cent cut and we hope that next year we will be able to do the same thing.[14]

The fiscal imperative of the council is: hold the line or, if possible, cut the property tax rate. The council and the mayor believe that Oakland citizens are concerned about the property tax rate; consequently, they pledged a 12-cent reduction if the people of Oakland would adopt a proposed charter reform.[15] The manager believes that Oakland is the first California city to make such an offer. On occasion, councilmen have run for reelection pledging a slight reduction in the rate. Thus, the property tax rate, as councilmen perceive it, is an important issue. If the councilman can put himself on the side of lowering the rate, he expects to accumulate considerable political support.

In the name of the taxpayer, the council seeks to defend and protect the tax structure by preventing other jurisdictions from encroaching, by not granting zoning variances to tax-exempt institutions, and by economizing with the salaries of city employees and other expenses. Councilmen concentrate their efforts on the traditional functions of the municipality, such as police, fire, and recreation. The school system, for example, is a separate governmental unit, so councilmen generally define school problems as outside their purview. For ceremonial occasions, they may wear a city-wide hat; but when it comes to money matters the hat suddenly shrinks. The fact that many local agencies use the property tax is an anathema to them. The indication that other agencies may get federal funds and interfere with the city's revenue hunt is a sign for council intervention. City in-

14. *Ibid.*, August 22, 1967, p. 18.
15. Oakland, City Clerk, *Proposed New Charter of the City of Oakland and Alternative Propositions to be Voted on at the Special Municipal Election Consolidated with the General Election to be Held November 5, 1968*, p. 3.

come must be preserved. Operationally, the self-preservation rule is most often seen in actions that relate to the property tax. Most of the councilmen's perceptions on city finance can be traced back to their tax rate attitudes and their role definition as defenders of city revenue.

Other governmental agencies do attempt to capture city revenue sources. For example, Oakland councilmen have defended against the Association of Bay Area Governments (ABAG), the Bay Area Rapid Transit District (BARTD), the local school district, and even the city's own Port Commission. In the case of ABAG, a regional government, the council's reaction has been mixed. Some councilmen recognize that in order to get federal funds, membership in a regional government is required and they recognize, in addition, that there are some functions, such as garbage disposal, which are regional problems. On the other hand, the council has been dubious about giving ABAG the power to tax Oakland property. In fact, at one time they passed the following resolution: "Oakland City Council opposes authorizing or empowering the Association of Bay Area Governments to levy taxes, to issue bonds or to acquire public property through eminent domain." [16] The port leases property and BARTD takes property off the tax rolls for its plant; both of these actions have reduced the tax base of the city. Therefore, councilmen are reluctant to see another independent taxing authority established:

Councilman: I, Mr. Mayor, . . . think this is a matter of protecting the interests of everybody in this community. I think that if you have been reading the papers you find there is quite a bit of opposition to the tax imposed by the Regional Parks; BARTD is another outstanding example of what the power of the [state] legislature can give to an organization once they get started and there is no end to what BARTD can do and there would be no end to what ABAG can do. The time to stop this is at the start. . . .

Mayor: This is really the crux of the problem. Do we want some sort of an agency that can handle regional problems or do we want to forget it and continue with special districts? . . .

Councilman: Mr. Mayor, that statement of regional problems is old hat.

16. Oakland, City Clerk, Council Minutes, March 23, 1967, p. 3.

Mayor: It may be old hat, but it is a reality.

Councilman: It covers a multitude of sins. What I am concerned about is what's going to happen to the taxpayers' investments in the city of Oakland. I don't care about the region.[17]

Thus, to be concerned about the taxpayer means to protect the property tax base so that it may be feasible to reduce the property tax rate. Sometimes the concern is more immediate when, for example, the other agency wants city funds to meet noncity expenditure requirements. BARTD has sought to use funds from the Port Commission in order to build its transportation headquarters center. When the Chamber of Commerce presented this request, a councilman responded: "I recommend that the city manager look into this thoroughly. In the first place, I would like to know why is BARTD backing out on what they originally promised? Why should the port, which is run on city funds, build this structure, and there are many facets of this that I think before we walk into a pig-in-the-poke that we better protect the taxpayers." [18]

Another example of the council resisting encroachments by other jurisdictions was its denial of the Oakland Board of Education's request for the council to levy a five-cent tax for the schools. This tax would have been in addition to the school district's usual sources of revenue. Some of the factors in turning down the request were the council's perception of the high tax rate and their own expenditure needs, as this councilman indicates:

I think we all sense the need for better schools and better education; however, there is one thing that is primary in my thinking and that is how much is this going to cost and I know what 5 cents on the tax rate means. We have to consider when we are considering the recommendations of the school board and its officials that we have an obligation to the police and fire departments that's going to necessitate many thousands of dollars.[19]

Tax-exempt institutions such as churches, old-age homes, and governmental agencies also take property off the tax rolls; so

17. *Ibid.*, pp. 6–7.
18. *Ibid.*, May 16, 1967, p. 5.
19. *Ibid.*, March 28, 1968, p. 7.

councilmen, where they can, try to discourage them from locating in Oakland unless the particular institution can bring in revenue or improve the economic condition of the city. Thus a large post office, because of prospective employment opportunities, gets the council's blessing while a small store-front church is likely not to get approval for a zoning variance. Councilmen are particularly unhappy with the state welfare exemptions for churches and church-sponsored old-age homes, as these councilmen state:

I am not against churches, but here is a case again where you are going to allow a church to take a piece of property, be tax free, and we have a man on there at the present time paying taxes and keeping the city going and we let the church come on and take more property off the tax rolls.[20]

I for one, voted, I think, for the first retirement home in the city of Oakland and at that time thought it was for the best of the community; however, since that time, there has been a tendency on the part of all religious orders, including my own, to become more political, which is not the basis on which they were granted tax exemptions. . . . If this attitude on the part of all denominations continues, something should be done to eliminate the tax exemptions which they now enjoy.[21]

If these retirement homes would pay an in lieu tax, then they would be exhibiting the proper attitude. Even though the state exempts these institutions, Oakland councilmen believe that the exempt should also help protect the property tax. The antipathy toward exempt institutions extends to their own city departments that lease space in downtown buildings and displace taxpaying occupants.

The councilmen value efficiency, but they would rather be inefficient if they can cut the tax rate. They are usually looking for ways to save money as a means of protecting the taxpayer. If they can cut down expenses, such as travel, they can relieve the pressure on the property tax. Some councilmen complain about the travel costs of the independent commissions and boards:

20. *Ibid.*, May 2, 1967, p. 10.
21. *Ibid.*, April 4, 1967, p. 2.

This is the old refrain. I do not believe it's of benefit to the city that the entire Planning Commission takes a leave and goes to this particular convention. In April, five members of the commission went on a junket to Philadelphia which cost the city $1,953.83. I have always believed that the head of the department and maybe an assistant or secretary could take notes by attending these meetings and bring back to the entire board the vital facts that are being discussed and I for one think this is another abuse of the taxpayers' money.[22]

Despite their efficiency notions, however, some councilmen are silent on travel expenses because they share with the commissions the same belief: travel is a reward for faithful service. One councilman, nevertheless, insisted that the mayor was going too far by having the taxpayers pay for the mayor's assistant's trip to Hawaii: "there comes a time when somewhere especially in the face of what we've just discussed in the last half hour, our tight budget. We're pinching pennies. We're doing everything to save the taxpayers a nickel. And here we take a man out of his office that's in an executive position, at an adequate salary, and take him on a jaunt to a Mayor's Conference." [23]

Save money where you can; fight exemptions; stop other agencies from poaching—all these are actions of men whose main perception of city finance is that the property tax rate is too high. The city manager has made councilmen financially aware, so they are wary of attacks which will increase expenses or decrease revenue. When employee associations petitioned the council for fringe benefits, the associations argued that the schools or other public agencies should not be given money until city employees were well paid. The council resolved to protect the tax base: our employees need a salary increase; therefore we cannot possibly give the school board five cents of our tax rate.[24] Once the school board was closed out, then the council proceeded to trim the employees' demands. Taxpayers, not employees, make up the constituency of councilmen.

COUNCILMEN HAVE A BUSINESS ORIENTATION

In the drive to clamp down on the property tax, councilmen defend and support the taxpayer. But some taxpayers, such as

22. *Ibid.*, September 8, 1966, p. 1.
23. *Ibid.*, June 15, 1967, p. 3.
24. *Ibid.*, March 19, 1968, pp. 10–11.

businessmen, get more support than others. The council supports business because, first, most councilmen are businessmen and, second, they believe that the long-run prosperity of Oakland is linked to the prosperity of business. The mayor directly expressed this prosperity perception in his "State of the City" message. "Economic development will continue to be of prime importance not only for its key role in the formation of jobs but also for the establishment of a more solid tax base. The city administration pledges to do everything possible to create a more favorable climate for the establishment and growth of business and industry in Oakland, and will continue to emphasize careful fiscal planning in its own operations." [25]

Support for business is carried, sometimes, to the point where the council seems to violate its own role definition as defender of the property tax base. For example, the council sent a resolution to the state legislature urging elimination of the business inventory tax.[26] Such a reduction would, if other revenue sources were held constant, increase the tax rate by twenty-four cents. Since elimination of the business inventory tax would seriously affect local governments throughout the state, councilmen expected that the state legislature would find some other revenue source to compensate for the loss. Obviously, a councilman will, on occasion, experience a conflict between his business and council roles. More often, he will tend to view the roles as coterminous; after all, government should be run like a business.

When there is trouble between the business community and some other group, all sides of the controversy will claim they are taxpayers; consequently, the rhetorical role, defender of the taxpayer, and the council's business orientation are conflicting and uncertain guides for decisions. Councilmen have to worry about which taxpayer they will defend. When Foremost Dairies appealed an unfavorable ruling by the City Planning Commission, the council denied the application for rezoning and found in favor of the neighborhood people who were opposed to Foremost's plans for plant expansion. Foremost said they might have to leave Oakland; the Milk Drivers and Dairy Employees Union argued they were taxpayers and might lose their jobs. The loss of tax revenue from such a business was a serious concern of the

25. *Ibid.*, January 12, 1967, p. 5.
26. Oakland, City Council Resolution no. 47131, passed August 25, 1966.

council. But the citizens of the neighborhood also emphasized the rhetoric of taxes:

The property owners in this area stand to suffer a great loss if this special privilege of spot rezoning is granted, whereas Foremost will suffer less in comparison if it is not granted. All of the homeowners have just as much, and more, invested in the area in question, and we also pay as much, or more, taxes than Foremost and we don't know of any special laws in our Constitution which grant special privileges to any one of us.[27]

After a series of arguments on both sides, a councilman pointed out that the people who opposed the rezoning had lived in the area for twenty years or more, that they had pride in the area, and that the issue came down to whether the council wanted people or business in the area: "Are we interested at all in the people who live in this area, if not, then we ought to tell them all to move out of Oakland and let's put more industry. If on the other hand, we are interested in them, we should do something to help them along." [28] The council decided the neighborhood people were also taxpayers and voted in their favor.

Business interests prevail when the city will not lose revenue from its support. Thus the council backed the Downtown Property Owners Association in a dispute with BARTD. The owners' appeal of "do not penalize your own taxpayers" was effective against the agency which was digging up the streets, cutting down on sales tax, and taking property off the tax rolls. Similarly, when a large bakery wanted a sign to include its slogan, the council reversed the decision of the city's Sign Review Committee and reinterpreted its own ordinance prohibiting slogans so that the phrase "Stays Fresh Longer" could be considered part of the name of the bread company.[29] On the other hand, the council rejected the Chamber of Commerce's appeal for a revision in the utility tax rates, which would favor business, because the city would lose too much revenue.

Councilmen's beliefs are fairly congruent with those of the city's business leaders. The councilman prizes efficiency. He tends to lose the service orientation of a public enterprise. He is not

27. Oakland, City Clerk, Council Minutes, March 14, 1967, p. 8.
28. *Ibid.*, p. 22.
29. *Ibid.*, April 27, 1967, p. 4.

unaware of the connection between taxes and services. On the contrary, he is aware of the increasing costs of government, but his emphasis is on taxes. He wants to keep the costs of government down and thus reduce the impact on the taxpayer. He has become a caretaker of the tax rate. As the social and economic problems of the city increase, he narrows the role of the city government to traditional functions. He no longer shuns federal funds and supports the Heller tax-sharing plan. He does not worry about equity; what is fair is to reduce the property tax rate. He feels that he is doing a fine job when the rate can be reduced by a few cents. The problem is to get other sources of revenue, as this councilman indicates: "Of course, everybody's for lower taxes; that's like being for motherhood, but everyone wants increased services too. I would like to lower the property tax further, but I just don't know where else we could get the money from; I'd like to know." [30] It is up to the city manager and his Finance Department to suggest where to "get the money from." The Finance Department works with the city manager to find revenue and to promote efficiency.

CITY DEPARTMENTS

Most of the operating departments of the city emphasize service and not revenue. At the Finance Department and city manager level the service orientation diminishes, which is functional for budget cutting and increasing revenue. At the operating department level, public needs, service, and regulation conflict with revenue considerations. Many department heads do not understand why they collect fees. As I discussed in chapter 1, there is an explicit city-wide policy norm that fees should be set to recover costs. City officials often cite the cost-recovery norm, but these statements are mostly rhetoric. Most department heads do not know their costs, and the manager does not apply sanctions to enforce the norm.

REVENUE BEHAVIOR DIFFERS BY DEPARTMENT

Generalizing about departmental revenue behavior is difficult. Revenue behavior differs by the kind of service the department provides. The Police Department is not revenue conscious,

30. J. Pressman's interview with Councilman P. Brom, August 25, 1967.

whereas the auditorium manager is a revenue maximizer who seeks to make a profit. There is also a disjunction between what department officials say they do and what they actually do. The Park Department claims it is very interested in making money but does not charge when it can do so and its fees are minimal. The Recreation Department says revenue is not as important as recreation but its fees can discourage the use of its facilities.

The variation in departmental revenue behavior is partially related to the diverse reasons for fee collection. Furthermore, these reasons may be obscure to department officials. In the Financial Capability Study, the departments were asked to explain why they charge and to justify the amount of the charge for each of their fees. Here are some of their responses:

Library: This fine, 5 cents per day, follows the national standard throughout public libraries.

Park: Fee established at a rate commensurate with ability to pay and the view that monies received would compensate for services rendered. The building facilities together with kitchen privileges are included in the fee charged.

Street and Engineering: Private work requires deposit per Section 6–2.02 Oakland Municipal Code. Permittee is billed for inspection rendered.

Traffic Engineering: This fee is charged to recover costs for providing red "no parking" areas adjacent to the entrance to driveways. Since this service is provided on an individual basis to particular properties and is a special benefit to them, it is recommended that the fee be continued so that payment is made by those benefitted rather than the public in general.

Police: Dogs have been licensed for many years as a means of identification and rabies control.[31]

Some officials, such as the librarian, only know how they arrived at the rate and not why they charge. Others, like the head of Street and Engineering, do not bother to search for a reason but quote the Municipal Code. Regulation and control of public

31. Direct quotations, unless otherwise noted, are taken from the various departmental Financial Capability Study submissions which were completed by the departments during the months of October through December 1966. Departmental submissions are available in the city's Budget and Finance Department files.

safety is an important rationale for fees, and this orientation is clear in the police chief's statements. Cost recovery for services rendered is another prevalent reason for fees. Both park and traffic engineering officials' statements employ this reason. The Park Department, however, compromises its stated rationale of compensation with the introduction of the conflicting criteria of ability to pay. The traffic engineer is sincere about recovering costs. He is one of the few city officials who has made detailed cost studies in order to charge people what the service costs. He uses the benefit principle to bolster his argument for cost recovery by assuming that the city's cost is equal to the individual's benefit.

Revenue behavior differs from one department to another because the officials provide different services and facilities, have different levels of understanding and ignorance, and are differentially motivated by the manager's pleas to be concerned about revenue.

DEPARTMENT HEADS MAINTAIN THE REVENUE STATUS QUO

The Financial Capability Study was not undertaken by the department heads as a happy chore. Although the manager believed the city should increase its revenue base, the incentive for the department heads to find revenue was not as clear. They were informed of the city's revenue problems and were encouraged to raise existing fees, drop nuisance fees, and suggest new sources of revenue for their own departments and for other departments. From Table 5 we can see that most department heads were not responsive to the manager's directions. If they had been responsive, then practically all existing revenue sources would have been modified, given the differences between fees and costs discussed in chapter 1. With some exceptions, such as the auditorium manager and the Fire Department, many departments maintained the revenue status quo. Another indication of departmental indifference or inertia to revenue increases is the frequency of fee revision; some revenue sources had not been revised for as long as ten to thirty years. In many cases, a department's costs had increased so that fees were recovering only a fraction of the city's expenses, but the department head was reluctant to suggest fee increases. One reason for this reluctance was the conflict between revenue and the service objectives of the departments. Another reason was the possibility that increased fees would be offset by reductions in general tax support for a department's program.

TABLE 5: Many Department Heads Maintain the Revenue Status Quo

Department	Number of Existing Departmental Revenue Sources [a]	Number of Modifications to Existing Revenue Sources [a]	Number of New Revenue Sources Suggested	Oldest Date of Last Change
CITY MANAGER:				
Police	13	0	3	1938
Fire	3	3	1	1947
Building and Housing	24	6	4	1948
Electrical	7	3	2	1949
Streets and Engineering	40	9	12	1955
Auditorium	30	24	1	1956
Traffic Engineering	9	1	4	1964
COMMISSION:				
Library	6	0	0	1952
Park	47	15	0	1958
Recreation	27	0	0	1963

SOURCE: Oakland, "Financial Capability Study," Departmental Submissions, October–December 1966.

[a] A revenue source might be a single fee or a grouping of similar fees depending on the department's discretion; therefore, the numbers are not comparable within a single column.

In any case, this lack of incentive and the conservative bias in department attitudes can only reinforce the reduction in the scope of Oakland's revenue base. If operating costs go up and the departments keep fees constant, then the city will turn once again to general tax revenues. From the city manager's perspective, conservative department heads who did not recommend increases or new sources are counterproductive. They are increasing, not relieving, the pressure on the property tax.

As I pointed out, Oakland's government is fragmented. At the time of the Financial Capability Study, not all departments were responsible to the city manager. The Library, Park, and Recreation departments were directed by independent commissions. The manager had some budgetary control over them, but generally they were more autonomous than departments reporting directly to the manager. The fact that these commission departments were not as responsive to the manager's exhortations is indicated in Table 5 by the total lack of suggestions for new revenue sources for themselves or for other city departments. In addition, the Library and Recreation departments suggested no changes in existing sources. There was a certain amount of hostility and rivalry between the manager and the commissions which these numbers reflect. The superintendent of recreation, who is the full-time professional in charge of the department, had actually submitted a comprehensive set of changes and suggestions to his commission for review. The commission felt that revenue policy and the setting of fees for the Recreation Department was their business and not the manager's. It instructed the superintendent to submit to the manager the existing rate schedule with no modifications. A few months after the departmental submissions were in the Finance Department for analysis, the commission directed a revision in its rate structure.

The problem of increasing revenue is related to the integration or cohesiveness of the *city* organization; I would expect that the greater the organizational integration of a public organization, the greater the potential for revenue maximization.[32] With an integrated organization more officials would be concerned about revenue, and maintenance needs would not depend on a few individuals. The lack of departmental response, particularly in the case of commission departments, is an illustration of the general problem of the maintenance of a fragmented public organization. Recently, the citizens' approval of a charter reform measure has remedied some of the fragmented aspects of the overall system, so that a test of the revenue maximization hypothesis will be possible.

32. This hypothesis is similar to Fenno's finding that the House Appropriations Committee's integration and unity increases its chance of floor success; see Richard F. Fenno, Jr., *The Power of the Purse: Appropriations Politics in Congress* (Boston: Little, Brown and Co., 1966), pp. 191–263, 460–71, 681–84.

In the following sections, two commercial departments and one service-oriented department, Recreation, all of which exhibit revenue concern, are discussed. The distinction between service and commercial is one of degree and is based on the department heads' expectations for self-support. A commercial department would like to be completely self-supporting. A service department expects a large subsidy from general tax revenues. No city department is self-supporting.

BUILDING AND HOUSING DEPARTMENT

The Building and Housing Department is supposedly in the public safety business, but charges according to what the traffic will bear; their officials check out their fees by examining practices in neighboring communities and by consulting the building and construction community. The money comes from permits and inspections made by a division of the department. This division is supposed to pay for itself. In a normal construction year the division will collect 90 percent of its costs; however, when there is a slump in construction, it will collect only 60 percent.

Within the limitations of building codes and what neighboring cities charge, inspectors are revenue maximizers. Fees are deliberately fragmented so that the inspector can charge by each appliance or fixture such as water heaters, stoves, and toilets. There is no single building permit, but rather a plethora of application forms and permits to cover a variety of trades and activities. Permits are issued for plan checking, building inspection, plumbing, electric wiring, heating, and ventilating. Rates for permits are set by a flat rate or by the value of construction.

Although the department is concerned about revenue, it is not concerned about costs. Inspections and permits are organized by trade; consequently, in one day several different city inspectors may visit the same construction site. The department conducts 9,000 to 10,000 inspections each month and has little idea what a single inspection costs.

The department does some free electrical inspections of vacant houses and investigations of dangerous or unsanitary plumbing and heating conditions, which is in the community interest. In addition, the department loses about $20,000 a year in fees for activities connected with governmental agency construction. Private work performed within the boundaries of the Port of Oakland is charged building and inspection fees, but work done for the port itself is not charged.

Since the department cannot control the level of construction, is not sensitive to its own costs, and must by the nature of its activity provide free services, the city manager does not find this department a dependable source for revenue.

OAKLAND MUNICIPAL AUDITORIUM

The auditorium is part of the Municipal Buildings Department. However, the auditorium director does not acknowledge this formality. The director perceives his role as maximizing profit and not just revenue. He is the most commercial city official on the payroll. The auditorium is one of the few examples in the city where revenue and service objectives do not conflict; therefore, the director can be commercial. He feels that most auditoriums on the West Coast charge enough to meet operating costs and a few even make a profit. He feels that auditorium managers, like himself, are more business oriented than most other government people.

Like many professions, auditorium managers have an association through which they know each other's facilities, costs, and charges. Thus it is a matter of professional pride that the director wants to break even (that is, revenue equals costs) on the operation of his auditorium. However, for the Oakland Auditorium, break even means covering about 60 percent of operating costs. The director is faced with a dilemma. He has been told by a previous city manager that his activity should be self-supporting, and at the same time he has not been allowed to adjust his rates. He feels that his costs are the same regardless of who uses the facility and would like to charge all users the same rate. Instead, as a matter of city policy, he has to maintain separate rate schedules for commercial, noncommercial, and city and governmental users. He feels the city is keeping him from breaking even.

In his view, charities, patriotic organizations, and conventions should not pay less. If the city wants to subsidize these activities, then it should find other funds for them. One of his recommendations in the Financial Capability Study was that conventions should pay the commercial rate and the city should subsidize the rent from the Transient Occupancy Tax. He resents the policy that a school district can use his facility at low rates. The Civil Service Commission, when using the auditorium for examinations, should also pay his costs. He does not think it fair that city departments do not have to pay.

In order to try to break even, the director attempts to get as much as possible out of his commercial clients, parking, and concessions. Commercial rates are higher than the other rate schedules. Parking used to make the difference in his profit and loss statement. Now he has lost his parking lots to the Peralta Junior College and he says, "without this additional source of revenue, it is extremely difficult for any public auditorium to break even, let alone make money." Concessions are his last hope and, as he says, "concession revenues are almost pure profit." Concessions must have been profitable because old-timers in City Hall tell the story about the director putting more oil into the heating system on a comfortable evening in order to raise the temperature in the building. As people would get thirsty from the heat, the concessions would sell more beer and thereby increase the city's revenue.

Fate has been cruel to the director. First, the city would not let him charge charities a commercial rate; then because of the local junior college he lost his parking lots. The final blow came when the city sponsored the building of the coliseum complex and he lost most of his clients. In Oakland it is hard to run a business like a business.

RECREATION DEPARTMENT

Recreation officials believe that the raising of revenue is an ancillary activity of their department. They believe they are not in the business of making money but of providing recreational services and facilities. There is little surface conflict between the stated purpose of the organization and the revenue demands, because revenue considerations are secondary. No recreation official believes that the department should be self-supporting. The department provides an important service to the community; so, it is quite legitimate to expect to be subsidized from general taxes. The Recreation Commission has incorporated this perception into a policy principle: "The Commission recognizes that its basic purpose is to provide a recreation service for all citizens of Oakland, with heavy emphasis on service to children and youth. . . . We anticipate that the large bulk of services will be provided with tax-supported funds on a free basis. Most activities for children are offered free of charge."

The dominance of the recreation function and the downgrading of revenue, however, is mostly camouflage, because the actions of the department indicate considerable concern with revenue. The superintendent of recreation is not an ex-dancing instructor who wandered by mistake into the world of construction paper and arts and crafts; he is a shrewd professional who is aware of the vagaries of municipal finance and pursues the last drop of fiscal blood out of a concession contract. In order to get the most out of tax-supported funds, he insists on a businesslike approach. The budget must include projects which can attract revenue to the department and where citizens will pay a certain amount. The superintendent tries to have departmental, nontax revenue run to 20–25 percent of his total budget. He believes that Oakland's Recreation Department sets the standard for many recreation departments throughout the country. In his view the Recreation Department cannot be a free country club; it should charge up to the 25 percent standard. In the last ten years departmental revenue has nearly doubled; for fiscal year 1968/69 it was expected to be $677,200. Even if officials do not emphasize it, the Recreation Department is in the revenue as well as the recreation business. Because the superintendent is aware of the city's revenue constraint and low assessment growth, he has to behave as if he cares. He must show he is a member of the team. If he does not indicate he is interested in revenue, he may not get his fair share of the general tax money.

I am not saying that the Oakland Recreation Department is being run by a commercial mercenary. Any Oakland department which has something to do with revenue must show concern about the money game. Each department develops a self-supporting standard. The superintendent's 25 percent standard shows the importance of the department's recreational purpose. If the

Recreation Department were, in fact, truly commercial, the standard would be closer to 100 percent self-supporting. The perceived service output of a public organization is a key variable for understanding revenue orientations. The greater the service orientation of the official, the less his concern with revenue.

Top officials of the Recreation Department undoubtedly feel some psychological conflict. To establish fees strictly for raising revenue conflicts with the objectives of recreation. Therefore, revenue is subordinated to recreation by establishing a diverse set of functional criteria for fees. The raising of revenue to recover costs is one function, and equity, administrative convenience, rationing, and regulation are all involved. Fees serve many functions.

Equity is introduced by the ability-to-pay principle and not by a consideration of benefit. Price discrimination, throughout most of the department's fee schedules, results from the official's notion of who can afford to pay. For example, organized school-aged groups are exempt from paying for recreational clubrooms, while most organized adult groups do pay for the same facility. The Recreation Commission states its policy for swimming pool fees as: "the amount of admission charged is based upon a study of the ability of the cross-section of people to pay." Operationally, ability-to-pay means that children should pay less than adults.

Sometimes the function of a fee is to encourage attendance. One way to provide for stability in the administration of programs is to charge. A fee, such as for the Swim to Live program, insures a certain minimal attendance. Consistency in attendance is important to the superintendent because of the high cost of skilled professionals involved in his programs. He would find it difficult to justify his personnel costs if people did not attend. When a client pays something for a service, he feels that he should get his money's worth, so he attends. The use of a fee to encourage attendance satisfies both client and official.

Fees are also set to discourage use, which is another way of saying that the skilled use of price mechanisms can ration scarce resources. There is only a certain amount of space on the city's golf courses, camps, and Lake Merritt; and fees are set to limit use. Rationing, however, is employed to discriminate between clients. The basic rule of children over adults is employed. In addition, nonresident fees are higher than resident fees; this price discrimination is particularly evident in charges for boat storage and summer camps. The justification for high nonresident fees is that these clients do not pay property tax to Oakland.

Regulation in the interests of the health and safety of Oakland's population is another function of fees. A recreation official cites learning to sail as an example of safety and a catering permit as an example of the health criteria.

Finally, fees are set to recover costs and to bring in extra revenue for enriching or broadening a particular program. High-cost programs are expected to partially pay their own way. A sailboat costs $1,200 and golf courses are expensive to build and maintain. Fees for sailing only partially recover costs, but golf courses are expected to pay for themselves. In some cases a golf course may make a profit from its green fees and concessions; for example, the Lake Chabot Municipal Golf Course made around $39,000 in 1965/66. Another city golf course, however, lost a greater amount.

The functional criteria we have been discussing tell why fees are used by the Recreation Department; they do not necessarily tell how. These criteria of equity, administration, and regulation explain which recreational activities are likely to have fees. However, the actual fee cannot be determined by this diverse set of policies or criteria. In any one situation the criteria will conflict with each other. How does one insure the attendance of poor children? The official wants the child to have a commitment to attend, but the child is too poor to pay the fee.

Even if we assume that only one criterion is operative, we will still not know how the fee is set. Recovery of costs is the dominant criterion for the operation of golf courses. But the separate green fees, locker room charges, and concession rates are not based directly on costs. Unlike many other city departments, the Recreation Department does know its own costs. The department can easily tell the operating cost, revenue, and attendance for each city swimming pool or golf course because the information is used for budget execution. However, prices are set by what other cities charge. Swimming pool fees are related to the "fees charged in nearby jurisdictions for similar services." Family camp fees

must take into consideration the charges made by other comparable municipal family camps such as Berkeley, Sacramento, and San Francisco.

Green fees are established in line with those being charged at comparable public courses in the area, such as Tilden, Alameda, and the Marine course in San Leandro.

Fees charged for lighted tennis courts are similar to those charged by other park and recreation agencies in the Bay Area.

The rule of competition, charge what your neighbor charges, is a useful shortcut. A city official does not have to worry about public acceptance when he knows the going price. But the use of this rule does result in anomalies in the department's application of its own criteria. Fees for the swimming pools are supposed to be set so as not to deter use, but since 1958 pool attendance has declined 30 percent. The reduction is directly related to the increase in "higher proportion of low income participants." If the main objective of the Oakland Recreation Department is to provide recreation particularly for children, then surely there is something wrong with its current pricing policies. Since low-income children are the biggest users of the pools, perhaps even the minimal fees are too high if the ability to pay criterion is taken seriously. Some adult activities generate a surplus while other adult activities do not begin to pay their way. The surplus is usually used to improve or enlarge the particular activity which generated it. The superintendent is happy as long as *total* revenue is between 20 and 25 percent of his budget; he does not insure that all adult activities pay their own way.

A flagrant violation of the department's norms is the support given to the Oakland Industrial Recreation Association. Founded in the early 1920s, this joint program provides recreational activities for forty-nine industries with about 50,000 *adult* employees. The OIRA is charged a minimal amount for clerical services but is not charged for the costs of the recreation director associated with the program. The Recreation Commission justifies this subsidy by pointing to the familiar rule, what is good for business is good for Oakland: "From an industrial standpoint, the OIRA presents one of the finest selling points that Oakland has to offer. Any industry contemplating relocating gives consideration to the organized recreation facilities of their employees. It is anticipated that this program will increase as the Oakland industrial growth continues."

Some of these inconsistencies are probably due to the complexity of a decision process which involves so many activities. The department keeps track of six swimming pools, fifteen club houses, Lake Merritt boats and launches, golf courses, camps, and a variety of dance, music, and craft classes. Another element of this complexity is that revenue criteria can change with the growth of an activity. Consider this description:

The Oakland Christmas Pageant was initiated in 1919 as a community service to celebrate the Christmas Season in Oakland. For many years the pageant was given free of charge. However, the attendance was large and it was difficult to anticipate the number of people who would attend. To exercise control over this problem, a very small fee was set and money was donated to the School Milk Fund. The costs of the pageant increased over the years and it was decided by the Recreation Commission to partially defray some of this cost by admission fees. Admission fees and reserved seat fees were established and the money was deposited in the Recreation Fund rather than serving as a donation to the School Milk Fund. It is the policy of the Commission to partially defray the cost of the pageant.

The pageant is a child-centered activity and originally it had no fee. Then because of the administrative need to stabilize attendance a small fee was set to regulate attendance. But costs became too high; so the cost recovery norm was introduced. Parents are charged $1.00 or $1.50 to see their children participate. What was once a wholly subsidized activity is now one-third self-supporting. Recreation Department officials' perception of the city revenue constraint and their desire to appear responsible and businesslike encourage them to compromise their professional recreational objectives and to attempt to recover costs.

CITY DEPARTMENTS CANNOT BE USED
TO MAXIMIZE REVENUE

The sections on the city departments have stressed their diversity of revenue behavior which differs by the services they provide, by their reasons for levying fees, by their knowledge of costs and expenses, and by their degree of autonomy from central control. Departments do have in common the violation of the city norm of cost recovery. In general, departments are not concerned about revenue, and they are not fiscal innovators. For those that are concerned, service objectives often conflict with or prevent revenue maximization. The revenue-service conflict can, as in the case of the Recreation Department, compromise the basic goals of the organization. Even when the revenue-service conflict is minimal, events outside the department's control can interfere with revenue objectives as was indicated by the discussion of the auditorium and the Building and Housing Department. Department officials in the city are the spenders not the providers. City departments cannot be used to maximize revenue.

SUMMARY

In this chapter, the effect of the city's revenue constraint on the behavior of its principal officials was examined. Pivotal among all city officials is the manager; he is the fiscal innovator and socialization agent. If city officials and the public are inclined to forget about the lack of money, he will remind them of Oakland's impoverishment. The revenue constraint intensifies his management beliefs in the separation of politics from administration, in the superiority of efficiency, and in his emphasis on fiscal realism in finding revenue to offset the property tax. The City Council's behavior reflects the influence of the manager. Councilmen are not initiators of tax policy, but they do protect the city's tax base and consider taxpayers their constituents. They have a business orientation and are knowledgeable about taxes. Councilmen worry less about service and more about cutting costs. The council is the caretaker of the tax rate. City departments live with the consequences of Oakland's revenue constraint, but they are not the key to the city's revenue problems.

Their service objectives conflict with revenue maximization. They do not always know their costs and set their rates by other criteria. Even commercial departments cannot break even due to events outside their control. Finally, the fragmented nature of Oakland's organization reinforces the lack of department concern and diversity of revenue behavior.

The city manager and his finance staff are the officials who have to worry about the lack of revenue. They play the important boundary function which helps the city maintain itself. Their search processes, decisions, rules, and tactics are crucial to an understanding of finance.

3

The Revenue Process
and Public Avoidance

Having discussed Oakland's fiscal discretion and identified its key fiscal actors, I will now present an analytical framework in which to integrate this material, using the concepts of the Simon-March-Cyert focus on "good enough" decision making and the perspective achieved by considering the city as an open system.[1] This framework has two major components: the stages of the revenue process from search and decision through administration; and the tactics which the revenue subsystem uses to cope with environmental uncertainty. When fully developed, the framework shows that Oakland officials withdraw from the public—that officials obtain revenue by public avoidance. First, it is necessary to define three terms: revenue subsystem, environment, and tactics.

1. For decision making, see Herbert A. Simon, *Models of Man: Social and Rational* (New York: John Wiley & Sons, Inc., 1957), pp. 241–260; James G. March and Herbert A. Simon, *Organizations* (New York: John Wiley & Sons, Inc., 1958), pp. 137–183; Richard M. Cyert and James G. March, *A Behavioral Theory of the Firm* (Englewood Cliffs, N.J.: Prentice-Hall, Inc., 1963), pp. 114–127. Lindblom's work is also relevant; see Charles E. Lindblom, "The Science of 'Muddling Through,'" *Public Administration Review* 19 (spring 1959): 79–88; David Braybrooke and Charles E. Lindblom, *A Strategy of Decision* (New York: The Free Press of Glencoe, 1963), pp. 37–110. For the open system approach see Daniel Katz and Robert L. Kahn, *The Social Psychology of Organizations* (New York: John Wiley & Sons, Inc., 1966), pp. 8–29; and James D. Thompson, *Organizations in Action* (New York: McGraw-Hill Book Co., 1967), pp. 6–10.

The *revenue subsystem* is the recurring role behavior that is associated with the supply of revenue to the city (the system).[2] One does not have to adopt the complete conceptual paraphernalia of general systems theory to observe that the city manager and his small finance staff help the city survive by finding new sources of revenue. At the center of the revenue subsystem's role network are the manager, the finance director, and a few analysts. Councilmen and some department heads are on the periphery. Councilmen act as legitimators of the subsystem's policies and occasionally provide informational inputs to the subsystem. Similarly, department heads (such as the traffic engineer) may suggest revenue opportunities; but for all practical purposes, the revenue subsystem is the manager and his finance staff.

The critical boundary function of the revenue subsystem is to maintain the city system by insuring adequate financial resources for task performance by the departments. The subsystem's function is not adaptation; the subsystem does not plan or conduct research seeking to anticipate extreme environmental change. Indeed, Oakland's revenue constraint drives out planning. Why devise elaborate capital improvement plans if there are no resources to fund them? City officials are just beginning to sense that their environment is changing, but they have not developed a social subsystem to cope with this change. Oakland's revenue subsystem is not directed toward obtaining large enough chunks of resources to deal with the extensive social and economic problems that exist. The subsystem looks inward and has a short-term time perspective of no more than three to four years. Expenditure and revenue policies, the output of the revenue subsystem, are directed to the preservation of the status quo and the meeting of the monthly payroll.

The *environment* is difficult to define, but it is not a residual category. It is definitely not some influential lump which political actors take into account. The environment is composed of some of Oakland's citizen-leaders (see chapter 6), heads of tax asso-

2. I am following Katz and Kahn: "role behavior refers to the recurring actions of an individual, appropriately interrelated with the repetitive activities of others so as to yield a predictable outcome. The set of interdependent behaviors comprise a social system or subsystem" (Katz and Kahn, p. 174).

ciations, city employee union representatives, state and federal officials, and heads of independent city agencies such as the port commissioners. Behind these actors who are concerned about taxes from time to time is a quiescent majority, unaware of taxes, that can be mobilized when a tax issue is salient.

Tax issues at the local level are salient only to small attentive publics. In Oakland the politics of local taxation is not intense and involves few actors. This low-intensity politics is character-ized by a fragmented environment and dominated by bureaucrats or professionals.

The environment is fragmented not only by the usual sources of cleavage (such as party, class, and race) but by the tax or revenue source itself. Chapter 1 discussed the myriad sources of local revenue. Now we will see that Oakland's fragmented tax structure contributes to a fragmented environment composed of many small tax publics. There is a transient-occupancy-tax public, and there is a cigarette-tax public. With the exception of tax association representatives, those people in the environment who care about taxes care only about specific taxes, and so the en-vironment becomes fragmented. For the sewer service charge, the attentive public is composed of actors from the few canneries and packing plants and their trade associations. These people are actively concerned about the charge because of its potential effect on their profit margins. Probably they would not be con-cerned about the cigarette tax or the transient-occupancy tax. The hotel and motel men were concerned about the transient-occupancy tax when it was adopted. The cigarette retail and wholesale distributors were concerned about the cigarette tax when it was adopted.

Although the attentive public for any tax may be small, it still is a source of uncertainty. The revenue subsystem is concerned about two types of environmental uncertainty: (1) What is the threshold of approval or opposition to a proposed change in the tax structure? In other words, what will the traffic bear? (2) Will there be any new expenditure demand which cannot be avoided and for which the city has insufficient resources?

Tactics define the relationship between the subsystem and environment. In the financial world, there are two basic kinds of behavior. A revenue subsystem can avoid the tax publics in the environment, or it can have contact with them. It can run away from the conflict which a tax public may generate, or it can face the tax public and bargain, exchange, and negotiate. This choice for public officials, between public avoidance and public contact, provides us with a useful way to classify tactics:

(*1*) *Consensual.* The subsystem perceives a consensus on tax matters and ignores the environment.

(*2*) *Negotiatory.* The subsystem, on a face-to-face basis, conducts transactions with elements in the environment.

(*3*) *Anticipatory.* The subsystem accepts the environment as given and attempts to manipulate it.

As Figure 1 illustrates, Oakland's revenue subsystem uses all three tactics to reduce environmental uncertainty and to avoid public conflict. Avoidance, paradoxically, links the revenue subsystem to the environment.

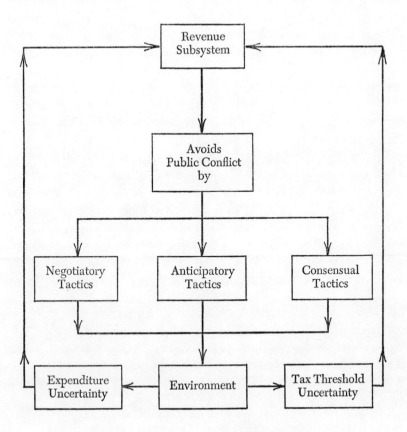

FIGURE 1. Tactics to avoid public conflict

Consensual tactics do not involve interaction with elements of the environment. Following the adage, "an old tax is a good tax,"[3] the revenue subsystem uses consensual tactics to make incremental changes in *existing* revenue sources. In one sense, a consensual tactic is a form of anticipatory tactics. The subsystem anticipates there will be no trouble with the public so it makes changes. The distinction, however, clarifies that financial behavior differs by whether the proposed action is associated with an existing or a new tax. Subsystem members adjust rates and extend the coverage of a tax without any public participation or consultation. The subsystem modifies the existing tax structure, which lacks public salience, with impunity.

In Oakland, negotiatory tactics are used with cooperative friends. Such negotiation between the subsystem and the environment involves quibbling over price. The issue is not whether a tax should be adopted but how much the public will pay, and there is not much conflict because the subsystem gives up fiscal discretion.[4] The revenue subsystem does not attempt to control or to bargain with uncooperative and abrasive elements of the environment. Instead, the subsystem contracts boundaries to reduce environmental conflict and avoid uncertainty. Such behavior is the antithesis of the system-expansion hypothesis of coping with environmental uncertainty.[5]

This withdrawing system behavior carries over to a heavy reliance on anticipatory tactics which substitutes for negotiation. The more the subsystem anticipates environmental change, the less it needs to negotiate with its environment through an exchange process, such as bargaining. The subsystem anticipates reactions so as to avoid having to negotiate. Better to lose and not fight than to fight and lose is the rule. The revenue subsystem does not seek to confront the taxpayer but prefers to hide taxes

3. James M. Buchanan, *Public Finance in Democratic Process: Fiscal Institutions and Individual Choice* (Chapel Hill: University of North Carolina Press, 1967), pp. 58–64.

4. In some cities, negotiation involves conflict; see Robert L. Peabody, "Seattle Seeks a Tax," in *State and Local Government: A Case Book*, ed. by Edwin A. Bock (Birmingham: University of Alabama Press, 1963), pp. 495–514.

5. For example, see Katz and Kahn, pp. 99–104 and Thompson, pp. 36–37.

so that they will not be felt. The subsystem manipulates the environment rather than transacts with it.

The revenue subsystem avoids the public and uses anticipatory tactics through each stage of the revenue process, as shown in Table 6. When the subsystem searches for revenue, it anticipates future expenditure requirements. The subsystem anticipates its revenue needs for the short term, making no attempt to optimize revenue input to the city over time. When the subsystem decides on a particular revenue source, it anticipates taxpayer resistance. The choice of a new tax is based on simplifying tactics. Looking for precedents takes the place of tax policy analysis. When the subsystem is seeking public acceptance of its new tax, it keeps the attentive public small by anticipatory tactics. For example, by proposing taxes sequentially the subsystem fragments the attentive public so that it can negotiate with friends. Even when the subsystem administers the tax structure, it seeks to avoid future confrontations with the public. Revenue is estimated conservatively, and the property tax is never cut to a minimum. Much administrative revenue behavior involves hedging, building financial surpluses, and other short-term contingency schemes.

TABLE 6: Oakland's Revenue Subsystem Relies on
Anticipatory Tactics

Revenue Process Stage	Subsystem Tactics
Search	Anticipatory
Decision	Anticipatory
Acceptance	Anticipatory, negotiatory
Administration	Anticipatory, negotiatory, consensual

Limited rationality also characterizes revenue behavior. The subsystem's limited rationality and its use of anticipatory tactics are related at various stages of the revenue process. Revenue is estimated conservatively because of the simple methods which are used and also because subsystem members want to hedge against expenditure demands. Search is simple and selective because the subsystem looks for taxes which are more likely to be accepted by the public. At each stage of the revenue process the subsystem cannot fully predict outcomes and copes with this uncertainty by attempting to anticipate public reactions. The subsystem's fear of the public and its limited rationality converge in the revenue avoidance process. From search, to decision, to acceptance, and finally to administration, the subsystem avoids the public.

SEARCH

Search initiates the process of coping with the city's revenue constraint and anticipates future expenditure requirements. The open-ended nature of the revenue problem encourages the recurrence of the search activity. The revenue subsystem attempts to look at many but not all revenue sources. Because of the subsystem's own tax preferences, resource limitations, and diverting environmental demands, search is fragmented and superficial. Some search efforts are not immediately useful because of environmental uncertainty. Search can be make-believe and ritualistic. Finally, since the subsystem has limited search resources, it relies heavily on information received from other cities and the League of California Cities.

REVENUE SEARCH IS A RECURRENT ACTIVITY

Because of Oakland's fiscal constraint, the search for revenue is a recurrent activity. Search behavior in Oakland departs slightly from Cyert's and March's concept of problemistic search.[6] It is true that search is stimulated by a problem, but in Oakland the money problem is always there; the revenue problem is never solved. Only in some vague systemic sense of a community level of expenditure support can we see an aspiration level being set and satisfied. Within perceived tolerances of support, city officials simply seek to increase revenue. The revenue subsystem does not specify an aspiration level, but it acts to anticipate short-term environmental demand or change by developing a menu of potential revenue sources. An approximate description of Oakland's dominant revenue search pattern is Thompson's concept of opportunistic surveillance: "It is possible to conceive of monitoring behavior which scans the environment for opportunities—which does not wait to be activated by a problem and which does

6. Cyert and March, pp. 120–122.

not therefore stop when a problem solution has been found." [7]

Related to the concept of opportunistic surveillance are Downs' notions of scanning and free information, which he includes as a minimal level of search in his model.[8] Downs believes that all officials conduct such scanning, while Thompson believes that opportunistic surveillance is infrequent. For Downs, scanning can be a jump-off point out of equilibrium into a more intensive search process. For Thompson, scanning is an opportunity, rarely taken, to cope with environmental change.

In Oakland the revenue subsystem scans the *Wall Street Journal*, various professional periodicals such as *Municipal Finance*, and the League of California Cities publications. Reading is supplemented by phone calls and other professional contacts. The city's documentary stamp tax on real property transfers was adopted employing such minimal search efforts. The League of California Cities sent Oakland a model ordinance for the transfer tax. After a few phone calls to neighboring cities and the league to find out what other cities were doing, a recommendation was forwarded to and adopted by the City Council. Opportunistic surveillance is used frequently and at minimal cost.

Oakland's search behavior emphasizes anticipation and not reaction to a specific environmental stimulus. City officials do not wait to be hit with a salary increase request to begin the search for money. Through opportunistic surveillance the revenue subsystem has its menu of suggested new sources from which the council can choose. Over a year after a utilities consumption tax had been identified as a possible revenue source, the council adopted it to meet police demands for wage increases. Occasionally, search will be of the specific stimulus-reaction type when the revenue is needed to finance capital projects such as the museum and major sewer replacement. But because capital projects usually are deferred, the dominant search pattern is oriented to future *operating* expenditures. This emphasis on the operating budget facilitates a generic revenue hunt separated from the specific stimulus of environmental demands. Subsystem members search for revenue irrespective of the projected use of the funds.

7. Thompson, p. 151.
8. Anthony Downs, *Inside Bureaucracy* (Boston: Little, Brown and Co., 1967), pp. 168–171.

Generally, Cyert's and March's assumptions that search is motivated, simpleminded, and biased fits Oakland behavior. However, problems and resulting search patterns should be differentiated, as shown in Figure 2. Open-ended problems, such as Oakland's revenue constraint, should be distinguished from closed problems, capable of short-term solution. Closed problems are related to simple stimulus-reaction types of search behavior. In the closed problem context, it makes sense to talk about alternatives and satisfying solutions. In the open problem context there are no satisfying alternatives; for example, no single identified revenue source is large enough in dollars to stop search behavior. For balancing the year's budget, sources on the revenue menu may be used additively or as alternatives. But balancing the

MODEL I: OPEN PROBLEM STIMULUS

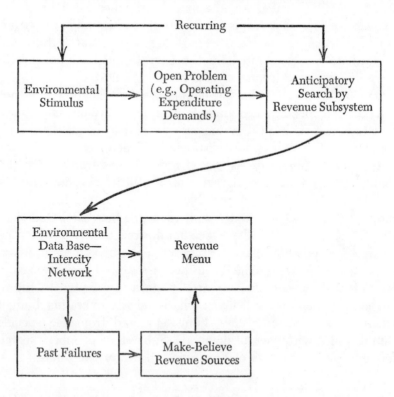

FIGURE 2. Two search models

MODEL II: CLOSED PROBLEM STIMULUS

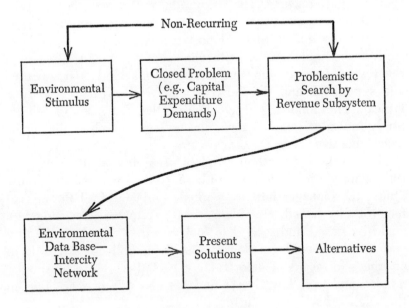

FIGURE 2. (Continued)

budget is a closed problem and the creation of the revenue menu is an open problem because it is designed to cope with the budgets of the short-term future. By anticipating that the city will require additional revenue, officials seek to control their environment. Recurrent, anticipatory search is one mechanism of uncertainty avoidance.[9]

REVENUE SEARCH IS FRAGMENTED AND SUPERFICIAL

The revenue subsystem has not the time, data base, or staff to conduct a comprehensive review of all city revenue. The Financial Capability Study, as it evolved in concept, was to undertake a comprehensive review. Departments would review their fees and minor charges and the Finance Department would summarize the departmental work and analyze the major sources of revenue such as sales tax and the business license. The total work load was spread throughout the city organization to officials

9. Cyert and March, pp. 118–120.

who were not in the revenue subsystem and had different perceptions and concerns. The study educated some officials about the city's revenue constraint, and major and minor revenue sources were added to Oakland's tax structure. However, the study was comprehensive neither in scope nor in the intensity of the review process. Revenue search in Oakland is fragmented and superficial, and the behavior associated with this study is typical. The following discussion of the Financial Capability Study indicates some reasons why revenue search could not be comprehensive.

The revenue subsystem conducts search operations from a rudimentary information system base. In the Financial Capability Study, the manager initially wanted a review of all the myriad fees the city levied. His advice was first to see if existing fees could be raised and second to look for areas in which the city was not but could be charging, such as collecting fees from attorneys for accident reports. He expected search to be simpleminded and to follow Cyert's and March's rule of searching "in the neighborhood of the current alternative." [10]

However, seeking information around the current alternative assumed that the current alternative was known and defined. In fact, the point of departure, the existing revenue structure, was ill-defined. Finance officials did not know who was responsible for what revenue source. Because they did not know, they made the departments responsible for omissions; thus some fees were sure to be overlooked. As the city auditor noted, departments collect fees when there is no legal basis for doing so and do not collect when they should. There was no manual listing all city revenues, which could be used to cut the subsystem's information costs.

The revenue subsystem does not have control over requisite informational sources. The subsystem attempted to determine the effect of the port's possessory interest practices and discovered that neither the port, the city, nor the county assessor had a complete list of city property which was under port control. Without knowing which land the city owned, the difference in assessed valuation, due to leasing arrangements was impossible to compute. The fragmented nature of Oakland's political system also contributed to the inadequacy of the data base. For example,

10. *Ibid.*, p. 121.

information from autonomous organizations such as the Redevelopment Agency and the Coliseum Corporation was difficult to obtain. Although these agencies received revenue related to city operations, they did not know their own revenue status and refused to project revenue receipts. Because these agencies did not want to commit themselves, there was an incentive not to cooperate.

The revenue subsystem excludes or downgrades some revenue sources to cope with the consequences of a comprehensive review. Concentrating on a review of the total revenue structure reduced the time for considering departures from the existing base and menu. Trying to review everything, the subsystem had trouble focusing on particular revenues. Departments did not make many revenue suggestions, but the number of particular sources which required attention inundated the subsystem. There was a tendency to aggregate or group revenue sources as means of coping with the detail. The more revenues were grouped to make the review manageable, the less it was possible to take action on single fees. Because of the information overload, the subsystem put aside many revenue suggestions for future investigation. Reimbursements were ignored because of the lack of a clear definition of what should be included under the rubric of revenue. Bonds and federal funds were downgraded in importance because of previous unreliability. State gas tax and other funds which are outside the city's discretion were also excluded.

The revenue subsystem includes its own tax preferences. Bias in the search process acted against comprehensiveness by excluding some revenue sources and including others. To have preferences was to create salience and some criteria for increased attention. Some revenue sources got more intensive search than others because the council or the manager had expressed an interest in them. In chapter 2 the manager's inclination toward fiscal realism and detail was described. The initial emphasis on fees in the Financial Capability Study was a product of his recognition of the city's narrow fiscal discretion and his detailed administrative style. The manager also drew the boundaries for search by stating where not to search. With his usual pragmatic flair, he cautioned not to bother with building inspection fees set by western building codes because they could not be touched politically. The finance director also introduced search bias. He felt that utility companies had an excessive tax advantage in California and should pay more money to the cities; so he had an analyst search the statutes to see if it was possible to levy an in lieu tax on local utilities. A councilman was unhappy about the city putting money into the coliseum and not getting any revenue and had openly advocated an admissions or amusement tax. The subsystem reviewed the admissions tax despite its concern for the possible effect on Oakland's obtaining a major league baseball franchise.

The revenue subsystem has many demands on its resources. The subsystem could not spend all of its time, energy, and expertise on revenue search. Budget preparation and execution, Model Cities grantsmanship, and other more pressing work intervened, so that search had to be cut down to the size of the subsystem's own resource constraint. Like many administrative situations, the agenda was set by environmental forces outside the control of the subsystem.

Given the limited resources which the subsystem can devote to revenue search, city officials are satisfied to find a few revenue sources which can be added to the tax structure. After identifying a likely revenue source, the subsystem concentrates its efforts on computing the yield for several rate schedules and roughly testing political and administrative feasibility. The subsystem does not conduct an economic analysis because it does not have the time, expertise, or inclination to trace the effects of a tax. Incidence is a word which is not in the vocabulary of most of the members of the revenue subsystem. The subsystem does not waste its few resources in studying revenue in depth but prefers to examine as many different revenue sources as it can. Small dollar sources receive as much attention as large dollar sources. Comprehensive search has to be limited because of the subsystem members' own tax preferences, the inadequate data base for the current tax structure, the lack of organizational control over informational inputs, and the diversion of subsystem efforts to more pressing assignments.

REVENUE SEARCH BECOMES MAKE-BELIEVE
WHEN THERE ARE FEW ALTERNATIVES

The effort devoted to gathering intelligence about revenue sources which the subsystem believes will not ameliorate the current revenue situation is ritualistic search behavior. Officials go through the same motions, perhaps with less intensity, but they do not expect much to happen: the tax will not be implemented and the grant will be too small. If officials had a choice, they would search only in areas of likely payoff. However, new acceptable revenue sources are hard to find; so the revenue subsystem searches for uncertain, less reliable sources and in areas of past failures. No one in the revenue subsystem expected the past failure, the municipal or payroll income tax, to be adopted by the council and accepted by the public in the near future. Nevertheless, on several occasions the subsystem has investigated the tax, computed the yield for Oakland, and submitted its findings to the council—to be ignored due to past opposition from the Chamber of Commerce and organized labor.

In developing their revenue menu, unreliable financing sources, such as bonds and federal grants, are ritualistically included within the scope of search. The revenue subsystem bias against these sources is not in using the funds but in relying on them. Bonds require elections, and a revenue source which relies on the voter introduces uncertainty. The finance director cites a primary advantage of lease-purchase financing as not requiring elections. Similarly, revenue bonds are preferred over general obligation bonds, because they may not require elections, or if they do, only a majority vote is necessary for approval.[11]

The mayor, manager, and several department officials go to Washington to get federal grants. They fill out the forms and play the game, but they are skeptical. Dealing with the federal government introduces uncertainty. The revenue subsystem has no way of predicting the amount of federal funds which the city will receive in the short-term future. Officials are content to know which funds are coming in, and they reduce their anxiety by looking at revenue that is tied to committed or ongoing programs.

Trying to anticipate the reactions of the council and citizens and whether the federal government will grant the requested funds are forms of environmental uncertainty. Generally, the more environmental uncertainty attached to a revenue source, the more the search behavior will be ritualistic. Sometimes ritual-

11. Oakland, Budget and Finance Office, *Financial Capability Study*, Part 1 (no date), pp. 14–15.

istic search is conducted for the sake of completeness so that officials can say, yes, we investigated that revenue source. Sometimes it is a testing tactic that assumes the revenue source will not be adopted the first time but might in the future. In most cases such search is a way of accepting uncertainty and living with it. Ritualistic search behavior cannot resolve Oakland's revenue problems. Of course sometimes a grant comes in, or a bond issue passes, or the council passes a tax when there is some vocal opposition; but most of the time ritualistic search behavior results in nothing except reducing bureaucratic anxiety.

REVENUE SEARCH RELIES ON AN INTERCITY COMMUNICATION NETWORK

City officials do not investigate any revenue sources in depth. Instead, they look for precedents as a way to cut their information costs. Either through the League of California Cities or directly, cities in California are continually exchanging revenue intelligence in search of precedents. By writing and telephoning, Oakland officials have an inexpensive way of screening revenue sources for political and administrative feasibility. For administrative practices, the subsystem is likely to check with smaller cities such as Sacramento, Santa Monica, Long Beach, and San Jose. For political testing, the subsystem waits for the leadership of large cities such as Los Angeles and San Francisco. The geographic boundaries of search are mainly within the state. Occasionally, due to professional contacts and reading, revenue subsystem members will be aware of revenue activity outside the state, such as a major review of goals and resources in Dallas, Texas. Since most California cities share much the same revenue headaches, search is not complex and involved. The fact that search is spread out geographically should not be interpreted as complicating the search process. Indeed, the city communication network facilitates search. By consulting with other cities Oakland's revenue subsystem extends its own meager search resources.

Search in Oakland is much closer to scanning or opportunistic surveillance than to a simple problem response. Sometimes search has a payoff; other times it is make-believe. It is never an intensive but rather an extensive revenue hunt. Thus search is an open-ended, minimal cost activity which anticipates generic revenue requirements for the short-term time period. The product of the search activity is the creation of a revenue menu for members of the revenue subsystem to select taxes when needed.

DECISION

In selecting a tax from the revenue menu, the revenue subsystem habitually applies anticipatory criteria. Justification to the council, maintenance of public acceptance, and ease of administrative execution are factors which the subsystem anticipates in making revenue decisions. Balanced against the benefits of projected yields are the counterweights of political and administrative convenience.

TABLE 7: The Subsystem Selects Low Yield-Low Political Cost Revenues

	Political Costs	
Yields	High	Low
High	—	0
Low	—	+

In Table 7, high and low political costs have been juxtaposed against high and low yields. From examining previous tax selection decisions, I expect that the low yield–low political cost revenue source has the greatest probability of choice by the revenue subsystem. The minus sign in the table indicates a low chance of selection and the zero indicates that no known tax source falls in this category.

Political costs are incurred when the subsystem activates a segment of the environment and is forced to negotiate.[12] These costs could be measured in terms of sacrificed resources such as time, adjustment in rates, earmarking of funds by elements of the environment, or council rejection of the legitimacy of the sub-

12. A good explanation of political costs is found in Aaron Wildavsky, "The Political Economy of Efficiency: Cost Benefit Analysis, Systems Analysis, and Program Budgeting," *Public Administration Review* 26 (December 1966): 308–309; see also Erik Lindahl, "Tax Principles and Tax Policy," in *International Economic Papers*, no. 10 (London: Macmillan and Co. Ltd., 1960), p. 50.

system. With no predictable constituency for increased taxes, the subsystem seeks to avoid conflict and to keep the public small and quiet.

I assume that a high-yielding source would add 10 percent to the existing revenue structure (currently about $5–6 million). Several years ago the sales tax probably was a high-yielding and low-political-cost revenue source. Today, the subsystem, unfortunately, has not uncovered any new revenue source which has a high yield but low political costs. A revenue source, such as the municipal income tax, which has high political costs and high yield is not likely to be seriously suggested for council adoption. A revenue source such as an entrance fee to the museum is not likely to be levied, because the expected political conflict is much greater than the expected revenue. The net result of the subsystem calculus is the selection of low-yielding taxes which involve minimal political costs and only a small segment of the environment.

The revenue subsystem faces a greater amount of uncertainty in estimating political costs than yields. The tactics which the subsystem adopts are designed to reduce this political uncertainty.

AVOID TAXPAYER RESISTANCE:
FOLLOW THE LEADER

The subsystem never pioneers a new tax. It uses other California cities to test the legality of a revenue source and to ascertain its political acceptance. Oakland adopts a wait-and-see stance for new taxes. If other cities get away with a new tax, then maybe Oakland can. In California there is tax leadership among the cities which is similar to price leadership in an oligopolistic economic situation. The subsystem watches what happens when Los Angeles or San Francisco passes a new tax, and then they wait for a smaller city to adopt it. For example, after Los Angeles and Pacific Grove had passed the utilities consumption tax, Oakland adopted it. Now several other cities are getting on the bandwagon.

By finding precedents in other cities, the subsystem can screen a new revenue source over time for political feasibility. The subsystem once seriously considered a property transfer tax. Both

Los Angeles and Arcadia had had some success with the tax, but then other cities such as Santa Barbara, Piedmont, and Berkeley ran into opposition from local real estate brokers' associations. The opposition in these cities was so strong that the property transfer tax was defeated by municipal referendum or repealed. Thereafter, Oakland's revenue subsystem dropped consideration of the tax. It was much easier to go along with the state documentary stamp tax which taxed the same base, real property sales, but yielded only a fraction (about 5 percent) of the property transfer tax. The subsystem traded potential political costs for a lower yield.

The subsystem's reliance on the California city communication network to find revenue precedents can be damaging, because it reduces the likelihood of radical departure from existing California revenue sources. For example, other cities throughout the country have adopted some versions of a municipal income tax, but this does not impress Oakland's revenue subsystem. A California city has to break the ice before Oakland will move. Obviously if all California cities wait for some other city to initiate a new revenue source, the financial condition of local government in California will not be significantly improved. Fortunately for Oakland, a few California cities occasionally are willing to fight political battles to get revenue.

AVOID TAXPAYER RESISTANCE:
INDIRECT TAXATION

The revenue subsystem chooses taxes to avoid public involvement. The subsystem's objective is to have the city adopt revenue sources which no one will know about until the tax has to be paid and perhaps not then. How to find taxes that will be paid but not felt is the problem. Evidently this is not a new problem, as Buchanan's discussion of Amilcare Puviani's work on public finance illustrates.[13] About seventy years ago Puviani suggested that rulers create "fiscal illusions" to minimize taxpayer resistance and "have the effect of making taxpayers think that taxes to which they are subjected are less burdensome than they actually are."[14] Puviani suggested several means for creating fiscal illu-

13. Buchanan, pp. 128–137.
14. *Ibid.,* p. 131.

sions. His emphasis on a fragmented tax structure with many small taxes and indirect taxation such as excises is congruent with the behavior of Oakland's revenue subsystem.

Oakland follows a nationwide trend of state and local government reliance on indirect taxation. In addition to the state sales tax and gasoline taxes, Oakland has levied a transient occupancy tax, cigarette tax, utilities consumption tax, documentary stamp tax, and has been contemplating the adoption of an admissions tax—all of which are indirect taxes on sales transactions.

Eckstein reports that the "American tax system has been gradually changing toward indirect taxation." [15] There are many reasons for this trend, such as the often stated preemption of the income tax by the federal government. I am not suggesting, therefore, that the nationwide trend toward indirect taxation is mainly due to the bureaucratic desire to reduce the taxpayer's awareness of his burden. For Oakland the explanation is simple. The revenue system has limited discretion to begin with, and by its follow-the-leader rule the subsystem has excluded, for the time being, municipal income taxes. Officials believe the property tax is exhausted. Other than fees and charges, what is left? Indirect taxes, chopped up by commodity to make them palatable, is the path of minimal taxpayer resistance. Oakland officials are conscious of looking for the path of minimal taxpayer resistance. A councilman, at an open meeting, declared his support for the admissions tax by stating that it was like the hotel tax (that is, the transient occupancy tax), because people do not know they are paying it. Oakland officials are not unique in their revenue behavior; using indirect taxes as the path of minimal taxpayer resistance is a historical fact of public finance. In discussing taxation in England during the eighteenth century, Barker states, "Here we touch an old issue of politics which is still with us. There is always a natural facility about indirect taxes. The payers of direct taxes, Walpole once remarked, were pigs that squealed if they were touched; the payers of indirect taxes were only sheep that let themselves be sheared in silence." [16]

15. Otto Eckstein, "Indirect Versus Direct Taxes: Implications for Stability Investment," in *Public Finance and Fiscal Policy*, ed. Joseph Scherer and James A. Papke (Boston: Houghton Mifflin Co., 1966), p. 165.
16. Ernest Barker, *The Development of Public Services in Western Europe, 1660–1930* (London: Oxford University Press, 1944), p. 57.

Puviani also pointed out the illusory effects on the taxpayer of paying a lot of small taxes rather than one large payment. Oakland has a fragmented tax structure composed of small, low-yielding taxes. Small taxes have two related dimensions. First, as Puviani suggested, the individual pays many small taxes which the subsystem expects the taxpayer will feel are nominal. Second, small revenue sources stimulate only a segment of the environment to pay attention to a particular tax. Oakland's fragmented tax structure splinters the attentive part of the public.

Small taxes are hidden taxes. Usually the taxpayer pays without complaint. Some resistance occurs at council meetings after the tax bills are received. In any case the subsystem has to cope only with token complaints. When the utilities consumption tax was being considered, the Chamber of Commerce made a perfunctory appearance at a council meeting. The chamber requested a sliding scale because business might leave Oakland.[17] The council turned down the request and adopted a flat charge of 5 percent on all utility bills other than water. Besides some grumbling from the utility companies who would do the collecting for the city, and a few letters from business and industrial groups such as the Oakland Wholesale Fruit and Produce Merchants Association, the tax was passed with practically no opposition. After the bills were sent out, some small consumers complained. The finance director received a total of fifteen letters and an average of five telephone calls a day for the first month and a half. The director expects to take to court about fifty citizens who refused to pay the tax. The revenue subsystem had chosen wisely. The tax was small enough not to activate a large vocal opposition. Taxpayers complied without much complaint.

When taxes are nominal, the taxpayer does not bother to complain. The costs of protest in terms of taxpayers' energy and time are probably greater than the charge. Small, hidden taxes work. Once, by mistake, the East Bay Municipal Utilities District billed Piedmont residents for Oakland's sewer service charge. Forty percent of the Piedmont residents who were billed paid

17. Oakland, City Clerk, Council Minutes, August 1, 1968.

Oakland the charge without question. One might argue that 60 percent of the Piedmont residents did not pay and therefore hidden taxes are not effective. However, for a Piedmont resident to pay an Oakland bill is similar to an individual paying a bill from a department store in which he knows he has no account. Most people would call the department store to complain. The fact that 40 percent of the Piedmont residents paid without complaint substantiates the effectiveness of nominal taxes.

If taxes are to remain hidden, then rates must be nominal. How does a member of the revenue subsystem know that a rate is nominal? How small is small? Where will be the threshold of political opposition? In considering a rate revision to the sewer-service charge, for example, members of the subsystem disagreed on what tactic to use. The finance director wanted to build up the charge slowly, making small changes each year until the charge was one dollar for residents. The manager wanted to go directly to one dollar. The finance director felt that the impact of the charge should be softened by piecemeal change. Each official had a different perception of what the traffic would bear. Finally, rates were revised to one dollar and no public opposition was encountered. The more desperate officials are for revenue, the more likely they are to raise their perception of the threshold of political opposition.

Officials can make adjustments, other than rate revisions, to keep the attentive public small. Cutting down the coverage of a tax is one way. For example, when the subsystem decided to include vending machine operators under the business license, it concluded that the tax would not apply to nickel and penny machines. The expected revenue was not worth the expected trouble.

As is shown in Figure 3, low-yielding taxes are the consequence of tactics that are designed to minimize taxpayer resistance. Follow the leader, use indirect taxes, encourage a fragmented tax structure, have nominal rates: these are tactics to keep the attentive public small, to avoid the public, and to cut off opposition before it develops. The subsystem prefers to anticipate the political costs of a revenue source. When it cannot estimate the political costs, it retreats to ritualistic behavior and suggests the source as a trial balloon with some other tax to see what happens.

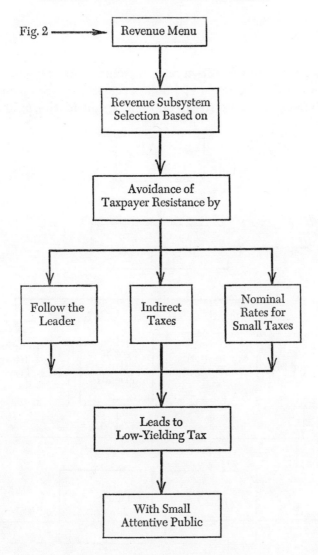

Fig. 2 ──────▶ Revenue Menu

Revenue Subsystem
Selection Based on

Avoidance of
Taxpayer Resistance by

Follow the
Leader

Indirect
Taxes

Nominal
Rates for
Small Taxes

Leads to
Low-Yielding Tax

With Small
Attentive Public

FIGURE 3. Anticipatory decision rules

If significant opposition develops, it will withdraw its suggestion and wait a few years for the fiscal situation to further deteriorate and then suggest it again. The choice of low yield–low political cost taxes satisfies the subsystem's concern with environmental uncertainty and fulfills its function of organizational maintenance.

ACCEPTANCE

If members of the subsystem have selected a new revenue source wisely, then the problems of public acceptance will be minimal. Nevertheless, the subsystem continues to avoid the public even

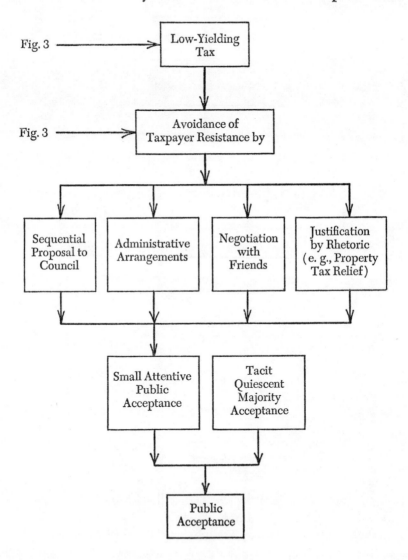

FIGURE 4. Public acceptance

in the public acceptance stage of the revenue process. As shown in Figure 4, the subsystem attempts to avoid taxpayer resistance by proposing taxes sequentially, by adopting administrative arrangements which make public participation difficult, by negotiating with friends to further resolve conflict, and by justifying a new tax with the rhetoric of property tax relief.

TAXES ARE PROPOSED SEQUENTIALLY

The attentive public can be kept small by fragmenting the council's decision process. The council, as gatekeeper, is the usual site for the final acceptance or rejection of a new tax. If there is going to be opposition, it will show up in some form at council meetings. The revenue subsystem does not submit its total revenue menu for approval at one time. It tries not to link taxes so that approval of one may be dependent on approval of another. Sometimes, because of the required dollar amount, the subsystem has to submit several small sources simultaneously. The usual tactic, however, is to submit revenue sources one at a time. Even if elements of the environment want to form a coalition in opposition, it is difficult to do so when the proposed taxes are submitted sequentially throughout the fiscal year.

ADMINISTRATIVE ARRANGEMENTS KEEP THE ATTENTIVE PUBLIC SMALL

After a tax passes, city officials will justify its adoption by pointing to the openness of the decision process: The tax was publicized in the newspapers; the tax ordinance was read three times in open meetings; public organizations were invited to testify. These statements are partially true.

Friends are usually invited to attend meetings. Official notices are buried in the newspaper want ads. Open meetings are scheduled at inconvenient times and in rooms in the City Hall which are not well known. When the sewer service charge rate increase was passed, only a few citizens were able to find the meeting. Besides the council, members of the revenue subsystem, a reporter, a neighborhood association leader, a few business organization leaders, and myself, there was only one nonaffiliated citizen who had come to complain about high taxes. The subsystem does not act to increase public consideration of taxes but adopts administrative arrangements which make public participation difficult.

NEGOTIATION WITH FRIENDS

Ironically, the importance of negotiatory tactics is that the subsystem generally avoids them. Negotiation means political interaction with perhaps antagonistic segments of the environment. The revenue subsystem has avoided conflict by giving up jurisdiction. As I pointed out in chapter 1, city officials have given away fiscal discretion for the certainty and efficiency of state tax collections and distribution. Subsystem members negotiate with friends not enemies. Oakland officials attempt to form coalitions with similarly situated governmental officials. The subsystem members negotiate with individuals by cooperation in which a clear quid pro quo can be established. Such tactics are characterized by minimal conflict.

Because the subsystem prefers to avoid trouble by anticipation, the instances of face-to-face negotiation on tax matters are infrequent. An example of negotiation by cooperation was when the subsystem asked a representative of the Chamber of Commerce to inform the council that the chamber supported an increase in the transient occupancy tax. The chamber supported an increase because the tax financed a large part of its program. A more dramatic example of negotiation by cooperation will be discussed in chapter 4. This example will illustrate the revenue subsystem's exchange of a rate modification for the concurrence of a segment of the attentive public.

Cooperation extends to the subsystem's attempts to form coalitions. Members of a subsystem believe that there is safety in numbers. If cities act in concert, they reduce opposition claims to tax discrimination and enhance tax acceptance. Since many of Oakland's neighbors are fiscally starved, it seems reasonable for the officials to get together and propose the same tax. Recently, the Oakland city manager wanted San Francisco to propose an admissions tax to increase acceptance in Oakland. Usually Oakland tries to get other East Bay cities to form a coalition. However, attempts at coalition formation have been abortive. After a few meetings, the other cities drop out and Oakland goes it alone. As I will discuss in chapter 4, Oakland formed a coalition of East Bay cities to force a public utility to collect a city sewer service charge. After a while, the other cities decided to collect through other means such as including the charge as part of the city's business license. Oakland, however, went on alone to use a utility company as its tax collector. Although the coalition may not accomplish its goal, the fact that it existed is still important. These short-lived coalitions are useful for justifying a new tax, and Oakland officials can properly state that other cities are considering the same tax.

TAXES ARE JUSTIFIED BY RHETORIC

For a new tax the revenue subsystem attempts to gain the acceptance of the public by using rhetoric: The tax is fair and equitable; there is an urgent need for the funds; the property taxpayer needs relief. Slogans are used to gain the concurrence of the attentive public and to keep the majority of people quiescent. Relief to the property taxpayer is the subsystem's central justification for new taxes. Does the slogan have any content? By cutting a few cents off the property tax rate to make a new tax palatable, does the sub-system relieve the property taxpayer?

If everybody wants relief for the property taxpayer, then it is reasonable to suggest taxes which will spread or share the burden. One way to cut down potential political opposition is to claim that you are doing what everybody wants. Unfortunately, the subsystem's claim to spreading the burden may not provide property taxpayers relief at all. Relief, when it works according to the subsystem's tactics, relieves the taxpayer of his money and not his tax burden. Relief is another fiscal illusion for reducing the taxpayers' *perceived* burden.

Any suggested new tax is explained at council meetings by its effect on the property tax. This new tax will cut so much off our tax rate. If we do not adopt this new tax, the property tax will have to be raised by so much. Consider the passage of the utilities consumption tax which cut eight cents off the tax rate. After the Chamber of Commerce representative, Mr. Sparling, made his pitch for a sliding rate for eighty-six large industries, the council responded:

Mayor: Thank you, Mr. Sparling. I am sure you know the purpose behind it, the theory behind it was that we are trying to relieve the property owner of tax and it appears that this is another method of spreading the tax on another basis.

.   .   .   .

Councilman: This tax was originally designed and recommended in order to relieve the burden of the ad valorem tax and if we don't get it from one place, we get it from another and the thought was, of course, to accomplish that purpose, we could put in this new tax instead of putting it on the real estate. It's got to come from some place.

.   .   .   .

Mayor: Elimination of it [the utilities tax] would amount to about 30 cents on the tax rate. . . .

.   .   .   .

Councilman: Mr. Mayor, Mr. Sparling, you are talking about 86 industries, do you have an answer to the 200,000 homeowners if we raise the tax on their property tax versus 86 industries.[18]

Without any study of the incidence and economic effects of this tax, the subsystem, council, and environmental spokesmen assume that the burden will be less on the small property owner. Such a study is beyond our purview, but there is no a priori reason for assuming that the small property owner will pay less. Depending on the property owner's consumption of utilities he might even have to pay more than if his property taxes were increased. Of course, some nonproperty owners do contribute to Oakland's tax resources, but this does not necessarily result in automatic relief to the property taxpayer.

Whether the property taxpayer is given relief by the subsystem's actions is an empirical question. Some indirect evidence suggests that the intent of the subsystem is not to provide relief but to reduce the taxpayer's felt burden. When the Port of Oakland agreed to repay its own airport bonds (which freed about eight cents on the tax rate), the subsystem included the money in the budget and did not suggest a cut in the tax rate.[19] When the subsystem was having problems with its sewer service charge, it seriously considered shifting the tax liability from the user to

18. *Ibid.*
19. See Oakland, *Tentative Budget Fiscal Year 1968/69*, May 1968.

the property owner. The irony of the suggestion is that the charge was originally justified and placed on the user to offset the impact on the property taxpayer. At one time, the subsystem also suggested a property transfer tax which would be a one-time cost to the property owner.

The basic rule which guides the subsystem is, never eliminate taxes but attempt to add. Spreading the tax base and relieving the property taxpayer are slogans used to obscure the fact that the level of taxation is being increased to keep up with rising costs. The property tax may be exhausted, but the property owner can still pay.

The tactics of rhetoric, negotiation with friends, administrative arrangements, and sequential taxes are integral parts of the general revenue model of public avoidance. These acceptance tactics keep the attentive public small. Public acceptance means acceptance by this small public. As long as the few businessmen and taxpayer association leaders concur, then the revenue subsystem does not have to be concerned about the majority of taxpayers. The majority's acceptance of a new tax will be measured by the low delinquency rates. Hidden tax decision rules usually work, and people pay without excessive complaint. The whole revenue process is geared to minimizing taxpayer resistance. Application of search, decision rule, and acceptance tactics to a new revenue source ensures public acceptance.

ADMINISTRATION

The administrative stage of Oakland's revenue process is characterized by a variety of tactics. The most important of these are the anticipatory property tax rate and revenue estimation tactics. These anticipatory tactics are used to hedge against unexpected expenditure demands. By estimating revenue conservatively and not cutting the property tax rate to its minimum, the subsystem creates a small financial capacity to cope with the short-term future. This capacity is another index of the subsystem's inclination to withdraw from conflict and avoid the public.

Negotiatory and consensual tactics are also employed at this stage. The use of these tactics involves minor adjustments to the existing tax structure and procedures for increasing revenue.

While making these adjustments, members of the revenue subsystem are not concerned about administrative costs. Their objective is to increase revenue with some measure of convenience.

PROPERTY TAX RATE TACTICS
AVOID UNCERTAINTY

Earlier I pointed out that city officials, by their own volition, had put the property tax outside their discretion. Officials do not look to the property tax to bail them out of their fiscal dilemmas, but not because of indifference. On the contrary, the property tax, and in particular the property tax rate, is quite important to officials. They believe that Oakland's tax rate is salient to the voters, leaders, and fellow bureaucrats. During the period when the rate is set, there is very little overt pressure to reduce the rate.

Elected and appointed officials, however, feel that the property tax rate must be cut. The problem is to cut the rate, and yet cope with other forms of environmental uncertainty. The tax rate decision is related to the desired level of expenditures and the amount of nonproperty tax revenue which is available for current and next year's budget. The official cannot depend on raising the property tax rate, and a convenient nonproperty tax revenue source may not be available to meet expenditures. The more the official cuts the tax rate, the fewer resources he has to cope with unanticipated expenditures. Therefore, the rate is cut minimally and the tax yield adjusted to protect a surplus. Although Oakland has meager tax resources, city officials attempt to build a surplus as a means of uncertainty avoidance.[20]

One can never be certain how long a decision will last. There is a transitory quality to the property tax rate decision. Unlike most other revenue sources, officials have an opportunity to review their position on the property tax each year. An examination of rates from 1926 to 1967 indicates that there have been eighteen years when the tax rate went down, thirteen years when the rate went up, and only eleven years when the rate stayed the same as the previous year. Half of the constant years occurred during the Depression when the rate was $1.97. Since the end of World War II, the rate increased, in an erratic fashion, to a high of $3.21 in 1962.

20. Cyert and March, pp. 118–120.

The variability of the tax rate through the years is directly related to the tactics adopted by the city. Indirectly, the choice of tax rate tactics depends on the affluence of the tax base and on economic conditions. Currently the revenue subsystem uses a fixed tax rate tactic in which nonproperty tax revenue and expenditures are adjusted to the implications of the fixed rate. To balance the budget, either nonproperty tax revenue is raised or expenditures are cut. The property tax rate is held constant and is not used to balance the budget. Previously, when the tax base was more affluent and the pressure on the property tax not as acute, the subsystem used a residual tax rate tactic. In that case, expenditures were cut to a "reasonable" level, nonproperty tax revenues were summed, and the property tax rate was set to balance the budget.

The frequency with which a decision is revised is an operational indicator of the organizational importance of that decision. For the organization, revision implies that various actors are introducing decision rules, "premises," which keep the decision in flux. For the individual actor, frequent revising of a decision may be an indicator of indecisiveness. But such behavior also signifies the personal importance of the decision. City officials believe that the setting of the property tax rate is a critical decision; consequently, during most of the fiscal year the rate is set and reset as officials interact with each other. The answer to the question, what will be the property tax rate, depends on when and whom you ask. The final property tax rate, which is set by council ordinance at the end of August, is the product of a set of tentative decisions.

Tax rate decision rules change with the officials and the point of tentative decision in the budgetary process. Without specific guidance as to what the rate will be, the Finance Department's analyst assumes the rate will be the same as last year and estimates revenue accordingly. The manager and the finance director postpone making a decision on the tax rate and claim that the setting of the rate is a council policy matter.

They submit the city's tentative budget with last year's rate. Keeping the rate constant is a means of uncertainty avoidance. It allows sufficient time to pass, during which the subsystem obtains a "better fix" on revenue estimates and assessment figures. The council adopts the tentative budget in June without having to pay attention to the tax rate. Between June and August more information comes in concerning major expenditure and revenue changes. With an adoption of a new revenue source, such as the utilities tax, or a major increase in the assessment base, or state takeover of a revenue source like the sales or cigarette tax, officials will have a sufficient stimulus for cutting the property tax rate. The problem then becomes how much to cut. From the manager's point of view, one advantage of submitting last year's rate to the council is that it provides him neutral ground on which to negotiate the amount of the cut.

The property tax rate is never cut to its minimum. Both the council and the manager want to cut the tax rate. As discussed in chapter 2, the manager wants a low tax rate because of professional norms, while the council wants a low tax rate because it is good for business and politics. Officials believe that elements of the environment assess Oakland's performance by comparing city tax rates.[21] And yet, even with all of the key city officials wanting to cut the tax rate, it is never cut to its minimum; it is cut by a few cents as a means of creating a surplus for future contingencies and to cope with uncertainty.

Token cuts are a means for officials to resolve psychological conflict. The manager is pulled by two different administrative criteria. He realizes his peers view a low tax rate as a sign of administrative efficiency. On the other hand something may happen next year where he will need money, and then he will not be able to raise the tax rate or find a new source. The council has similar feelings over the perception that it is harder to raise the rate than cut it. City officials believe that they live in a goldfish bowl in which irate taxpayers are sensitive to fluctuations in the city's rate. It is better not to cut the rate to the point of having to fight political battles next year. A preferred course of action is to cut a little bit each year.

This administrative and political caution can be made clearer by an example. In 1967, assessment practices had changed so that officials expected an above average increase in the tax base.

21. City behavior in this instance is quite similar to Thompson's proposition 7.4: "Under norms of rationality, complex organizations are most alert to and emphasize scoring well on those criteria which are most visible to important task-environment elements" (Thompson, p. 90).

In addition, due to conservative estimating procedures, sales tax revenue had been considerably understated. At the same time debt servicing requirements had been reduced by about five cents on the tax rate. With the prospect of a significant revenue surplus of over a million dollars and less interest and principal to pay, the expectation of an eight-to-ten-cent tax rate cut was not unreasonable. But because the manager knew he was going to need this money over the next few years for capital improvements such as the Central Yard, he submitted his budget with the previous year's rate.

During the budget review councilmen were surprised that the manager had not recommended a cut. They felt that the newspapers had publicized the new assessment procedures, and it was common knowledge that Oakland's tax base was going to increase. The council adopted the budget; when it came time to set the tax rate, the council had received about a dozen postcards from taxpayers saying the rate should be lowered. The manager suggested a one-cent cut, but the council wanted to cut it more. Finally they agreed and in the finance director's words, the manager had "held it to two cents."

After the agreement on a two-cent cut, a public letter with the recommended tax rate was sent to the council by the manager.[22] As a way of "absorbing" the surplus and justifying the token cut the letter stated that original revenue estimates of the sales and property taxes had been too high. The letter explained that owing to increased state and federal taxes people would spend less so that the sales tax yield would be lower than expected. Delinquencies on property tax payments would also increase; so the manager had increased the delinquency percentage. With fewer people paying their property tax, the property tax yield would be lower. Thus the subsystem explained the two-cent cut in the tax rate. The subsystem had lowered its revenue estimates to protect the surplus. In his work on municipal budgeting Crecine found that tax yield estimates are not changed to balance the budget.[23]

22. Letter from Jerome Keithley, city manager, to City Council, subject: "Recommended Tax Rate, 1967–68," August 22, 1967.
23. John P. Crecine, *Governmental Problem Solving: A Computer Simulation of Municipal Budgeting* (Chicago: Rand McNally & Co., 1969), pp. 32, 68–69.

With the minor exception of adjustments to fund balances, yields are not changed to balance at the time of the adoption of the tentative budget and appropriation ordinance. However, yields are adjusted when the property tax rate is being set which is also a point of balancing the budget. In Oakland, yields are adjusted to protect a surplus. Both the sales tax yield and the delinquency percentage which affects the property tax yield were changed to obscure the extent of an anticipated surplus.

REVENUE ESTIMATION TACTICS

AVOID UNCERTAINTY

Adjusting yields in connection with the property tax rate decision is related to the general phenomena of conservative revenue estimation. The subsystem is not afraid of making an error as long as the error is in the right direction of creating a surplus. Officials estimate conservatively by the application of a few simple rules, and they see no need to be sophisticated; the present method is good enough.

Revenue estimating depends on the purpose of the estimate. Not all estimates require the same accuracy. The context of the estimating process is as important to understand as the rules by which estimates are made. What the estimator does depends on the purpose of the estimate, the particular point in the fiscal year when he makes the estimate, and the time he is given to make it. For the preparation of the city manager's budget in May, the estimator separately projects 150 different revenue sources. Most of these sources are projected by slight variations of last year's actual figure. For most other financial activities the subsystem requires estimates for only about thirty major revenue sources ($100,000 or more).

The nearer it is to the end of the fiscal year, the more the estimator feels his computations will be accurate. The passage of time allows more information, more "experience" with an existing source to come into the process. Similarly if the estimator is allowed only a few hours a day to make an estimate, he will feel his estimate is "just a guess" or the best he could do under the circumstances. Whether it is true or not, the estimator feels there is a trade-off between search and computational time on the one hand and accuracy on the other.

Revenue estimating depends on access to information. For both existing and proposed sources of revenue, the estimator's informational resources are generally meager. Special information about environmental events stimulate the revenue analyst to modify his estimating behavior. In Oakland most revenue sources are estimated by percentage changes in terms of yields; consequently, when special information is known which affects the base, the revenue estimator is in "trouble." How will a new hotel affect the transient occupancy tax? How will the construction of the rapid transit system affect downtown sales? Seldom does the estimator have time to calculate the potential effect on the particular base; so he fudges his estimate up or down depending on whether he considers the special information to be optimistic or pessimistic.

The estimator must search when a change in the property tax base is involved. When assessment practices were changed, Oakland's analyst read the local newspaper to find out how the county was going to project the change in assessed valuation. He then called the school district to find out how they were estimating the change in assessment. Finally he called the county assessor and was told that he could probably use the county figures for the city, which he did with some minor modifications.

The paucity of information is particularly evident for new or proposed revenue sources. Although the estimator does refer to other cities for information from their experience, he usually has to extend the search process within Oakland to achieve a more accurate estimate. Originally, for the transient occupancy tax, the estimator had to gather information on hotel and motel occupancy rates. Even after the city had gathered the necessary information, the transient occupancy tax yield was underestimated by 30 percent. Estimates for a proposed utilities consumption tax were based on information obtained from the utilities. While the council was considering the tax, new information was received. The gross receipts from the utilities indicated an underestimation of half a million dollars.

Although the city manager dislikes errors (inaccuracy can be interpreted as an index of incompetence), he is unwilling to pay the costs of extensive search to improve accuracy. The Finance Department's one part-time revenue estimator is expected to be accurate with little or no information. However, the standards for accuracy are not rigid, as long as the error is in the direction of underestimating revenues.

Estimating errors can arise from the application of the basic revenue rule: estimate revenue conservatively. Burkhead calls this rule the "principle of conservatism" and explains it as follows: "Governments were supposed to underestimate their revenue and overestimate their expenditures. Then, when reality caught up with the estimators, there would be an automatic budget surplus." [24] Although Burkhead discusses the principle as if it were a historical fact, the rule is still operative in Oakland, and for good reason. If the property tax rate were set and actual revenue receipts did not meet expectations, then the council would have to cut expenditures to avoid a deficit. Officials do not like to be in the position of cancelling purchase orders or perhaps firing somebody. The manager believes it is wise to estimate revenue low and have more revenue rather than less. Error in the pursuit of a surplus is "good" management. Conservative estimating provides a cushion for contingencies and minimizes the risk of public criticism.

The conservative bias in estimating revenue is cumulative. Each level in the hierarchy does not want to overestimate; thus estimator, budget officer, finance director, and city manager in turn tend to lower estimates. The manager does not have to cut an estimate directly. He can suggest that perhaps the finance director is optimistic about the sales tax. Anticipated reactions, an occasional exercise of supervisory authority, and the individual's own tendency to follow the conservative norm contribute to the cumulative conservative bias in revenue estimation.

By emphasizing previous experience, the estimator's techniques complement the conservative bias of the revenue process. Burkhead identifies two estimating techniques, "the rule of the penultimate year" and the "method of averages," both of which originated in the nineteenth century.[25] The first rule means that

24. Jesse Burkhead, *Government Budgeting* (New York: John Wiley & Sons, Inc., 1956), p. 378. Conservative revenue estimating also occurs in a school district. See Donald Gerwin, *Budgeting Public Funds: The Decision Process in an Urban School District* (Madison: University of Wisconsin Press, 1969), pp. 29–31, 127, 148.

25. Burkhead, pp. 378–379.

the last completed year's revenue is the next budget year's estimate. The "method of averages" means the application of a rate of change, such as a percentage, to each revenue source. Both rules, though modified by "judgment" and special information, are Oakland's predominant techniques.

A simulation of the municipal revenue process would be quite detailed. The model would probably consider each revenue source or a grouping of revenue sources. For example, some cities estimate the sales tax by paying attention to projections of automobile retail sales; therefore, the estimating equations would emphasize the estimation of the base rather than yield. In Oakland, because most revenue sources are estimated by changes in yields, the estimator ignores a great many independent variables. For the minor sources, last year's actual yield is the estimate. For the major sources, the "method of averages" is applied as Figure 5 illustrates. Rounding down is the estimator's final conservative touch.

The problems of estimation for budgetary purposes are reduced by a process of selective attention. The estimator, for example, is more concerned about large dollar revenue sources than small ones. Another selection rule is to emphasize general fund revenues. Special fund revenues, such as the gas taxes, are included only for the sake of completeness. The Street Department will spend whatever gas tax money is allocated to the city. However, the general fund—including revenue from the property tax, sales and cigarette taxes, licenses and permits, fines, interest, and service charges—is viewed as the main resource pool for the city program. The estimator and his supervisors feel that the general fund provides the money which the subsystem can actually control and spend.

Related to the general fund concern, the estimation of unexpended balances receives considerable attention. Once money is allocated from general fund revenues to a special fund such as the Park or Recreation Fund, the money stays in the special fund until it is expended. The department head tries to obscure the actual amount. The Finance Department's estimator guesses what the amount is in order to protect next year's general fund revenues. The rule is to try to use the department's balance for its own future program. The problem is that no one in the city

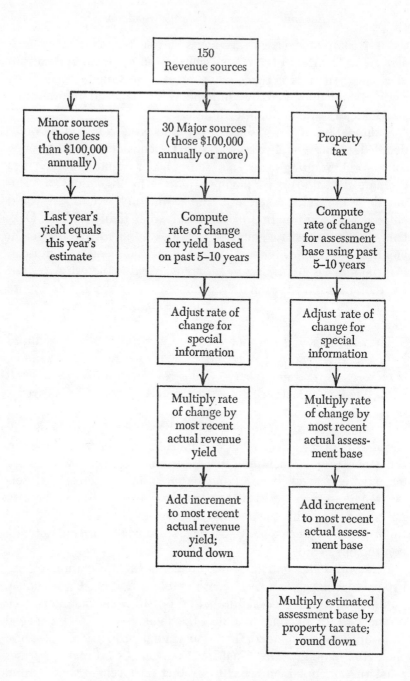

FIGURE 5. Oakland's revenue estimating procedures

really knows what the amount in the fund balance is. The Finance Department estimates the balances in February for the submission of the budget in June, but it is not until the following December or January that actual accounting information is available. Total fund balances in any year can vary from two to four million dollars. A further complication is estimating how much of the balance has actually been obligated but not yet expended. In the past some departments have used open-ended construction work orders as a way of reserving funds and creating their own checking account.

Finance officials say they guess at these balances, but like in other decisions involving uncertainty in which the official says he uses judgment and experience there are mechanical rules that are actually used. The estimator, for example, develops an "error" factor by computing the difference between his estimate and the actual fund balance for the previous year. He also computes a percentage which shows how much of their appropriations the departments spend. He has his own conservative revenue estimate; so it is a simple matter to apply the spending percentage to the revenue estimate and then adjust the amount by his error factor. If there is time, he can gather the outstanding work orders and check for suspicious projects. From the analysis of work orders he can trim about $100,000 from department surpluses.

Fund balance estimating procedures are not designed for accuracy but as a means to relieve anxiety over guessing. Finance officials appreciate the grossness of their fund balance estimates. When a balanced budget is to be presented, fund balances provide levers for adjustment. Thus, revenue is estimated selectively by paying attention to large dollar sources, to general fund revenues, and to fund balances.

City officials are not terribly concerned about the accuracy of their revenue estimates. Given the static economy and stable population, their estimates are conceived as being "good enough." Total revenue changes slowly through time and compensating errors tend to cancel out the risk of a major mistake. Most of the time, conservative estimating rules work. Rarely must the council meet to reconstitute the budget. By assuming the minor revenue sources will remain constant and estimating conservatively on the major sources, the subsystem minimizes the risk of overestimation. In the previous decade only once did the council override these bureaucratic norms. Under the pressure to grant a salary increase, it decided that the finance director's sales tax estimate was too conservative and raised the estimate to meet the salary increase. During the fiscal year capital and nonpersonnel operating expenses had to be cut because sales tax receipts were close to the finance director's original estimate.

City officials have not developed more sophisticated estimating procedures because they see no need to do so. The only major estimating error in several years contributed to the creation of a significant surplus which was kept as a reserve for future use. Although the city has a small electronic computer which could be used for regressions and correlations, Finance Department officials do not use the computer because they believe their present procedures are adequate. In this respect, Oakland is similar to many cities throughout the country. A 1965 survey of forty-three cities found only a few cities using correlation analysis and computers for estimating revenue, and as the authors said, "Revenue estimates in major cities are based predominantly upon analyses of historical trends, tempered by judgments about changes in the specific factors which affect the particular sources." [26]

By estimating revenue conservatively and creating a surplus by design, the subsystem copes with unanticipated budgetary requirements. At the same time the conservative bias in estimating compensates for defects in the subsystem's informational base.

NEGOTIATORY TACTICS IN ADMINISTRATION

In the administration of the city's tax resources, the subsystem negotiates with the environment. The basis of the negotiation is cooperation, not conflict. Revenue subsystem members seize opportunities to make cooperative exchanges throughout the fiscal year. Although such negotiatory tactics are not dramatic and exciting, they do marginally enhance the city's financial capability.

26. A. M. Hillhouse and S. Kenneth Howard, *Revenue Estimating by Cities* (Chicago: Municipal Finance Officers Association of the U.S. and Canada, 1965), p. 14.

Cooperation with members of the environment means exchange. In chapter 1, I pointed out that city officials agreed to a rate increase for the local refuse collector in exchange for an increased payment to the city. Tax-exempt organizations also require council legislation and approval. In exchange for such approval, officials can suggest a payment of in lieu taxes. Such negotiations are obscured because they are illegal. Tax-exempt organizations are not supposed to pay taxes. Nothing stops the official, however, from pointing out the drastic condition of the city's tax base. If the organization could make an in lieu payment, it would certainly help the city. When a church-sponsored organization wanted to build tax-exempt apartment units for the elderly, its offer of a small in lieu tax payment paved the way for council financial and zoning support. Although the manager was quick to point out that the in lieu payment would not be equal to the lost property tax, he still complimented the organization for their "willingness to break through the barrier that exists where there is no payment whatsoever. Inasmuch as this is a low cost housing project . . . it is of interest that we do have a nontaxable facility offering to make payment even though it is not total in lieu." [27]

The manager would also like to use the cooperative device of special assessment districts for lighting, street, and sewer improvements in order to get revenue from tax-exempt organizations, like hospitals; but he has not been successful. Special assessment districts come into existence because most property owners in an area want the improvements. Special assessments are not meant to be money-making devices for the city but a means to get the property owners to share the cost of the improvement and its maintenance. For example, the special assessment for a business area, the Washington Street Mall, covers less than one-third of its maintenance costs. However, in the case of lighting districts the city is receiving special assessment funds for a level of lighting which is now provided without extra charge in other areas because of an increase in lighting standards.

Negotiation also takes place with other governmental officials. The finance director will meet with his counterparts in Alameda

27. City of Oakland, City Clerk, Council Minutes, August 30, 1966, p. 2, and April 2, 1968, p. 8.

County to see if the county can speed up its tax payments to the city so that interest payments could be increased. A more financially rewarding negotiation has been the manager's gentle persuasion of port officials to pay their own airport bonds. By writing a letter to the port, having lunch with the port officials, and attending Port Commission meetings, the manager was able to convince the port that it was much better off than the financially impoverished city. Since the port on occasion needs the cooperation of the city and it has been doing well financially, the manager hoped that his negotiation with the port would set a precedent for an annual $600,000 donation. So far he has not been disappointed.

CONSENSUAL TACTICS IN ADMINISTRATION

Members of the subsystem and environment agree about many tax matters: The property tax cannot be raised; bonds will never pass; the municipal income tax is not feasible in Oakland; hidden taxes on consumption are preferable. The subsystem's spreading the tax base is equivalent to the citizen-leaders' perception that everyone should pay their fair share. Where possible, business should not be hurt.

Agreement on tax matters and the *existing* tax structure indicates minimal uncertainty and conflict. Consensual links are significant because they lead to introverted tactics in which the environment is mostly ignored. The subsystem turns its attention to the existing tax structure and administrative convenience.

"An old tax is a good tax" because people accept the old tax or are not conscious of it. As Buchanan points out, "The adage is useful as a rule for government, considered to be divorced from the individuals in the jurisdiction. The old tax generates less reaction than the new tax." [28] Small changes can be made to the existing tax structure and administration with little fear of activating the taxpayer. Furthermore, there are many small levers which can be adjusted to increase revenue: rates, measures of tax liability, tax coverage or scope, frequency of billing, and auditing and enforcement procedures.

The subsystem's attitudes toward the administration of taxes is particularly interesting. Couched within the context of effi-

28. Buchanan, p. 62.

ciency is a peculiar indifference to high administrative costs. Members of the subsystem are not concerned with maximizing the net difference between revenue and administrative costs. The subsystem follows this rule: when you have a tax with high administrative costs, raise the rates. Even in the selection of new taxes, a projected administrative convenience is not ignored. Convenience is much more important than costs.

The drive toward administrative convenience results in shifting the burden of enforcement to the taxpayer, which means self-policing taxes. The subsystem does not have adequate resources to audit and enforce the payment of taxes. Officials talk about court action and include stiff penalties in tax ordinances. In practice they do little except make judgments about who is not likely to pay; for example, in revising the business license, officials are thinking about charging professionals (doctors and lawyers) a flat rate instead of a charge based on gross receipts because officials feel that professionals have low tax-paying morality. The subsystem designs tax ordinances to make it easy on themselves. A flat rate is more convenient to administer than a gross receipts based tax.

Another tactic to insure payment of the business license fee is to have an applicant deposit it at the same time he applies for necessary permits. Thus the city receives the applicant's money before the police and other departmental personnel investigate. No doubt this administrative improvement will enhance the existing confusion between regulation and revenue.

Some ways of charging for the *same* city service or privilege seem better than others to officials; for example, the finance director feels that the charges for city manager permits should be treated as rezoning applications, which would result in more revenue. Similarly, having a daily charge for peddlers does not work because peddlers do not bother to come in and pay the charge. The finance director is presently thinking of some way to include door-to-door people such as peddlers, solicitors, milkmen, and Avon ladies under the provisions of the business license.

Sometimes a change in one existing tax can be used to justify an increase in another existing tax. When the state raised the sales tax from 4 to 5 percent, the finance director submitted a recommendation, later approved by the council, that the transient occupancy tax be raised from 4 to 5 percent. Similarly the 5 percent rate for the utilities consumption tax was established by linking it to the sales tax. Such behavior is a variant of the follow-the-leader rule, except the leader in this case is a tax and not a city.

The existence of consensual links between members of the subsystem and environment should not be construed as setting rigid boundaries for official action. The boundaries of perceived fiscal discretion are fuzzy for the city official. If the manager and

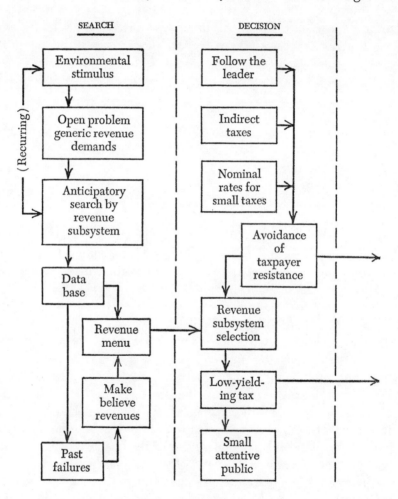

FIGURE 6. Oakland's public avoidance revenue process

finance director always knew what the traffic would bear, they would not have to resort to testing the environment with trial balloons.

Because members of the subsystem know that certain taxes are accepted and are no longer conspicuous to taxpayers, the subsystem can look organizationally inward and make minor adjustments to increase revenue and convenience. Consensus operates to slightly increase the discretion of the subsystem.

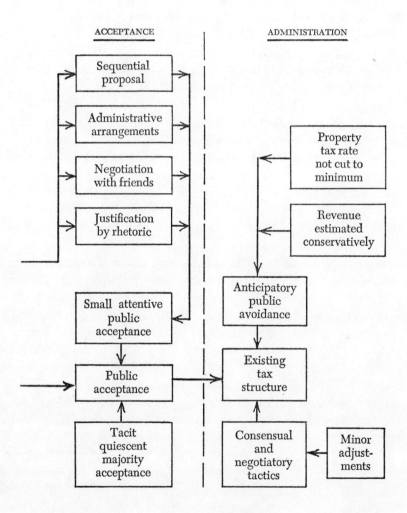

FIGURE 6. (Continued)

SUMMARY

The subsystem avoids the public while coping with the city's financial problems. Avoidance of the public motivates the subsystem's anticipatory behavior: Anticipate short-term expenditures; anticipate taxpayer resistance. As summarized in Figure 6, anticipation is part of each stage of the revenue process. Since the subsystem cannot fully predict outcomes, it attempts to anticipate expenditure demands and taxpayer reactions.

The inference that Oakland officials anticipate the reactions of environmental segments or tax publics is not an indication of a healthy democratic process. It is possible that officials are not accurately perceiving the threshold of tax opposition. By direct negotiation with taxpayers, the subsystem could be more assured of the accuracy of their perceptions. By making taxes salient, the subsystem could enlarge the attentive public and possibly receive support for expansion of services. Nevertheless, city officials seek to avoid the conflict and uncertainty of negotiating with possibly hostile taxpayers. Their behavior manifests what Downs calls the "shrinking violet syndrome." [29] The boundaries of political actions shrink, and revenue decisions are dominated by the manipulation of bureaucratic actors.

Manipulation starts with anticipatory search tactics. Revenue search anticipates short-term expenditure requirements. Because the revenue problem is open ended, search is recurring. The subsystem, in fragmented and superficial ways, intermittently scans sources which can be added to the revenue menu. Because there are relatively few revenue sources which satisfy the subsystem's criteria for low yield–low political cost taxes, some search will be ritualistic or make-believe. Contrary to the model of problemistic search, the problem is never perceived as being solved; search does not stop, and search is just as likely to be conducted in areas of failure as well as success.

Avoiding taxpayer resistance connects the decision and acceptance stages of the revenue process. Reducing the tax consciousness of the taxpayer is a key subsystem objective. How does the subsystem know what the traffic will bear? The choice of which

29. Downs, pp. 216–217.

tax to present for public approval is simplified by following the leader, by finding precedents in other cities. Promoting indirect taxes and encouraging a complex of nominal nuts and bolts taxes, the subsystem reduces the tax consciousness of the taxpayer. Such behavior results in low-yielding taxes and small attentive publics. By proposing taxes sequentially, making public participation difficult, and justifying all actions in terms of property tax relief, the subsystem keeps the attentive public small, fragmented, and quiet. After some cooperative negotiation with friends, the subsystem has achieved public acceptance for the new tax.

The administration of the existing tax structure is also characterized by public avoidance and anticipatory tactics. The cautious attitude toward the environment is carried over to critical property tax rate and revenue estimating decisions. Since the revenue subsystem is also responsible for budgetary calculations, it never cuts the rate to its minimum. Instead, it slightly cuts the rate to satisfy attentive elements in the environment and creates a surplus to handle future contingencies. Similarly the subsystem estimates revenue simply but conservatively. Each member of the subsystem depresses the estimate so that cumulatively a surplus is certain to be created.

Whatever negotiation with the environment takes place, after city officials have spent so much energy in public avoidance, is infrequent, trivial, and usually with cooperative friends. Consensus on tax matters, furthermore, encourages officials to look inward at their own organizational requirements rather than outward toward a changing environment. Slight changes are made to the existing tax structure not to reduce costs, but to increase revenue and administrative convenience.

The subsystem, by these various tactics, admirably meets the recurring requirements for organizational maintenance. By scraping the fiscal barrel and attempting to control the environment by avoidance, enough resources are gathered to keep up with price changes and salary raises. However, it is unlikely that such a withdrawal from direct political participation can ensure adequate resources for system adaptation.

4

The Sewer Service Charge

The ten-year history of the sewer service charge illustrates the continuity of subsystem behavior throughout the stages of the revenue process. At each stage from search to administration, there are examples of the revenue tactics discussed in chapter 3. During the search and decision stages, the subsystem resorted to anticipatory tactics. The subsystem did not pioneer the sewer service charge; instead, it modified other cities' experiences to fit the Oakland context. The subsystem also negotiated with segments of the environment. A local utility district had to be convinced that it should be the tax collector for the city. The subsystem had to negotiate the rate schedule with the large industrial users. At the administration stage, the subsystem maintained the consensus by anticipating the reactions of the large users to a rate increase.

Because of their anecdotal nature, case studies are too often relegated to the social science ashcan. When the social scientist looks at an organizational process at a point in time, he may miss the dynamics of the observed behavior. Even for the relatively static city of Oakland, one might expect a modicum of change in the revenue process. Certainly environmental pressure on the property tax has increased, and the subsystem's search for non-property-tax revenue has intensified. I had thought that a case study of a revenue source would reveal modifications in the revenue process. This was not true in Oakland.

Instead of documenting modifications in the revenue process, this case study demonstrated continuity in revenue behavior. During the ten-year period in which the charge was suggested, adopted, and revised, the occupants in subsystem roles changed; but even with a new city manager and new finance director, revenue behavior remained much the same. The subsystem used the solutions of the past to cope with present problems. At the beginning of the case history, the subsystem wanted a utility district to be the city's tax collector; and at the end, the subsystem achieved that objective. Throughout all stages of the charge's history, the subsystem used the same justifications. The property taxpayer always needed relief. The subsystem regularly resorted to the camouflage of the equity of a user-based charge. Avoiding taxpayer resistance was a key criterion in both the initial and revised rate selections. Regardless of which particular official played a role in the subsystem, revenue behavior was the same.

No doubt during the ten-year history the environment changed dramatically; but the attentive public for the sewer service charge continued to be a handful of industrial taxpayers and their trade associations. Thus, one condition for continuity in the behavior of the subsystem—stability in the attentive public—was fulfilled in this Oakland case study.

THE PROBLEM AND SEARCH

A recognized service need is a tactical opportunity for members of the subsystem. The revenue subsystem is usually engaged in a generic revenue hunt; it searches for financial resources without being concerned with the potential use of the funds. Occasionally, revenue search is put in focus because of a specific service need, and in such cases the subsystem has a unique opportunity. In addition to explaining an increase in taxation by its potential offset to the property tax, the subsystem can justify an increase by pointing to a crisis of need. The members of the subsystem do not necessarily share the service orientation of line officials. Although the members may be indifferent to the service need, they use it to fulfill their primary function of increasing revenue. Thus, when it was possible for Oakland citizens to smell that the city sanitary sewer system needed extensive repair, it was the ideal time to suggest a new tax. It took longer, however, to sensitize people's noses to the financial problem.

In the budget, capital items are treated as a residual, and major improvements are often deferred. It is either make do or do without. The small amount of money which can be used for capital items is placed where the subsystem thinks it will do the most good. Shortly after World War II, Oakland, like many other cities in the United States, started to catch up with the backlog of public works improvements that had been postponed because of wartime constraints. City officials decided they would put as much money as possible into paving the streets. By covering over streetcar tracks they hoped to make the city attractive on the outside, develop more business, and create a favorable economic climate. At that time the sewer system was in a state of disrepair and needed considerable replacement and maintenance, but there were few funds available to apply to underground, or less visible, activities. As the years went on, the situation worsened and complaints increased both from individuals and from various public health authorities. Personnel of the Underground Section of the Street Department finally brought the problem to the surface by presenting briefings that exposed the emergency in the city sewer system.

In searching for ways in which to finance this major sewer replacement program, the subsystem began to look for a precedent. On June 18, 1958, one of the secretaries in the city manager's office suggested to J. Locke, the manager's assistant, that it might be possible for the city to tax various utilities such as telephone, water, and perhaps sewer connections. A month later, the city manager, W. Thompson, asked Locke to research a sewer use fee. The secretary had heard about a sewer charge used in Oklahoma. When Locke was on vacation, he visited Oklahoma City to investigate. Locke also gathered relevant ordinances from Santa Cruz and Sacramento, California, and from Portland, Oregon. At the end of July, he reported his research to the city manager.

During this period, Locke found an extensive survey of the sewer service charge in the April 1958 edition of *Western City* magazine. The survey covered seventy-eight cities. The fact that other California cities were using the charge was important, because Oakland has tended not to be a pioneer, at least in fiscal matters. Bolstered by the acceptance of sewer charges elsewhere, Locke felt that Oakland should proceed with the charge. The information on other cities was used as evidence for widespread acceptance of the revenue source. Later on, other cities would be used as sources of information for standards and procedures.

The revenue subsystem wants to receive revenue but prefers to avoid collecting it. Locke suggested that working through the East Bay Municipal Utilities District (EBMUD) might be the best way of collecting the charge. EBMUD charged on the user basis of metered water consumption. Why not have EBMUD collect the city's charge? As Locke saw it, the city could get the revenue by having Special District No. 1 of EBMUD bill for its own services and, at the same time, collect the city revenue with a certain deduction to cover its administrative costs.

A program would have to be worked out so that the cities in the District (Alameda, Albany, Berkeley, Emeryville, Piedmont, and Oakland) would use EBMUD as a tax collector. Locke coordinated his ideas with J. Morin, superintendent of streets. Morin agreed that the city should have a sewer charge and that EBMUD would probably be interested in doing this job because it would solve some of its own sewerage disposal problems. On September 8, 1958, Morin, in his Capital Improvement Program for streets and sewers, emphasized the difficulty of financing sanitary sewer construction from existing budgetary revenues and suggested the use of a sewer service charge. City officials at that time were convinced that EBMUD would be happy to be a tax collector. No one considered the possibility that EBMUD might not want to assume the role.

NEGOTIATION WITH FRIENDS: COOPTATION

One of the tactics of gaining public acceptance for a new tax is to use a citizens' committee to propose it. Such a committee is staffed with members of the revenue subsystem who feed facts, write drafts, and orient the product of the committee. The subsystem uses the committee as a conduit for its own objectives. At the same time the committee produces a report which sets the frame of reference for future bureaucratic action. For the short term the city manager uses the committee report for justification to council and citizens. As time passes and new actors assume the roles of the subsystem, the report's recommendations constrain action and reduce the number of alternatives the subsystem will consider.

In December 1958 Mayor C. Rishell invited a group of citizens to form a committee to aid in the evaluation of the city's capital needs. This Citizens' Executive Committee on Capital Improvements was organized into subcommittees according to the type of improvement. The report of the Streets and Sewers Subcommittee of February 4, 1959, documented and recommended the alternative that the subsystem had previously chosen. The subcommittee's report emphasized need, eliminated alternative financing sources, and selected EBMUD to be tax collector for a sewer service charge. According to the subcommittee, Oakland needed $800,000 a year to replace sanitary sewers. New areas in the city were to be taken care of through assessments of the property owners, but these new areas placed additional stress on the rest of the sewer system. The sewers were old, worn out, and undersized. To back up this point the report cited replacement information provided by Morin. The city had 894 miles of sanitary sewers with a replacement cost of $53 million and their ages were as follows:

90% over 10 years	53% over 40 years
80% over 20 years	28% over 50 years
69% over 30 years	12% over 60 years

The subcommittee emphasized that: "Replacement and restoration of these old sewers is mandatory in that a health problem immediately arises which seriously endangers the welfare of the community when these sewers fail or overflow during periods of heavy use."[1]

In this report the subcommittee selected the basis for financing. Since a sewer's service life was sixty years, replacement would be a continuing problem. A yearly replacement fund set up on a pay-

---

1. This chapter is based on informal and formal interviews with Oakland officials and on memoranda and reports obtained from the files of the Budget and Finance Department and City Manager Office. Since this is a case history I thought it preferable not to clutter the text with citations; anyone who wants further documentation can have access to my files.

as-you-go basis was preferred to a bond issue, because as a rule Oakland avoided bonds. The subcommittee eliminated other sources of funds. Grants-in-aid were not available. Special assessment district proceedings would be inequitable because sewer system maintenance was a community responsibility. The general fund provided for minimum maintenance only. The property tax rate could not be raised to increase the general fund for sewer replacement. After eliminating alternative means of financing, the subcommittee recommended a sewer service charge similar to EBMUD's. The report indicated statewide acceptance of the charge by citing the *Western City* article. Only a sewer service charge would do.

The subcommittee recommended that EBMUD collect the city's charge, suggesting that EBMUD could simply increase its charge and turn over the increment in revenue to the city with a minimum of administrative and collection expense. The report did not indicate whether EBMUD would agree to such an arrangement.

To substantiate its recommendations the subcommittee included with its report a legal opinion from the city attorney: "Although the collection and treatment of sewerage affects the public health of the entire community, and is more commonly supported by general taxation, the same as other matters of public health and safety, such as police and fire protection, there is precedent for levying a charge against the users of such service." City Attorney Melby also believed that other sources of revenue such as special districts, special assessments, or revenue bonds were not applicable in this situation. Furthermore, the city should avoid taxpayer claims of double taxation; therefore, Melby pointed out that it would be better as a matter of policy, and not strictly from a legal viewpoint, to have EBMUD increase its charge and then pay a certain percentage to the city. EBMUD was singled out not only for ease of administering the charge, but also as a way of reducing legal conflicts.

SEARCH AND NEGOTIATION ON DETAILS

Previous administrative decisions act as constraints and limit the alternatives considered in present decisions. By this time in the history of the charge, the revenue subsystem was committed to charging the user of the sewers. The basis of the charge had been chosen. The subsystem now perceived its problem as how to bill and collect from the user. Locke noted in a memo, for example, that the Street Department had suggested billing through the property tax. But, as Locke said, "Problems are apparent in this approach since tax bills are sent to property owners and the sewer service charge is to be assessed against the user, not necessarily the owner of the property." Although administrative arrangements were in flux, the subsystem's objective of charging the user remained fixed. Not only would the subsystem get money for sewers, but it would be able to relieve the property taxpayer and collect from tax-exempt organizations. Everyone would pay. It was an ideal revenue source from the viewpoint of public acceptance even though it might create some administrative problems.

On June 4, 1959, the city manager initiated a series of meetings to work out the mechanics of the charge with the superintendent of streets, finance director, city attorney, and auditor-controller. The manager emphasized the recommendation of the citizens' committee report and directed Morin to work out the details. In his response to the city manager on July 16, 1959, Morin noted that he was not able to procure administrative costs from EBMUD. A few weeks later at another joint meeting, department heads and the city manager decided not to press EBMUD. Instead, the billing would be accomplished by the city auditor-controller, and the finance director would be responsible for the receipt of funds. The city would still have to obtain consumption information from EBMUD in order to develop a rate structure based on use.

Over the following months, discussions were held with other cities and with EBMUD to survey procedures, facilities, and costs of administration. In this review, city personnel gathered comparable ordinances and gained some understanding of what would be involved in administering a sewer service charge. In December 1959, Locke and several city officials visited Sacramento, where the sewer service charge was administered as part of other utilities services (including garbage collection and water) under a superintendent of water and sewer. The billing was handled by the Sacramento auditor-controller. Collections were no problem; delinquents were forced to pay by cutting off their water service. Sacramento also could place a lien on property for nonpayment. Such information was not entirely applicable to Oakland, which intended to rely on a separate utility district for some of the requisite information. Sacramento administered its sewer charge along with its regular water operations; Oakland was intending to rely on EBMUD.

In February 1960, Morin was again asked to provide a summary report. For this report Locke computed collection costs for the sewer service charge. He noted that the city should expect a higher delinquency rate than EBMUD. The city would only be able to place a lien on the property of delinquent users, but would not be able to cut off their water service. Morin felt that EBMUD should handle the collections. As he said in his report:

All that would be necessary would be to add another statement to their existing bill. If this were done the city could pay the additional billing and collecting expense necessary because of this additional statement and, also, share proportionately in the present administrative costs and result in material savings to the taxpayer by preventing costs of duplicate service by two tax supported agencies. The city's sewer service charge could be plainly indicated as such on the EBMUD bill. If the savings to the taxpayer, both from the city and from EBMUD were generally known, it is possible that the taxpayers would demand this service from the EBMUD.

But would EBMUD help? During this period, regardless of the numerous discussions between EBMUD and the city, there was no definite understanding as to what the utility district would provide. Hamb, the finance director, pointed this out in a letter to the city manager: "We do not appear to have . . . a commitment . . . that the information we desire would be furnished to us, although there is an availability of such information, and indeed, some collateral services." Morin asked the city manager to make a formal request to EBMUD. The manager wrote J. McFarland, general manager of EBMUD, on March 7, 1960, and "in the interest of economy for the city and district taxpayers" requested that EBMUD perform billing and collecting services for the city.

The EBMUD issue was still not resolved by August 31, 1960

when the manager made his progress report on the sewer service charge to the council. He reviewed the citizens' committee recommendations for the introduction of a charge to provide $800,000 a year for sewer replacement. The city manager defined the problem as one of recurring replacement, not a one-time capital improvement. Therefore it was reasonable to raise the money through a sewer service charge "whereby the cost would be referred back to the users of the sewer system in proportion to the extent of their use and contribution to the deterioration of the system."

City Manager Thompson informed the council that at a minimum the cost of administering the charge would be $131,000, or approximately 10 percent of the gross revenue yield. This would be the case if the city itself would administer the charge. However, as the manager put it,

It was hoped that the East Bay Municipal Utility District could, by simply including in their water bill the amount of the sewer service charge and, handling the collection as part of their present operation of collecting water and sewer disposal service charge, do this work for the city. The administrative cost of the East Bay Municipal Utility District for this service would be less than the cost for the city to provide its own billing and collection service.

He then stated that he had a committee of city personnel working with EBMUD to ascertain how this service could be provided. The district thought that its equipment and space were inadequate to provide this additional billing service, and so city personnel were exploring the possibility of using district consumption data as a basis for the city doing its own billing.

The city manager's report was equivocal, a statement of progress rather than a request for action. The draft of this report, however, was explicit. It contained a recommendation that the City Council approve a sewer service charge and "request the EBMUD to cooperate in the billing and collection of these charges," and it stated that "both the city and the EBMUD are governmental agencies receiving their support from the citizens of our city and it seems only logical that the agency which can do the work at least cost to the people who must eventually pay the bill, should assume the responsibility." It took many years, however, for EBMUD to accept this view of the situation.

NEGOTIATION WITH FRIENDS: COALITIONS

Once the subsystem gave up the notion of trying to administer a sewer service charge by itself, it could concentrate on getting the reluctant EBMUD to cooperate. At the horizontal level of intergovernmental relations, the influence of any one governmental unit over another is severely limited due to a lack of resources. The subsystem could neither order nor persuade the district by itself. What it could do was to bring more actors into the political arena and form coalitions. Some of these coalitions would be with citizens' groups which shared the common objective of saving taxpayer money. Another coalition would be with similarly situated city officials who also required new sources of revenue. These coalitions were formed and lasted long enough for Oakland to get some small measure of cooperation out of EBMUD. As it turned out, Oakland was the only city in the East Bay area to pursue a sewer service charge with the direct participation of EBMUD. Other cities found less costly ways of levying a tax on sewers.

At a meeting of the Greater Oakland Communities Council in November 1960, the manager singled out the need for sewer replacement and stated that the city could save $150,000 annually if EBMUD would bill and collect the city's charge. At about the same time a subcommittee of the Oakland Industries Committee for the sewer service was proposed. The subcommittee's strategy was to present a complete program for the Alameda County mayors' approval which could then be discussed with EBMUD. The objective was to include all the cities and to explore the possibility of uniform charges so that it would be economical for all participating governmental units.

On December 9, 1960, mayors from Piedmont, Oakland, Alameda, Berkeley, and Albany met and decided that they should call a policy level meeting with EBMUD as soon as possible to determine how the district could administer the sewer service charge for all of the cities. The group agreed that a uniform rate for all cities might be established. The mayor of Alameda pointed out that his city had taken care of its sewer replacement needs and if Alameda participated in the program he would have to

sell it on the basis of capital improvements rather than maintenance. This approach would be the exact opposite of Oakland's.

Shortly afterward, the mayor of Piedmont called Mr. Breuner,
president of the board of EBMUD, to set up a meeting. Breuner
requested that a legal opinion be obtained on whether EBMUD
could collect a service charge for the cities and whether the
district could discontinue water services as a means of enforcement. The Oakland city attorney provided this information, and
the meeting was held on January 4, 1961. After this policy conference, Oakland sent the district a proposed ordinance establishing a sewer service charge for the city. A few months later
technical representatives from Oakland, Piedmont, and Berkeley
met with district personnel and agreed that EBMUD would
provide billing services on a proportional cost basis but would
not do any collecting. The revenue subsystem was content to
get its foot in the door. EBMUD submitted cost estimates for its
billing services on May 2, 1961.

COUNCIL JUSTIFICATION

Having gotten its foot in the door, the revenue subsystem presented the sewer service charge for council adoption. Justification to the council followed the usual story line. There is a
continuing need for sewer replacement. Other California cities
have a sewer service charge. The user would pay, not just the
property owner. In fact, property tax requirements for the general
fund were to be reduced by $200,000 once the charge was
adopted. Charitable institutions, hospitals, and state and federal
organizations would have to pay because the levy was a user
charge, not a tax. At the same time the revenue subsystem
minimized the existence of alternatives, the high administrative
costs of the charge, and the possibility of a high delinquency
rate.

On June 19, 1961, the city manager presented his recommendations to the City Council. He reviewed the history of the charge
by reminding councilmen of the citizens' committee report of
February 1959 which had complained that Oakland's sewer
system was deficient. He emphasized the recurring need and the

pay-as-you-go financing. In 1959 the committee had reported that there were over 894 miles of sanitary sewers which required a continuing program of maintenance. The city manager reminded the council that this report by the citizens' committee was over two years old, and that in this period the sewer system had continue to deteriorate. To further emphasize the need for immediate action, he went on to say: "Failure to initiate such a program could result in an extremely dangerous health situation involving a complete breakdown in sanitary sewer service in some areas as a result of failure in event of heavy rainstorms or other natural disasters."

The city manager pointed out that the charge would be based on use of the sewer system and that this method was employed by 212 of the 366 cities in California. To document this, he attached the April 1958 *Western City* survey to his written report. Further substantiation of the general acceptance of sewer service charges was provided to the councilmen in the form of tables indicating that cities within Alameda County (Hayward and Berkeley) and nearby counties (Contra Costa and Marin) had adopted the charge.

Sewer service charges throughout California employ a variety of bases for computation. They can be computed on a fixed percent of the water bill, the number of employees, the number of rooms, the number of sewer connections, a flat rate, metered water consumption, or the size of the meter. Billing methods also differ. Sewer service charges can be billed separately or as an item on the tax bill or as part of the water bill. Finally, the recipient can be either the occupant or the owner. Thus, there is a wide variety of alternative approaches to this type of charge. This variety was not emphasized in the manager's presentation to the council. The council was not encouraged to examine alternatives.

Budget sheets were attached which revised the budget, showing the administrative cost for the rest of the fiscal year and a projected administrative cost of $92,000 for the next fiscal year, 1962/63. Although these costs were stated (about 7 percent of gross revenues), they were not in any sense highlighted, nor was there any effort to point out possible problems with delinquencies. Relations with EBMUD were expressed as part fact and part expectation. The manager stressed that most California cities incorporate their sewer service charges in a water program and that 75 percent of the cities bill the charge as part of a water bill. He also pointed out that it had been Oakland's intention to have EBMUD, on a contractual basis, do both the billing and collecting to avoid costly duplication. Since EBMUD had agreed only to the billing, the administrative cost for the city would include approximately $52,000 for collection and another $40,000 for the district's services.

The manager recommended the adoption of the charge with the rate of 50 cents per family unit for residences consisting of four or fewer family units, and a commercial-industrial rate of 6-⅔ cents per 100 cubic feet of water used. This would result in a gross revenue of $1.2 million. The rates had been structured so that about 50 percent of the total revenue would come from the residential users and the other 50 percent from the commercial-industrial users. Splitting the burden down the middle seemed fair to members of the revenue subsystem.

A week later, according to the *Oakland Tribune* of June 28, 1961, the city manager was instructed to present a proposed ordinance for the sewer charge. At the meeting the manager said it was "a special charge for a special service." A councilman added, "It's the painless way to tax." Another councilman said he was for it because he didn't know where they were going to get the $20 million in the next few years for sewers. The mayor said the levy was justified only if residents of Piedmont would also pay a similar fee because its sewerage runs through Oakland lines. Morin, now assistant city manager, reported that Piedmont was prepared to share in the cost of sewer replacement. A councilman said that Piedmont would quickly adopt the sewer service charge to "circumvent the necessity of going to the people for a raise in the tax rate." Only one councilman raised the question of the high administrative cost—almost $100,000 a year—and thought it might be better to get the necessary funds through a direct tax levy. As he put it, "If you put it on the tax bill it doesn't cost a penny." No one listened. The sewer service charge was the painless way to tax.

CONFLICT OVER EQUITABLE RATES

Once the adoption of a particular tax is likely, taxpayer opposition will focus on modifying the subsystem's recommended rate structure. In local revenue situations, organized interests such as industry and business do not escape paying taxes but may pay less than the amount originally suggested by the revenue subsystem. In Oakland, organized industrial interests sought a favorable rate structure for the sewer service charge in exchange for their concurrence.

The problem of paying less is related to the general question of who should pay. Since the sewer service charge was to be based on use, the subsystem expected little trouble in determining what the tax burden should be. The charge was to be based on the benefit principle in which there is an explicit quid pro quo between the city and the taxpayer. The user is expected to pay for the benefit of the goods or services he receives. However, if benefit is equated with use, how does one measure the use of a sewer system? Oakland's revenue subsystem had adopted EBMUD's standard of water consumption as a suitable measure. Water consumption, however, has little known relation to cost of sewer replacement, and organized groups have their own notions of measures of use. Since the participants in the conflict over rates had inadequate cost and engineering information, there was considerable opportunity for diverse interpretations. Equity shifted with the point of view and its underlying interest.

As the months passed, a difference of opinion developed between Councilman Reading, who was chairman of a council special committee for the charge, and the revenue subsystem. Reading, representing industry's viewpoint, wanted heavy commercial-industrial users such as canneries to pay less than residential users. Subsystem members wanted all users to pay the same or equivalent charge, reasoning that the city's cost increased in direct proportion to the user's water consumption. A flat charge tied to water consumption was the way to connect the city's cost and the taxpayer's benefit. The more water a taxpayer used, the more he should pay for sewer service. Costs were equated to benefits. To simplify administration of the charge, the subsystem had converted a rate of 6-⅔ cents per 100 cubic feet of water consumption into a monthly charge for residential users, based on average residential consumption. The manager's recommended rate schedule of 50 cents per month for residential users was considered equivalent to the 6-⅔ cents per 100 cubic feet of water consumption for nonresidential users.

When Reading urged that residential users pay 75 cents a month and nonresidential users pay a maximum of 3 cents per 100 cubic feet with a sliding or decreasing scale for the heavy users, the subsystem was in a dilemma. Members of the subsystem wanted industry's support for final approval of a sewer service charge ordinance. Yet the provision of a sliding scale and Reading's other changes would reduce the revenue yield and would discriminate between residential and nonresidential users. The sliding scale and the increased residential rate would distort the equity of the charge. Small users would pay more than large users.

At a meeting on September 19, 1961, some of the main contenders in the conflict asserted their positions. Attending were McFarland of EBMUD, representatives of various packing companies such as Erickson of the California Packing Corporation, a representative of Owens-Illinois Glass Company, representatives of Alameda County Industries Incorporated, McKnight of the Alameda County Taxpayers Association, Councilman Reading, the city manager and several members of his staff, and a reporter from the *Oakland Tribune*. Assistant City Manager Morin opened the meeting by pointing out the need for getting on with the job because of the tremendous health problems.

Reading interjected that the council would not approve the proposed rates. He objected to the recommended policy of charging industry the same rate as residential users. The city should consider that the cost of sewerage disposal is much less for larger quantities than for smaller quantities. He stressed that the council had taken a stand to do everything to attract industry. The flat rate recommended by the city manager would discourage industry from coming to Oakland. Reading felt that the rate should be adjusted so that the residential areas would carry a heavier load than industry.

McFarland of EBMUD countered Reading by stating that there was no relationship between the sliding scale water billing of the district and sewerage disposal; the theory of sewerage disposal did not require a sliding scale. McFarland had previously stated in the public hearings that the flat rate "was the only sound means of computing a sewer service charge equitable to all." This had to be the case for him because the subsystem's proposed method was the same as EBMUD's. In addition, the introduction of a sliding scale presented EBMUD with special billing problems for the charge. He felt that billing for the heavy consumption industries, where there might be a possible inequity, would have to be handled separately by the city.

Erickson of the Alameda County Industries Incorporated and manager of a packing corporation, held out for a sliding scale and was strongly opposed to the original recommendation. The association he represented included a group which accounted for approximately 15 percent of the use of city sewers. His own organization, California Packing, was the largest single user. Erickson pointed out that in order for the charge to be acceptable to industry, the rates must not be higher than if the property tax were used to raise the required revenue. Industry argued that a flat rate would be excessive. Other utilities such as water, gas, and electricity employ sliding rates for large users. A flat rate would be too expensive for canneries, hotels, dairies, hospitals, and bakeries. Certain canneries which were marginal producers might have to shut down or move closer to their suppliers. Seven canneries within city limits would be affected by the proposed plan, and in many cases they were so close to the district's main interceptor lines that the use of the city's sewers was not in proportion to the volume of sewerage placed into them. In addition, the cost of sewerage disposal to service industrial plants was less than the cost for an equal volume of sewerage to serve residential areas; for example, a ten-inch sewer line has three times the capacity of a six-inch sewer but does not cost much more to install. Business and industry felt that the flat charge was inequitable, would put a heavy burden on them, and would act as a deterrent to Oakland's industrial development.

City officials had no information on the economic condition of these firms and were sympathetic to the problems of business and industry. The manager defended the proposed rate structure because it was based on the original recommendations of the 1959 citizens' committee report and on engineering studies by both EBMUD and the city. There would be too many taxpayer complaints if the sewer service charge was ruled out or reduced and the tax rate increased. Furthermore, all federal installations in Oakland, although exempt from the property tax, would have to pay the sewer use charge. A member of the revenue subsystem summarized the disadvantages of industry's sliding rate proposal as follows:

(1) The relation between residential and non-residential rates are changed from a direct relationship based upon equal rates to a relationship set arbitrarily to favor one group of users;

(2) By allowing special consideration for a special group, the city would set precedence for all other groups of special users (hotels, theatres, governmental units, apartment house owners) to petition for reduced rates now and each year in the future; and

(3) The administrative cost for operating the sewer service charge program would be increased by an unknown amount to handle the special groups.

Thus the small nonindustrial and residential users would be paying more for the same benefit based on water consumption than the big users.

COMPROMISE

If taxpayer resistance is of sufficient intensity, the revenue subsystem will usually withdraw its recommendation for a particular source. It is an all-or-nothing situation if the issue is the proposed adoption of a new tax. However, once the revenue subsystem and attentive segments of the environment agree to a new tax, then compromise can be accomplished in terms of the measures of tax liability or the rate structure. There are not enough sources on the revenue menu to enable bargaining over different taxes; therefore, compromise is more likely to occur in terms of rates or some other aspect of a particular tax source. The more intense the opposition to a new revenue source, the more the rate will be adjusted to satisfy the opposition and gain its concurrence.

Shortly after the September 19, 1961, meeting, the conflict over the sewer service charge rates was resolved by Councilman Reading and Assistant City Manager Morin. The residential rate would be increased to 60 cents per month and there would be a sliding scale for heavy users from 5 cents to 1½ cents depending on the volume of water consumption. City officials discussed this compromise rate structure with representatives of Alameda County Industries and the Apartment House Owners Association of Alameda County, who offered no objections to the charge. The precedent was established that residences would pay more than nonresidences.

THE RELUCTANT EBMUD

Throughout the negotiations on the sewer service charge, EBMUD was an unwilling participant. From an economic viewpoint it was logical that EBMUD should completely administer the charge. From a political viewpoint, however, EBMUD was an independent governmental organization with its own perceptions of constituency, image, and interest that directed its relations with the city. City officials felt EBMUD's position was as follows: (1) EBMUD was concerned about its public image. It did not want to be a tax collector for any city. It was afraid that, if it helped Oakland, other cities would ask for similar assistance. It did not want to be in the position of shutting off the water to help the cities collect their delinquencies. EBMUD shut off the water to collect its own bills, but to do it for Oakland might create adverse public relations. (2) EBMUD was concerned about its own profit and loss statement; helping the cities might affect its profit margin, ability to pay off indebtedness, and bond rating. (3) EBMUD was concerned about its constituency. It operated in the public interest; however, its public was not Oakland but rather the utility district. EBMUD officials were responsible to the district and not to Oakland.

A member of the subsystem correctly assessed EBMUD's position when he said, "The basic problem with regard to the installation of a sewer service charge is *not* administrative but *political* in nature." EBMUD would express administrative reservations to mask political concerns. The utility stated that it lacked office space and machine capacity as an excuse for avoiding a negative public reaction. It tried to keep Oakland's bill separated from its own so that the public would not feel that it was being charged twice for the same service. EBMUD did not under any circumstances want to be identified with the city's charge; it did not want the charge on its bill no matter how clearly "Oakland" would be designated.

This conflict between the two governments was more apparent at the policy level than at lower administrative levels. During the proposal and operational stages of the charge, technicians and accounting supervisors were able to work quite closely together. They solved the identification problem by developing a completely separate bill which the district could mail but which would be identified only with Oakland.

The Morin-Reading agreement on the sliding scale rate structure allowed Oakland to complete its arrangements with EBMUD. The city would do all collections. EBMUD would do the billing with the exception that the city would bill the large users from district consumption information. The district was unhappy about the location of the breakpoints in the sliding scale as they were the same as those in the district's water service rate structure. McFarland, concerned that the district would be confused with Oakland, wrote the city manager: "the breaking points proposed by the city for its special billing suggest a similarity and relationship to the utility district's schedule of charges for water service that may make the participation of the utility district in this entire program very awkward and perhaps even unacceptable."

At a meeting with EBMUD personnel, a compromise was reached whereby these breakpoints for the sliding scale would differ. The new sliding scale was incorporated in the ordinance which City Council passed on March 20, 1962. A few days later the city and EBMUD signed a final agreement. The city would pay all direct costs of the billing operation—such as material, postage, and labor—and would pay one-third of the costs "which are indispensable to the performance of the billing operation by the district for the city, but which are not performed exclusively for the city." Under this agreement the city would pay one-third of EBMUD's costs of meter reading, computer system rental, and overhead. In other words, the city was subsidizing activities for which the district would have to pay, whether EBMUD provided the billing service or not.

PUBLIC ACCEPTANCE

When levying a new tax, officials expect the worst and are pleasantly surprised when only a miniscule segment of the community complains and when they have to fight only a few taxpayers in court. One reason that this pessimism is not confirmed in Oakland is that members of the revenue subsystem tend to overestimate the intensity and salience of public opinion on revenue sources. Another reason is that, having negotiated a favorable sewer service charge rate for the large users and set a nominal rate for the small users, members of the subsystem had already assured a large measure of public acceptance.

At the time of the passage of the ordinance, various press releases emphasized that city officials felt the sewer service charge was not a tax. All users would pay their share, including many who do not pay taxes at all, such as military bases, schools, hospitals, and public agencies. In brochures printed by the city of Oakland to explain why people would be getting a bill for sewer service, the theme was repeated: the charge was not a tax, and all users would pay their fair share. The city pointed out that the charge was a result of a citizens' committee, that there had been public hearings and debates, that the mayor and City Council agreed with the citizens' committee, and that the fairest way of meeting the sewer replacement problem was to introduce such a charge. Furthermore, money from the sewer service charge would go into a special fund that could be used only for maintenance and reconstruction of existing sanitary sewers, not to install new sewers.

Regardless of this attempt to indicate the importance of the charge and its supposed equity, the council received complaints and the subsystem answered them. For example, one person wrote his councilman: "I would like to know since when the City has the right to pass laws that affect all the people without putting it to a vote by the people. I can understand property owners that would be very happy about this but a tenant pays for everything such as this in their rent. This sewer service charge I can't understand."

In answering the letter for the councilman, the finance director responded that a special committee of the council had met with many groups and that these groups had included the Alameda County Taxpayers Association, the Apartment House Owners Association of Alameda County, and the Alameda County Industries Incorporated as well as the Chamber of Commerce. He continued by pointing out that public hearings were also held, that they were open to anyone who wished to express his opinion, and that there were newspaper and legal notices telling the citizens of Oakland about the ordinance and hearings. In addition, he bolstered his argument by pointing out that the wording of the ordinance which the city adopted was taken directly from that part of the state of California General Code which gives cities the permission to levy such a charge.

The sewer service charge became effective on July 1, 1962, and the first bills were mailed July 9. After a year of operation, in June 1963, the *Oakland Tribune* reported that officials felt the sewer service charge had gained public acceptance and were pleased with this and with the replacement of sewers. The finance director emphasized that federal and normally tax-exempt properties were paying the charge, and that the great majority of Oakland residents "are paying cheerfully . . . because they realize it is one of the most equitable 'taxes' ever levied."

ADMINISTRATION: DELINQUENCIES

Some people will not pay a new tax. Since the subsystem judges public acceptance by the number of people who pay, it must ascertain the point where a taxpayer's revolt turns into acceptance. Delinquency rates could be convenient operational measures of acceptance. One problem, however, is how to interpret the meaning of the rates. If 40 percent of the people do not pay their tax bills, does this constitute revolt? If the delinquency rate is 10 or 20 percent, does this constitute acceptance? The delinquency rate for the sewer service charge was quite high—16 percent in the first year—yet members of the revenue subsystem felt that the public had accepted the charge. Subsystem members defined the high delinquency rate as an administrative problem. For five years they kept track of the delinquency rate, tried to soothe irritated taxpayers, and worried about how to collect the charge.

Table 8 shows that not everyone was happy to pay the sewer service charge. The finance director's cheerful taxpayer was an example of administrative hyperbole. Delinquencies leveled off in 1965/66 to about 5 percent of the dollar value of billing. When delinquencies, for the same time period, are computed in terms of accounts rather than dollars, 18 percent of the residential accounts and 13 percent of the nonresidential accounts were delinquent; in other words, there were over 17,000 citizens who had not paid the charge.

TABLE 8: Delinquencies as a Percentage of Dollar Billings

Fiscal Year	Charges Billed	Actual Collections	Percent of Delinquency
1962/63	$1,198,109	$1,006,330	16.0
1963/64	1,165,254	1,054,455	9.5
1964/65	1,143,831	1,089,089	4.8
1965/66	1,155,706	1,098,567	4.9

SOURCE: Oakland, Budget and Finance Department.

It is not true that all federal agencies are paying the charge. The Department of Navy operates a supply depot which makes use of the city sewer system. As of fiscal year 1967, the city figures that the navy owes it over $40,000. The navy refuses to pay because of a 1953 council resolution in which the city agreed to maintain a certain sewer if the navy would pay for the sewer's installation. The navy did pay for this particular sewer and now believes it should not have to pay the city's charge. The city attorney believes that the city has a good case but is reluctant to sue the federal government; consequently, the city's Collection Division keeps adding up the bill without much effort to collect.

One of the unfortunate consequences of EBMUD'S not agreeing to collect the city's charge is that the city included in its sewer service charge ordinance a lien provision. If the user did not pay, then several years later the property owner would be informed that he was liable for the charge plus penalties. The combination of a lien on the property owner and late notification had precipitated a public relations mess. In and out of court, people claimed violation of due process. Practically every time the property owner was informed that he was responsible for a delinquent account, the City Council received a bizarre letter like this:

Dear Sirs: I am paying the enclosed $3.60 under protest but knowing you use dictatorship methods, I can do nothing about it. The water at this property was on in our name for the total sum of 5 days and we end up paying for 6 months of your so-called services? If this is not the signs of communism in which we people have no rights, no vote, no appeal, and no consideration, I do not know what it is. . . . Well, it's about time we honest citizens wake-up and find a way to out-rule your group that put this . . . charge . . . into effect.

Or an irate landlord would feel that the city is highhanded and unfair:

Dear Mayor Reading: Does the fact that they cannot locate the party responsible for these charges make me, the landlord, responsible? Maybe I am responsible. I don't know how the city runs things. But that is not the reason why I am so irritated and very angry.

26 dollars will not make me any richer nor any poorer. What makes me really mad is the fact that if you will notice these charges go back to 1963! If I am responsible for these charges why was I not billed for them in 1963 or 1964 or 1965? Why didn't they wait until there were sufficient charges and penalties accumulated to take over the real property and get it over with?

Although 17,000 taxpayers had not paid the charge and property owners are incensed at being held responsible for delinquencies, officials feel the charge has gained public acceptance. They view the problem as one of efficiency in collection procedures and administration.

ADMINISTRATION: COSTS AND CONVENIENCE

High administrative costs by themselves do not inhibit Oakland officials from suggesting a new tax or keeping the tax in the existing structure. The arrangement whereby EBMUD would bill and the city collect was bound to incur high administrative costs. The subsystem, however, could not continue tolerating the inconvenience of delinquency enforcement.

In fiscal year 1962/63 administrative costs were $95,000, or about 10 percent of revenue collections. For fiscal year 1967/68 the subsystem expected administrative costs to be approximately $240,000, or about 22 percent of estimated revenues. In the intervening years administrative costs ran about 14 percent of revenue receipts; about half of these costs were for payments to EBMUD and the rest for the city's own Sewer Service Charge Collection Division. The city's cost figures are understated, because the subsystem usually does not include personnel fringe benefits and overhead costs in its computations.

Technicians from EBMUD and the city have a friendly but costly relationship. They have to cooperate, otherwise the administration of the charge would not be feasible. Gradually EBMUD has put aside its initial feelings of reluctance concerning its partnership with the city. Although EBMUD originally insisted that the city bill the high consumption accounts because of the sliding rate agreement, it has taken over most of the billing for these accounts. The costs for EBMUD's services have increased, however. One of the reasons for this increase is that EBMUD upgraded its data processing capability. It replaced its small accounting machines with a large electronic computer. Oakland was paying for one-third of the district's IBM 360 installation.

In 1966 a new city manager, J. Keithley, and a new finance director, R. Odell, assumed their roles in the revenue subsystem. At about the same time the cost and delinquency problems converged. Administrative costs were rising. Citizens were irritated and complaining to the council. The lien provision against the property owner was being tested in the courts. High delinquency rates continued. The subsystem knew the problems but not what to do about them.

Should the city try to do the billing with its idle computer? Perhaps EBMUD would reduce its charges to the city? Should the city again ask EBMUD to do the whole job? But would EBMUD shut off the water to enforce collections? While going around in circles the subsystem came up with some utopian solutions. Instead of the charge, the city could levy a gross receipts tax on EBMUD's operations. Or the city could do the whole job itself by charging the property owner instead of the user. Forgetting about property taxpayer relief, the subsystem searched for an administrative solution.

Without resorting to equilibrium notions, it is interesting to observe how the subsystem solved its administrative headache. After superficially exploring a variety of alternatives, the subsystem returned to the 1958 solution: EBMUD should be the city's tax collector. At the beginning of 1967, Reading, now mayor, and City Manager Keithley met with the top officials of EBMUD, who came prepared to defend their billing charges. Instead, Keithley asked them to take over the complete operation for the city.

A few months passed and the city had not received an answer from EBMUD. Members of the subsystem were pessimistic; they did not expect EBMUD to agree because the district was concerned about its public image. Everyone was surprised (including me) when McFarland of EBMUD told Keithley and Odell on March 23, 1967, that EBMUD would do what the city asked. No one in City Hall knew why EBMUD stopped worrying about its public image and agreed to become a city tax collector. Officials speculated that EBMUD did not want to lose the city's money that subsidizes EBMUD's computer operation. EBMUD officials were not available to verify this speculation. In any case, EBMUD agreed to bill, collect, and shut off water to ensure payment—for a price. The district's services would cost an estimated $200,000 a year plus a one-time charge of $50,000 for reprogramming.

The subsystem agreed to EBMUD's price. It had taken five years for Oakland to get what it wanted. No members of the subsystem questioned whether the new administrative arrangement would be worth having. High administrative costs would continue, approaching 18 percent of revenue receipts. The city might receive an additional $50,000 a year due to the district's enforcement procedures. The decision to use EBMUD, however, was made not on the basis of costs or additional revenue but on convenience. The agreement with EBMUD would allow the subsystem to escape the difficulties of enforcing the lien provision, and the embarrassment of high delinquency rates would be avoided. The subsystem was happy to go along with the approach which for years it had tried to arrange. No one seriously tried to explore any less costly alternative. Besides, if the costs were too high, then the rates could be increased.

The agreement with EBMUD provided the subsystem with an opportunity to propose a rate increase. The council could approve the EBMUD agreement and an increase at the same time. The subsystem followed this basic rule: if a tax has high administrative costs, raise the rates. A rate increase would also relieve the general fund. All sewer maintenance and city overhead expenses could now be paid out of the Sewer Service Charge Fund. The subsystem could also argue that existing revenues were inadequate to fund the planned modernization of the city sanitary sewer system. Existing revenues were inadequate because of high administrative costs and the subsystem's tendency to transfer general fund expenses to the sewer charge fund. Thus, the subsystem could use a variety of justifications for a rate increase. The efficiency appeal of the EBMUD agreement would be the opening wedge, and justification on the basis of property tax relief would insure the adoption of a rate increase.

In planning its proposal to the City Council the subsystem had to calculate what the traffic would bear. For residential users the manager decided that the city should charge a minimum of one dollar a month. The finance director, in devising the rate schedule for the commercial and industrial users, looked for a rate structure that would minimize taxpayer resistance. He thought at first that fifteen large users should pay more than the 13,000 small business and industrial users, feeling that it would be easier to deal with fifteen unhappy taxpayers than 13,000. Then he remembered that it was the large users who had insisted on the sliding rate.

While the subsystem explored alternatives, E. Hayden, the spokesman for Alameda County Industries, suggested a rate schedule that would soften the impact of an increase for the fifteen large users. His suggestion was added to the subsystem's list. By March 1968, the subsystem had eight different rate schedules to present for council consideration.

The finance director presented all the alternatives but recommended number five, which the council adopted. Number five provided for a two-thirds increase in the residential rate, a two-fifths increase for the small commercial and industrial users, and a one-third increase for the large industrial users. When the finance director chose number five, he was conscious of making a political decision. In a letter to the council, he stated, "In pricing governmental services, an economically scientific approach cannot be utilized. Political considerations must be part of the pricing effort. By political considerations, it is meant that each segment of the business and social environment which might be affected by the establishment of rates must be considered." The political consideration which the finance director mentioned was that the large users might leave Oakland. He said that an across-the-board increase gave an appearance of equity, but equity was not as important to Oakland as these large industries. In reality, he did not care if a few canneries left Oakland so long as they did not complain too loudly. Although he left the decision to the council, the finance director did not want the consensus on the charge disturbed. Number five was not Hayden's suggestion but would be accepted by him.

In the *Oakland Tribune* of March 24, 1968, reporter B. Martin called attention to the proposed increase and to a meeting which would be held to discuss the charge the following Tuesday afternoon. The council held this open meeting in a small room in City Hall. Only a few members of the attentive public attended: Martin of the *Tribune,* Hayden of Alameda County Industries, and McKnight of the Alameda County Taxpayers Association, one neighborhood association representative, and one nonaffiliated citizen.

After a general complaint about high taxes from the citizen and a complaint about sewer contracts from the neighborhood representative, the mayor asked the finance director to give the council a presentation. Odell explained that most of the city's administrative problems and costs were with the residential accounts; therefore, it was appropriate that residential rates be increased more than industrial rates. In other words, all residential taxpayers should be penalized because some of them do not pay their bills.

City Manager Keithley avoided the details of the proposed rate schedule. Instead, he pointed out the advantages of the charge: charitable organizations, rest homes, and federal agencies paid the charge; the tax exempt did not escape. His basic argument was that the rate increase would provide property tax relief. He reminded the council that it had recently decided not to support sanitary sewers out of the general fund. The city would not be increasing taxes but merely cutting one tax while increasing another. Throughout his discussion, the manager indicated that he knew the history of the charge. He might have been the manager ten years ago. While most of the participants lacked a contextual knowledge of the charge, the manager knew the original justifications, the details of the EBMUD agreement, and the sewer service charge's interrelations with other tax and budgetary policies. His continuity with the past and his effective performance encouraged the council's adoption of the rate increase.

The subsystem expected that by summer 1969 EBMUD would have completed its arrangements to accept all billing and collecting responsibilities for the city. At that juncture, the lien procedure would be replaced by EBMUD's threat of shutting off the water. It was expected that delinquencies would go down, and that the sewer service charge would become like the rest of Oakland's hidden taxes. Unaware taxpayers would pay without pain.

SUMMARY

One of the interesting features of this case history is the continuity of revenue behavior. The decisions of the past guide the solutions of present problems. Once the subsystem develops a story which facilitates taxpayer acceptance, there is no good reason to change it. It would waste the subsystem's time to conduct an intensive information search every time the council considered the sewer service charge, and thus the subsystem used the *Western City* article advantageously to cut search costs. An old justification is as good as a new one. The property tax always needs relief. The subsystem continued to explain the sewer service charge by quoting the 1959 citizens' committee report. City officials continued to minimize taxpayer resistance; for example, the finance director took care not to disturb the consensus on the charge by recommending a rate acceptable to the attentive public composed of large users. Finally, continuity of revenue behavior is best expressed in the subsystem's perseverance in trying to get EBMUD to be a city tax collector. For the subsystem the administrative convenience of using EBMUD outweighs the excessive costs of its services.

Members of the subsystem see many advantages to the sewer service charge. It is a painless way to finance sewer replacement. General fund costs are transferred to the sewer service charge fund, and the property taxpayer is relieved. The tax burden is spread among users who pay the nominal charge without complaint. Organizations exempt from the property tax pay the charge. Other sources of financing are not as attractive for the subsystem; for example, Oakland voters seldom approve bonds for sewer replacement. The adoption of the sewer service charge is consistent with the general city norm of financing capital improvement projects on a pay-as-you-go basis.

The case history of the sewer service charge shows clearly how the subsystem minimizes political costs while incurring economic costs. Are there alternatives to low-yielding, painless taxation? Do city officials have a choice? Is it possible to raise the property tax? Just what are the limits of taxpayer support and resistance? These are complicated questions and there is little empirical evidence on which to base a definitive answer. In chapter 7, I will try to explore possible policy alternatives open to city officials.

5

Budgeting Without Money

One of my main interests in exploring revenue is that I believe it is an important factor in explaining budgetary behavior. In the previous chapters, I noted that the city's revenue constraint encourages building a budgetary surplus through conservative estimating rules and that Oakland uses its limited resources mostly for self-maintenance but not for an expansion of services. In addition, other aspects of budgetary behavior indicate the importance of revenue. Departmental officials often use revenue as a justification for expenditure requests; for example, the Recreation Department argues that its subsidization of Lake Merritt activities helps downtown business and increases the sales tax yield. The city's budget officer believes his analysts should know about revenue because it provides insight to a department's program. Another example is similar to a "strategy" Wildavsky identified at the federal level: in budget review, an expenditure request is more likely to be approved if it will pay for itself by generating its own revenue or decreasing costs.[1] Thus, revenue influences behavior at a number of points in the budgetary process.

To say that revenue influences budgetary behavior is not particularly helpful because this conclusion approximates the empty statement that cities spend the money they have. It is

1. Aaron Wildavsky, *The Politics of the Budgetary Process* (Boston: Little, Brown and Co., 1964), pp. 117–118.

more interesting to focus sharply on the nature of the influence. Brown and Gilbert, for example, point out that federal and state funded projects are given preference in Philadelphia's capital programming process, and this finding suggests that the kind of revenue (i.e., free money) may bias resource allocations.[2] Crecine found, in testing the sensitivity of his simulation model, that the type of revenue pattern (constant, accelerating, and fluctuating) over time does differentially affect allocations between salaries, expenses, and equipment accounts. An increasing revenue situation, for example, decreased the "share" of resources going to salaries.[3] Probably budgetary behavior also varies by the wealth of the city; certainly those students who use aggregative statistical approaches have found that measures of income and assessed valuation are important determinants of local expenditures.[4] Hence, the kind of revenue, the pattern of funding over time, and the level and distribution of wealth in a city are some of the influential links to budgetary behavior.

In Oakland revenue clearly influences budgetary behavior, but the relationship is obscured if one views budgeting only as a resource allocation device. For the most part, Oakland's resources were allocated years ago when the present governmental structure was established. Previous decisions determine present allocations: the decision to have a manager-council form of government, the decision to have a free library, and the decision on the fire insurance rating of the city were made by other participants but govern today's actions. If one allows for slight increases in the cost of Oakland's employees and expenses, then last year's

2. W. H. Brown, Jr. and C. E. Gilbert, *Planning Municipal Investment: A Case Study of Philadelphia* (Philadelphia: University of Pennsylvania Press, 1961), p. 270.

3. John P. Crecine, *Governmental Problem-Solving: A Computer Simulation of Municipal Budgeting* (Chicago: Rand McNally and Co., 1969), pp. 179–185.

4. See, for example: Alan K. Campbell and Seymour Sacks, *Metropolitan America: Fiscal Patterns and Governmental Systems* (New York: The Free Press, 1967); John C. Bollens et al., *Exploring the Metropolitan Community* (Berkeley and Los Angeles: University of California Press, 1961), pp. 331–352; Harvey E. Brazer, *City Expenditures in the United States*, Occasional Paper no. 66 (New York: National Bureau of Economic Research, 1959); Stanley Scott and Edward L. Feder, *Factors Associated with Variations in Municipal Levels: A Statistical Study of California Cities* (Berkeley: Bureau of Public Administration, University of California, 1957).

budget is this year's budget. Although the participants will argue for marginal increases, no one expects there will be enough money to make a dramatic change in a particular budget. The acceptance of the no-money premise by most participants reinforces Oakland's incremental budgetary behavior.

If the budgetary process should not be interpreted strictly as an allocation device, then how should one interpret the effort which most city officials put into it? Certainly the budgetary process is not a meaningless ritual but does have some use to officials. The department heads use the budget to communicate to the revenue subsystem, to the council, to segments of the community, to their professional associations, and to their employers. The revenue subsystem will appreciate their problems and the other groups will know that they tried. Department heads do not expect to get what they request, but they assume there is nothing to lose by asking. Since the departmental requests exceed available revenue, the subsystem chooses to balance the budget by cutting, and enough cutting can postpone revenue increases. Line-item budgeting and the inexperience of the budget analysts facilitate the cutting. Besides having to force expenditures to fit a conservative revenue estimate, the subsystem uses the process to control city operations: the manager finds out what is going on and encourages the department's cooperation by making marginal changes in the budget. Communication and control are two important reasons why Oakland officials take budgeting seriously.

The title of this chapter could easily have been: Disjunctions in the Budgetary Process. When one examines the influence of revenue on the budgetary process, the city bureaucracy appears to be dichotomized into budget spenders (the departments) and budget cutters (the revenue subsystem). The continuous fiscal deprivation in Oakland sharpens the difference between these two groups of officials. The subsystem has to reduce its service orientation and emphasize revenue considerations. The departments, on the other hand, have to disregard the revenue constraint and concentrate on their service-performance function. As a result disjunctions occur: the departments ignore revenue limitations in formulating their programs; and the revenue subsystem ignores program and service considerations in balancing the budget. The subsystem worries about input (revenue) while the departments worry about output (service).

Members of the revenue subsystem seek to hold down costs, while operating officials seek to improve service and indirectly to expand costs. The budgetary interaction between these two sets of officials is one of latent conflict and is related to functional differences: throughout the budgetary process the maintenance function of the subsystem conflicts with the service-performance function of the operating departments. This conflict is particularly evident when one examines the guidance part of the process. In the fall, the revenue subsystem issues instructions to the departments for budget preparation. One of these instructions is the manager's guidance letter which states his assessment of the city's probable fiscal condition for the future budget year. How do budget spenders respond to the guidance of the budget cutters?

If experience from other studies was applicable, one might expect that the city manager's guidance letter, which reflects the subsystem's revenue concerns, would influence the department's budget preparation. The manager would state his no-money premise and operating officials would lower their requests accordingly. Yet in Oakland most officials do not pay attention to budgetary guidance. In other cities, however, operating officials appear to be more responsive to guidance. In Crecine's simulation work he found that the mayor's letter sets in motion the budget process, but more importantly it structures the department head's decision problem; from the "tone" of the letter the department head estimates what the mayor will allow in terms of an increase in his present budget.[5] Supposedly, a pessimistic financial tone tends to depress budget requests, and therefore department heads ask for more but not as much as they would if the financial situation were optimistic.

The explanation for the differences between Oakland and these other cities might lie in the degree of centralization of the city,

5. Crecine, p. 54.

the city's political structure, and economic conditions. Conceivably a strong mayor, who has some control over his departments, could insure that departments would be responsive to changing economic conditions and revenue resources. In Oakland, there is a history of autonomous departments and commissions, and only in the late 1960s has the manager attempted to control the fragmented organization. Furthermore, there is the continuing problem of no-money, which I termed "fiscal atrophy" earlier. Is there any incentive for a department head to pay attention to guidance letters in an impoverished city, like Oakland, which has been pinching pennies for years? As we shall see, some department heads pay more attention to the guidance than others, but no official holds the line even though all are asked to do so.

GUIDANCE WHICH IS NOT GUIDANCE:
REPETITION AND AMBIGUITY

The important thing to understand about the manager's letter is that it contains nonoperational guidance, or decision rules that are not decision rules. Because everybody knows there is no money, the letter does not express anything new. The city's head librarian, for example, complains that for twenty years he has listened to the same old story from a variety of managers and budget officers: there is not enough revenue and the budget must be cut. City officials have cried wolf too often.

The librarian is correct in his observation that every year the manager says the same thing. An examination of the guidance letters since 1957 reveals two themes. The first is the "teamwork" theme which states that the city has financial problems and everyone must work together to cut costs and be efficient. This theme appeals to the conscience of the department head to give the taxpayer the most for his money; if the departments can be efficient, then the city might avoid revenue increases. Here are some selections from the guidance letters to illustrate this teamwork theme:

Fiscal year 1957/58: Our goal is to maintain the present high level of services at a decreased cost. It is requested that . . . each department head and board review its operations and make suggestions that will assist us in reducing costs. With your assistance, we may avoid increasing the tax rate or seeking new sources of revenue.

Fiscal year 1960/61: Your fine team effort in helping us meet the financial problems of the city in these difficult times is greatly appreciated.

Fiscal year 1962/63: As you know, the main source of revenue that keeps our city's operations going is the property tax. Please remember that every $65,000 that you are responsible for spending is equal to 1¢ on the tax rate. Approximately 90% of our city's budget pays for day-to-day expenses. . . . You can see the importance of reducing our day-to-day costs by increasing efficiency.

The second theme is more dismal; it stresses the revenue-expenditure gap. It states the no-money premise and emphasizes that services cannot be expanded. Although the letters do not use the hold-the-line term, the subsystem's expectation is that the departments will submit expenditure requests similar to their current funding levels:

Fiscal year 1958/59: No substantial growth in Oakland's population can be predicted. Significant revenue increases cannot be expected, but the cumulative effects of increased employee benefits . . . must be met. . . . Expenditures are increasing at a rate which exceeds the ability to raise additional revenues.

Fiscal year 1963/64: Your budget estimates are to be based on the existing level of services as approved . . . for the 1962/1963 year. . . . Requests for new personnel will only be considered in extreme emergency situations. . . . Expenditures are increasing at a rate which exceeds the ability to raise additional revenues.

Thus there is justification for the charge of crying wolf. In Oakland it is not a question of pulling in your belt one year so that next year you will do better. Department heads soon get cynical and adopt the stance that they have nothing to lose by asking.

Even during a fiscal year, members of the subsystem continually remind departmental officials that the city is financially impoverished. The manager, at every possible opportunity, points out the revenue constraint. Hence, department heads are well aware of the city's financial limitations before they receive the formal guidance letter. In the summer of 1967, the manager told the department heads that they would have to hold the line. By the fall (October) no one was surprised when the manager said it again: "As I have stated earlier . . . the 1967/68 year will be a most difficult one, financially. Consequently, it is not possible to plan any major changes in the level of services provided, or that any major additions will be made in the amount spent by any department beyond what is absolutely essential."

In a situation of continuous fiscal deprivation, to be told to cut costs and not to ask for more loses all significance. Furthermore, the guidance is ambiguous:

Fiscal Year 1968/69. As you begin the preparation of your departmental budget request, I would ask that you bear in mind that the city of Oakland continues to face a difficult and debilitating financial problem. The economic condition of the community is such that we as professional administrators must be constantly aware of the fiscal limitations within which we must function.

The department head who receives this guidance can say, yes, I am aware, but so what? Lacking specific instructions, department heads are free to interpret the guidance according to their own spending inclinations. Oakland does not make use of ceilings or acceptable percentage levels of deviation. Since the subsystem does not quantify the hold-the-line guidance, department heads see the guidance more as a request rather than an order. Ambiguity provides maneuver room, and department heads do not want the guidance to contain ceilings and be specific.

Another interesting feature of the hold-the-line guidance is that the subsystem does not make much effort in developing it. When they write the city manager's letter, members of the subsystem do not try to estimate revenue for the coming fiscal year. Detailed revenue estimates are not computed until late March and April when the subsystem must balance the budget. Considering the importance of revenue to the municipal budget, one might expect that guidance would be based on some investigation of future revenue conditions. Instead, members of the subsystem assume that they are not going to have any significant increases in money and write the letter on the basis of their general feeling of financial pessimism.

Thus, both sides in the budgetary arena, the members of the subsystem and the department heads, are well aware of the city's financial problems. The subsystem does not have to estimate revenue to put out the guidance, and the department heads do not need the guidance because they already know. The guidance letter simply initiates the budgetary process; it does not structure or delimit the actor's decision problem because it is ambiguous and because the no-money premise has already been accepted by city officials.

DEPARTMENT HEADS DO NOT HOLD THE LINE

One could think of guidance as structuring the department head's decision problem if, when the manager said to hold the line, the department head did so. To the manager, "hold the line" means that, because there is no money, do not waste your time on budgeting; submit this year's budget for next year. Although department heads accept the no-money premise, they do not accept the manager's conclusion to hold the line. In many cases the difference between a department's 1967 budget request and its 1966 budget appropriation is quite substantial. In Table 9 this

TABLE 9: Department Heads Do Not Hold the Line
(in percent)

Department	(*1967 Request minus 1966 Appropriation*) ÷ *1966 Appropriation*
Museum	−12.7
Police	+ 5.9
Library	+ 6.0
Fire	+ 9.5
Building and Housing	+11.8
Municipal Buildings	+13.8
Street and Engineering	+17.3
Park	+32.3
Traffic Engineering	+34.1
Recreation	+38.7

SOURCE: Oakland, Budget and Finance Department.

difference is shown as a percentage of the 1966 budget appropriation. Departments certainly vary in their responsiveness to the manager's guidance, and it is reasonable to conclude that the large departments that are responsible for providing services and meeting public demands do not hold the line. The one major exception is the museum's reduction of 12.7 percent. Such reductions are quite atypical, and this situation was the result of a decision to postpone the opening date of Oakland's new museum. Minor exceptions to the conclusion occurred in some of the staff offices such as the city clerk and the manager's own office which requested slightly less than their previous budget. If department heads were trying to hold the line, one might expect a slight increase in the requests as a result of price changes; but certainly one would not expect a 30 percent increase.

To students of organizational behavior, the conclusion that officials do not do what they are asked to do is trivial. The interesting question is, Why do heads of departments, like Dickens' Oliver, ask for more, particularly when the fiscal barrel is empty?

DEPARTMENT HEADS IGNORE THE GUIDANCE
TO GET MORE MONEY

There is no doubt that department heads believe that by asking they increase their chances for getting more funds. They usually can cite examples of putting in an item and getting it. Moreover, some department heads feel they are competing for funds. If they do not ask, they might lose the money to another department and not get their fair share. From their perspective, submitting a bare-bones budget is giving an advantage to those officials who do not follow the guidance.

But does it pay to ask? I do not have a definitive answer to this question, because it is difficult to isolate the effects of the request patterns. But I feel that, in a fiscally deprived situation, asking for more probably has some minor short run payoffs, but in the long run it does not make much difference in the expenditure level of a department. Asking for more in itself is not enough to dramatically change what a department gets. For example, in examining budget request and expenditure patterns since 1960, I found that the Police Department was consistently lower in its requests than the other major departments. On the average, the police chief asked for a 3.4 percent increase (over the previous appropriation), while the recreation superintendent asked for a 32.7 percent increase. Through the years with different actors, these two departments maintained their patterns of budgetary request. But the average increase in expenditures for both departments was about the same: the low-asking Police Department's expenditures increased 8 percent per year while the high-asking Recreation Department expenditures increased 6.9 percent per year.

Furthermore, events outside of a department head's control influence expenditure levels more than his request patterns. A grant from the federal government, a new gas tax from the state, the voters' approval of bond issues for a museum—all of these revenue events dramatically affect expenditure levels. Even for those departments that grow gradually through the years, the request pattern is not a satisfactory explanation. For example, salary increases, an important factor in the growth of expenditures, are determined outside of the system of requests. Sometimes the council approves salary increases as a result of organized employee pressure, but usually salary increases are computed according to a formula and are granted automatically. Hence, asking for more may occasionally get a department a minor equipment item, but that item will be lost in the other forces which increase the level of expenditure over time.

DEPARTMENT HEADS IGNORE THE GUIDANCE
TO EXPRESS NEEDS

Department heads may have the expectation that it does not hurt to ask, but hoping for additional funds is not the only explanation for their behavior. The typical department head explains his response to the guidance as: I am a professional; no one, not even the manager, can understand this job unless he sits here; I know our needs, and I would not be doing my job unless I expressed them. Department needs are assumed to be coterminous with community needs when the department head mixes professional standards and community demands in his budget request. Whatever the source of these needs, the budgetary process is used to communicate needs and to put the problem where the money is. The department head, like a doctor, prescribes medicine for good health, but he cannot force the patient to take it. His professional responsibility stops when he writes the prescription. Similarly, the city engineer states a path needs a railing or someone might be hurt, the fire chief feels the level of fire protection is in jeopardy because the city should have a new pumper, and the recreation superintendent believes the golf course should be reseeded as the city is competing with other courses. Department heads feel they have done their jobs and relieve their own anxiety when they express their needs. Not only do they satisfy their own professional norms, but by passing the buck to the manager and council, department heads satisfy their employee and community constituents.

Although department heads do not hold the line, they do exhibit different degrees of responsiveness to the subsystem's guidance and can be classified into three types: ignoring, compromising, and following.

The "ignoring" department head accepts the no-money premise but completely disregards its implications. He acknowledges that the city is living within a severe revenue constraint; however, because it is his responsibility to express the needs of his department regardless of the revenue problem, the guidance letter is meaningless to him. His budget requests are a device to make these needs salient: the budget is an educational process and an opportunity to express needs and problems. Although he wants more money, it is equally important for him to get the manager and the council to appreciate the nature of his problems. If these officials do not get the money this year, they hope that maybe they will next year. They say they would submit the same budget regardless of the financial warning in the manager's letter.

The "compromising" department head does not play it straight but manipulates his budget to get all that he can without alienating the manager. He tries to strike a balance between what he thinks he needs and what he thinks he can get. For example, holding the line may mean not rapidly expanding the staff, not requesting excessive equipment, and cutting out some programs. On the other hand, the compromising department head wants as many opportunities as possible to explain his problems and press for his programs. If he keeps his budget stable, there might be less opportunity to gain the manager's appreciation of his problems. Considering the lack of incentives for a strict interpretation of the hold-the-line guidance, the compromising department head looks for some middle ground where he can feel that he followed the guidance and presented his problems. In short, he believes it does not hurt to ask as long as he does not ask for something extravagant. Holding the line for compromising department heads means keeping the lid on expenditures but not maintaining the same budget level. It means looking for funds for some needs and keeping quiet about other needs.

The "following" department head is cautious about using the budget to gain an appreciation of needs and problems. Only a few of the major department heads fall in this classification. The following department head unequivocally states that he seriously follows the manager's guidance letter. He has a reputation for not padding budgets, and he is anxious to maintain this reputation with budget and finance officials and the manager. Therefore, when he receives the manager's letter, he has his subordinates use it in preparing their budgets. Furthermore, this official and his immediate budget assistants feel that they conduct a detailed review by each minor item, so, as they put it, "there is no water in the towel." The following department head looks to cut costs wherever he can, and the aura of "turn in your pencil stub before drawing another pencil" is prevalent. His predilection for following the orders of a superior to maintain the department's reputation gets in the way of an expansive use of the budget. On the other hand, he believes his budget can be used to express a few operating problems even though he expects that his requests will be cut.

DEPARTMENT HEADS IGNORE THE GUIDANCE
BECAUSE IT DOES NOT HURT TO ASK

Ironically, the subsystem wants the departments to hold the line but encourages them not to do so. Subsystem members excuse noncompliance. They believe it is unrealistic to expect a budget to remain flat, and that some change is likely. They know that occasionally departments cannot help themselves. For example, the scheduling of a project may be out of their hands: because of their renewal plans, the independent Redevelopment Agency may call for a heavy street-lighting expenditure in a particular year; similarly, the chief engineer has to request construction funds because of previous commitments. Particularly for those departments whose budgets rely on state and federal funds and involve capital expenditures, the subsystem does not expect them to hold the line. Department heads sense that the subsystem's expectations are not firm, which provides leeway to ask for more.

Since the subsystem does not mean business, there is no punishment for noncompliance and no reward for adherence. Given the city's fragmented organization, it is difficult to enforce any orders of which adherence to guidance is a specific case. The manager cannot fire a department head because of noncompliance. All the department head loses is the time he spends filling out requests which will not be approved. Moreover, department heads realize that their personal potential rewards (such as a raise) are related to the subsystem's general evaluation of them and are not a function of a single year's budgetary request.

In any event, for the subsystem to reward or punish a department head, the members have to perceive that the official did not follow orders. Given the ambiguity in the guidance, I had expected that the higher the official was in the city hierarchy, the more negatively he would perceive department responses; members of the subsystem would feel that no one held the line, and department heads would feel that they had done so. However, as Table 10 shows, perceptions as to who held the line were much more uniform among officials than I had anticipated. Department heads more often than not agreed with subsystem members. But what is more interesting, there was agreement on the positive responses even when objectively these departments did not hold the line (see Table 9). Furthermore, when the data in Table 9 are compared with the responses in Table 10, it is clear that the department's recent budget request is not the only influence on these perceptions. For example, the library's modest increase of 6 percent is similar to the Police Department's figure. But while everyone agrees that the police held the line, there is no such agreement among members of the subsystem about the library. The museum submits a budget decrease and both the subsystem and the department head agree that the museum did not hold the line. It does not make much difference how much the director requests; subsystem members believe the museum is living in relative luxury. The museum director is puzzled about this reaction because he does not believe that the manager's guidance applied to him. He is under the impression that he has been given a mandate to develop the finest museum on the West

Coast, and he has developed the spending norms that everything (including the ashtrays) must be first rate. The museum has the reputation of being a big spender.

TABLE 10: Did the Department Hold the Line?

| | | Revenue Subsystem | | | |
Department	Dept. Head	Budget Office Reviewer	Budget Officer	Finance Director	City Manager
Museum	No	No	No	No	No
Police	Yes	Yes	Yes	Yes	Yes
Library	No	No	Yes	No	Yes
Fire	No	Yes	No	No	No
Building and Housing	Yes	No	Yes	No	No
Municipal Buildings	Yes	Yes	Yes	Yes	Yes
Street and Engineering	Yes	No	Yes	No	No
Park	No	No	No	No	No
Traffic Engineering	No	No	Yes	No	No
Recreation	No	No	No	No	No

Why do members of the subsystem perceive some department heads as big spenders and others as holding the line? Since the perceptions reflect evaluations of the individual department heads, a broader range of behavior probably influences their formation. In other words, the subsystem member develops these perceptions through years of contact with the department head on a variety of budgetary and nonbudgetary matters. The perceptions are built up out of a general pattern of behavior not as a reaction to a single budget request. Because department heads do have spending reputations, the manager congratulates the police chief on doing a good job on the budget while he comments on the recreation superintendent's performance, "that's par for the course, recreation departments never hold the line."

One explanation for the members' perceptions which appear inconsistent with budget requests of the department lies in a distortion of an old saying: familiarity breeds understanding and tolerance. Through the years some subsystem members, by working with department heads on a variety of projects, have come to appreciate the department's problems. The subsystem member adopts the service orientation of the department head. He starts believing that the budget should express needs, and it is hard for him to cut a budget because he becomes concerned about the cut's impact on service. Such a situation existed with the city's budget officer who was finally fired because the other subsystem members felt that he had been coopted by the departments. The budget officer, more than any other member of the subsystem, thought the departments had held the line (see Table 10).

Although the budget officer's behavior may be exaggerated, the same factor of tolerance also affects the other members of the subsystem. In the case of Municipal Buildings Department, the members know that the department houses the city architect and the auditorium director who, for reasons which no one remembers, feel they are autonomous. The department head has no control over these people, so his budget requests come in high (13.8 percent increase). However, since all members of the subsystem are aware of the department head's organizational difficulties, they agree with him that he held the line.

Subsystem members also transfer their negative evaluations of a department head's performance to their perceptions about budgetary response. For example, subsystem members believe that the library has the highest cost and the lowest service in the state. They feel that the library did not hold the line because of their general negative evaluation of the library's performance, and their feeling is not related to its current budget request. Similarly, members of the subsystem view the Building and Housing Department with suspicion, so most of them perceive this department as not conforming to guidance. According to them the department head has not held the line because he had not fired the people who had been cut from the previous year's budget. The department head thought he could let the people go by attrition, and he feels that he held the line.

Members of the subsystem evaluate department heads not from a single budget request but from exposure to a broad range of behavior. Department heads know that their own evaluations are not tied to a single budget request, so there is every reason to ask for more. Since the subsystem does not, at least openly, punish noncompliance or reward adherence, department heads are free to use the budget to satisfy other demands on them. Without getting substantial amounts of additional resources, department heads still feel there are enough incentives to ignore the guidance. It does not hurt to ask.

Under conditions of continuous fiscal deprivation, budgeting at the departmental level ceases being fiscally realistic because programs, the department's plans and aspirations, are insulated from the city's revenue constraint. Responses which ignore budgetary guidance demonstrate a critical disjunction in the process.

BALANCING THE BUDGET

Although the departments ignore the city's revenue constraint in their requests, the revenue subsystem cannot ignore the reality of not having enough money to meet these requests. Subsystem members know they must follow Oakland's basic fiscal rule: the budget must be balanced. Every year the subsystem faces the problem of cutting the budget to match the city's revenue constraint; for example, for fiscal year 1967/68, the total amount requested was about 10 percent more than estimated revenues. Cutting is an intrinsic part of any budget process. It occurs at the national and state levels. But what is interesting about smaller governments, like Oakland, is that the people who do the cutting are the city's revenue maximizers. Cutting the budget is a form of revenue behavior. In Oakland this behavioral tendency is reinforced by the lack of money. The motivation for the revenue subsystem is clear: the more it can cut, the less it has to worry about finding new sources of revenue. The first line of defense against budget spenders is to balance the budget by cutting.

The simple fact that budget cutters are revenue maximizers creates another disjunction in the process: the revenue subsystem ignores program and service considerations in balancing the budget. In practice, balancing does not mean the explicit determination of services by considering available resources. In fact, most of the balancing is a matter of paring the budget down to what the base was in the previous year by getting rid of incremental requests and not by making major reallocations in terms of the utilization of resources or the adjustment of the operating configurations of the departments.[6] The world would have to be

6. Wildavsky defines the base as "the general expectation among the participants that programs will be carried on at close to the going level of expenditures but it does not necessarily include all activities" (Wildavsky, p. 17).

very different than it is to make such major reallocations: for example, (1) all resources could be used (no constraints on transferring personnel because of civil service); (2) officials would agree on goals; (3) officials would know the relation of current programs to those goals; and (4) the public would agree completely with the officials. In such a world, officials probably would not have to worry about a revenue constraint either, but they do have to worry, so budgeting proceeds by cutting, and the city's output in terms of goals and services is mostly disregarded.

City officials, as compared to the general public, certainly understand that there is a connection between taxes and services. Intellectually, they see the tax-service nexus, but in their behavior they have to emphasize only one-half of the relation. City officials expect the departments to express service needs and the members of the subsystem to express revenue needs. Fairly insulated from community demands and service needs, the subsystem balances the budget with impunity. Although members use the rhetoric of any cut means a cut in service, the fiscal situation drives them to cut.

INEXPERIENCE FACILITATES CUTTING
IN THE BUDGET OFFICE

The Budget and Finance Department—the analysts, the finance director, and the budget officer—would like to balance the budget by allocating and reallocating within and between the departments. In practice, they seldom have the knowledge to be able to do it. Balancing the budget in the Budget Office is accomplished by a lack of information. Because of his own lack of experience, the analyst is not aware of the impact of his acts on service or on policy; he is free to make cuts and to identify items for which the city manager must make decisions. The more experienced and knowledgeable an analyst becomes about his department and the more aware he becomes of the impact of cutting on that department, the more reluctant he is to make rash suggestions. Thus, for the budget analyst to be a defender of revenue, inexperience is a great help.

To put this balancing by cutting in an organizational context, it should be recognized that the Budget Office is small, containing a handful of analysts. During the past few years, it has become relatively isolated from the departments which view the Budget Office suspiciously as a necessary evil, as a compiler of other people's numbers. Besides worrying about revenue, the Budget Office spends its time fighting small fires, taking care of minor transfers of funds or getting involved in meaningless detail; consequently analysts have limited opportunity to do studies before the budget season and during the season it is impossible to do anything in depth. Since each analyst is assigned three or four departments and has a heavy workload during the rest of the year, he is unlikely to learn much about any department. The few experienced analysts in the office have left for other jobs, and the considerable turnover in the office has reinforced this lack of experience. Budget officers usually worry about their analysts becoming captive by the department to which they are assigned, but this is not a worry in Oakland because of the low level of experience. How does an inexperienced budget analyst, who knows little or nothing about the department he is reviewing, cut that department's budget?

Inexperience in itself forces upon the budget analyst the use of a set of rules of thumb. The analyst first looks at last year's appropriations to identify any significant changes. It is the changes or incremental requests which get his attention. Without going into detail, here is an outline of the rules of cutting:

(1) Cut all increases in personnel

(2) Cut all equipment items which appear to be luxuries

(3) Use precedent—cut items which have been cut before

(4) Recommend repair and renovation rather than replacement of facilities

(5) Recommend study as a means of deferring major costs

(6) Cut all non-item operating costs by a fixed percentage (such as 10 percent)

(7) Do not cut when safety or health of staff or public is obviously involved

(8) Cut departments with "bad" reputations

(9) When in doubt ask another analyst what to do

(10) Identify dubious items for the manager's attention

The analyst, by looking for enough items to cut, proceeds until the budget is balanced within the existing revenue constraint. Ironically, the very existence of the city's revenue constraint facilitates expenditure cuts. The analyst does not have to be persuaded or convinced that certain things should be cut or that economy is a necessity when he is told there is no choice. For example, consider personnel. Usually, departments will request a total of over a hundred additional people (about 3 percent of the city's current personnel strength). These requests will be turned down without any investigation because the point of departure is, What was the budgeted personnel strength last year? If there were no revenue constraint, then someone might have to consider seriously the validity of personnel requests. But because personnel are the main costs of the budget and for every person the subsystem adds, the city incurs a fixed cost—once hired never fired—the rule is: cut any incrementally requested personnel.

In addition to inexperience and the effect of the revenue constraint, the line-item form of Oakland's budget facilitates the cutting. The analyst does not have to worry about the effect on service when cutting line items, because he does not know the effect. Budget requests do mention services in the narrative and sometimes in the workload statistics. Budgeting cost information, however, is not related to the measures of services or workload statistics; in fact, requests from departments obscure services so that the revenue subsystem cannot adjust programs even if it wants to. A program budget would be much harder to cut and would conflict with the subsystem's short-term revenue objectives. This is not to argue that inexperience and the lack of program information are virtues, because obviously the ability to perform analytical studies about a department can aid in making reallocations. But, given that the analysts do not have the resources to make such studies, then line-item budgeting coupled with inexperienced review does facilitate the process of balancing and the protection of revenue.

THE CITY MANAGER: BUDGET REVIEW
FOR CONTROL AND EFFICIENCY

The city manager often asserts that budgeting is a waste of time because there is no money. He says that officials should not spend much time on budgeting, but in fact he spends a great deal of time on budgeting. After the analysts review the submissions from the departments and focus on items for his decision, the manager reviews all the budgets and makes most of the decisions; he feels that it is his budget. The manager contradicts his own budgeting statements because of his definition of what a city manager should do. He makes budgeting decisions within the context of his *total* job. Since he is trying to centralize administration in the city, the budget becomes a crucial point of control. In order to introduce efficient administration, the manager must control the city bureaucracy. The more the city is efficient and the more costs can be cut, the less the pressure on scarce revenue sources. Revenue protection, efficiency, and control converge when one examines the budget behavior of the city manager.

Although the city is in a financial straightjacket, there is enough leeway in budgetary procedures for the city manager to enhance his control. For example, there has been the prevalent feeling that the auditor is wasting the city's money on a computer which is idle most of the time; therefore, in the 1968/69 budget, the manager recommended transfer of $340,000 from the auditor's budget to a special account, under the manager's control, in order to encourage the auditor to give up responsibility for the city's automatic data-processing equipment. Another example is the manager's use of contingency accounts, such as contractual services, to hold money which would ordinarily go to a department; in the case of the furnishings for the new museum, the money, rather than going directly to the "extravagant" Museum Commission for allocation, was kept under the manager's control in a special account to be allocated as needed.

To increase his control, the manager tries increasing his information while decreasing the information of the other participants. Secrecy in budgeting becomes an important means of control. He does not want the analysts to communicate with the departments when they review the budget. If the departments do not know what the manager is considering, he can prevent end runs to the council. In review sessions when department heads explain their requests, he asks questions about their operations, but does not tell them where he is going to cut. He even deletes the department request figures from the formal budget. All these actions stifle department communication (a fact which once autonomous department heads are upset about); but when the manager submits the budget to the council, it is indeed *his* budget. He also uses the budget to find out whether department heads are doing what they said they would do. The budgetary process provides a great deal of information to him, not so much because of the form of its submission, but because it serves as a stimulus for further inquiry into the status of various projects. These informational cues help him control and identify areas where costs can be cut.

The manager has a simple three-stage process of examining the budget. First, he sees whether the revenue estimate is as pessimistic as his own expectations. Then he asks that those fixed costs, which the subsystem can do nothing about (such as automatic pay raises), be subtracted from the budget. And finally he gets down to looking, as he says, at the nitty-gritty details. The details, however, are not just in the budget submissions. In addition to the budget, the manager asks the budget analysts to prepare a set of ancillary data, including detailed analyses of personnel requests, overtime, and travel. Although he does not want to get involved in details, he continually does so. When the submissions reach him, many of the items for decision have already been identified; but the original department submission budget is also there, and he will often glance through page by page to pick up an item and consider it. One important aspect about his review is that it does not involve any type of meat-ax cutting—no 10 percent here or 5 percent there. It is strictly a line-item deletion, determined by his own set of preferences.

In cutting, the manager pays attention to small dollar items as well as the lumpy or big dollar items. Somehow he is cued to pay attention to certain items—and dollar amounts are not the only index of saliency. He cuts and adds small items; for example, he once tried to cut business cards out of the mayor-council's budget. Large dollar items are generally important as cues to inexperienced budget analysts, but for the manager's detailed screening, the large dollar item is only one cue among many. The manager feels this is the only way to avoid using meat-ax approaches. Considering that city officials do not have reasonable measures of what operating costs should be, the only way that he can deal with this problem is to pay attention to as much of the nitty-gritty detail as he can. Because he is only one man, a great deal slips by in the process. There is never enough time to review the base intensively. However, many items within the base and incremental to it are reviewed if they are given sufficient saliency. The Budget Office provides saliency in focusing certain items for decision. The dollar amounts focus others. A more important source of saliency is the manager's own experience in operating city government. He has certain expectations concerning what things ought to cost and what departments ought to do; and these come out, at times, when he is looking at the budget. The language of social psychology—selective perception and the provision of cues—adequately describes the decision process which occurs in the city manager's review.

No doubt, the manager's review exhibits a greater concern with program than the blind cutting of the Budget Office. But because of the lack of information, the time constraint, and the volume of minor cuts which are made, it is never possible to trace out the effect of any particular cut on a department's output. Moreover, the manager feels the revenue constraint more than any other official in the city and will often cut where other officials are too timid to do so. Based on his experience, he quickly makes judgments as to what a department can realistically use. In the case of one department, for example, the analyst had cut back the submitted budget to the previous year's level. The manager felt this was not sufficient, because he remembered that the same department had a disproportionately large share of the previous year's resources. Furthermore, he felt that he should not give money to departments that may have had insufficient time to absorb what had been previously allocated. By cutting a department's budget, he determines its absorption rate. Thus, he cuts into the base and demonstrates a time perspective which is not usually associated with incremental budgetary behavior.

The specter of revenue is apparent throughout the manager's review. Regardless of the dollar amount of an item, he is always trying to protect the general fund. The subsystem usually seeks to protect the general fund because of its concern with the property tax. The more the subsystem can reduce demands on the general fund, the more likely the property tax rate can be cut; and a low tax rate is a good sign of efficient management. By adjusting fund balances and finding new sources of revenue, the subsystem protects the general fund. The manager also contributes to this activity by constantly looking for ways of moving various costs from the general fund to the special funds. If he can charge a half man-year off to a special fund, he will be quite pleased. His concern with the general fund is also related to his desire to stop the fragmentation of local government because in some cases the special funds are governed by independent commissions that do not share his interest in cost cutting.

The manager spends a great deal of time preparing his budget for presentation to the council. He spends this time because he does not want to be cut up by the council. To be "cut up" in this context means that the council will be fiscally irresponsible and approve expensive projects or excessive salary increases. He makes his budget so tight that, if the council wants to increase an item, they also will have to find the revenue to pay for it. Before approaching the council he must get the council's Budget Subcommittee on his side. The manager operates as this subcommittee's gatekeeper for fiscal policy issues. In its many informal sessions he tells the councilmen what he considers to be the key issues and gains their support. Frequently, he points out the importance of avoiding fixed costs and policies which will automatically increase future budgets. When the Police Department requested fringe benefits for motorcycle policemen, one alternative was to have a bonus which would be tied to the officer's basic salary. The manager pointed out that in such cases the amount of fringe benefits would change as the basic salary went up and that it would be better to use an absolute amount.

The manager knows that councilmen do not have time to pay attention to the whole budget, that they tend to have pet projects. In his previous assignment a former councilman had told him, "You've got to give the man a bone to play with, and then the rest of it goes by without review." The bones, in the case of the Oakland City Council, are the community improvement projects. This is the city's giveaway program to local civic organizations such as the symphony and flower societies. In this case the manager simply recommends a total for such activity and allows the Budget Subcommittee to allocate within this total.

Careful preparation by the manager with the subcommittee results in a rubber-stamp council action on the budget. Budget

Subcommittee agreement with the manager operates as a strong lever with the council. On the other hand, the meetings with the Budget Subcommittee have certain mutual advantages to both participants. By their interaction, the city manager feels out what the council might possibly accept, and at the same time the council gains more confidence that the manager is running the city efficiently. Usually the manager defines the sequence of city manager–council relations as: the manager is supposed to cut the budget and the council is supposed to act as the liberalizing agent. But he has been so successful with the council that he will have to revise his rule. For example, for fiscal year 1967/68 he did not expect to have his budget increased because he had spent the whole year informing the council about the severe fiscal constraints that the city faced. Generally his expectations were borne out, because the council did not change his budget but accepted it as is.

A great deal of the manager's budget cutting takes place in the context of administrative efficiency and is motivated by the desire to avoid revenue increases. While cutting satisfies the revenue constraint, it is an open question whether the cutting is efficient. To answer the question the subsystem would have to examine the effects of their cuts on departmental output. But this is rarely done because of scarce informational and time resources. Both subsystem members and councilmen talk about balancing the budget by introducing administrative efficiencies. With some zeal, they assert that the same level of service can be provided at lower cost. The finance director conservatively estimates that about $2 million a year could be saved by being more efficient. Such an amount, however, would not be enough to cover annual wage and price increases. Nor could this amount be achieved at one time. At best it is possible to introduce a few administrative improvements during the fiscal year. Because efficiency is a distant goal which one approaches in a piecemeal fashion, the call to balance the budget by cost reduction may be sincere but not practical. In any event, ascertaining a desired *service level* and reducing costs is not the same thing as the subsystem's budget cutting.

SUMMARY

Usually, revenue is viewed as an afterthought, as something which pays for public demands that filter through the budget process. Demands lead to budget actions which in turn lead to revenue. The notion behind such a sequence is that if there is sufficient pressure for public services, revenue will automatically follow. But what happens when a city has to live with a severe revenue constraint? Under conditions of fiscal atrophy, revenue can have an independent influence on the budget. I have discussed two disjunctions in the no-money budgetary process which are directly related to the city's continuous revenue constraint. Departmental behavior reflects a service-performance function which conflicts with revenue imperatives. The subsystem's budgetary behavior reflects its revenue-maintenance function. Balancing the budget and the use of the budget as a control and efficiency device are alternative forms of revenue behavior. The same people who have to find revenue also have to balance the budget. No wonder they have minimal service and program orientations.

6

Citizen-Leader Perceptions
of Oakland Finance

From a systemic viewpoint, the public is the ultimate provider of the resource input to the city system. It seems reasonable to get some insights into public opinion on taxation; however, taxes, like many policy issues, suffer from public inattention. In spite of newspaper coverage of public conflicts over assessment or a new source of revenue, most people are unaware of taxes most of the time. The exceptions are the few times a year the taxpayer receives his property tax bill or fills out his income tax form. From previous survey work we know that there is a general confusion over the relationship of expenditures and tax policy. Poor people, for example, generally want more services and fewer taxes. They want someone else—the government—to pay for these services. Taxation is not only dull but it is hard to understand. A college education does not guarantee that the citizen will understand the possessory interest tax or the difference between secured and unsecured property tax rolls.

Does it make sense to talk about public opinion on taxation when only small segments, the tax publics (see chapter 3), of the community articulate such opinions? The average citizen will have opinions on taxation, but his opinions may be neither differentiated by revenue source nor bolstered by actual knowledge. On the other hand, the city official is concerned about the political feasibility of specific sources of revenue. Just what the public will support is an important criterion in the official's calculus. For example, the city manager maintains that the property tax rate must be kept stable or lowered as there is no support for a raise. The problem of political feasibility rests in part on those citizen-leaders of the community who care enough to know about the city's social, economic, and financial problems. I have designated these leaders as the potential support nucleus for increased levels of taxation and services. Tax support, in my view, must start first with the leaders of a community; therefore, it is important to understand the conditions under which leaders will support increased taxes. Obviously, one of these conditions is the particular city service which requires improvement and financing. However, there may also be a set of conditions which incline leaders to support general increases in taxation without reference to specific services. The first half of this chapter discusses some of these conditions and the number of leaders who might be in the support nucleus. It will be shown that, as of now, this nucleus is quite small, since only a minority of Oakland's citizen-leaders are aware of the financial and social problems that confront the city.

The first half of the chapter is organized by a series of questions: Why is tax comprehension important? Who should pay? Why will citizen-leaders pay? Who will pay? The second half of the chapter deals with the question: What type of tax would leaders prefer to pay? The leaders' preferences for alternative forms of taxation are discussed. Starting with the most favorable, the sales tax, and proceeding to the least favorable, the payroll or municipal income tax, seven different revenue sources will be explored.

CITIZEN TAX OPINION

DESCRIPTION OF METHOD AND CITIZEN-LEADERS

Community citizen-leaders were interviewed at the beginning of 1967. I expected that leaders, unlike the general public, would have a differentiated set of opinions on specific tax sources and city expenditures. The respondents were selected at random from lists which city officials use; they were the formal leaders of garden and social clubs, and professional, business, and neighborhood organizations. Recognizing the methodological disadvantages of such a "positional" approach, I felt it would be adequate as a first step, in view of the exploratory nature of my research activity. Open-ended questions were used and the interviews were nondirective. Sixty-six usable interviews were obtained, coded, and analyzed. (The questions used are set forth in the Appendix, p. 287.)

I attempted to achieve some balance with respect to geographic area, sex, race, residency, and organizational type. The demographic breakdown in percent is:

Race		Sex		Residency	
White	85	Male	71	Resident	76
Nonwhite	15	Female	29	Nonresident	24
N = 66	100		100		100

The typical citizen-leader interviewed is white, middle to upper class, Republican, a resident of Oakland and a professional or businessman. Among the ten nonwhite respondents, nine were Negro and one was Chinese. Eight of the nonwhite respondents were associated with neighborhood associations. The neighborhood organization category, composed solely of residents, is made up of improvement associations, parent-teacher associations, and poverty program Target Area Advisory committees. They were grouped together because they tended to serve or work for a particular geographic area of the city. When an organization worked for a particular target population—like poor children, senior citizens, youth athletics—it was classified as a service organization. Among these were the Kiwanis, Optimists, Oakland Jaycees, Zonta, and the Oakland Council of Churches. Those organizations that tended mainly to serve themselves were grouped under the category of social/professional. They included the Elks, Athenian-Nile Club, Certified Public Accountants, Credit Women's International, Music Teachers Association of California, and the Oakland Businessman's Garden Club. The largest group was composed of business organizations and several tax associations. This group consisted of such organizations as the Chamber of Commerce, Real Estate Board, Kaiser Industries, *Oakland Tribune,* Alameda County Industries Inc., Alameda County Taxpayers Association, Downtown Associations, and the Apartment

House Association of Alameda County. Finally, the "other" category included an executive from Mills College, a noncity governmental official, and leaders from the Civic Affairs Council of Oakland, AFL-CIO Labor Council of Alameda County, and the Oakland Education Association. Usually the respondents occupied positions such as president, chairman, or executive director so that they could speak for their organization, when appropriate, as well as for themselves. The breakdown by organizational category is:

	Percentage, N = 66
Business	29
Social/Professional	23
Neighborhood	21
Service	20
Other	8
	101

THE RELEVANCE OF TAX COMPREHENSION AND

THE TAX–SERVICE NEXUS

Most people are uninformed about taxes and financial matters. When I rated the respondents for their tax understanding, I did not expect to find a group of lay experts. On the other hand, since most of our respondents are middle or upper class and many are college educated, the sample should indicate greater tax comprehension than that of the general population. In Table 11 the leaders' tax comprehension is classified into three categories: good, average, and poor.[1] On the whole, citizen-leaders score fairly high on the tax comprehension rating. As in other aspects

1. A word of caution about the tables is in order. The purpose of the tables is to suggest hypotheses for future testing and not to imply evidence of verification. I tried to be assertive in the titles of the tables and in the discussion to communicate with the reader and not to claim that I am right. On the contrary, I would expect that with more rigorous methods than I used, many of my "findings" would not stand up. For example, the sample was often not large enough to employ adequate controls for exploring alternative hypotheses. Some readers may object to the omission of significance statistics from the tables, but since the interview data were used to generate the hypotheses, I felt that it would be misleading to indicate verification by such statistics. See Hanan C. Selvin, "A Critique of Tests of Significance in Survey Research," *American Sociological Review* 22 (October 1957): 525–526.

of political participation, there are sex differences. Males have higher tax comprehension than females. What I find encouraging is that only 26 percent of the citizen-leaders have poor tax comprehension. A sample of the general public probably would show at least a majority with poor tax comprehension.

TABLE 11: Males Have Higher Tax Comprehension than Females

Tax Comprehension	Male		Female		Total	
	No.	%	No.	%	No.	%
Good	20	43	2	11	22	33
Average	21	45	6	32	27	41
Poor	6	13	11	58	17	26
Total	47	101	19	101	66	100

The classification categories used for tax comprehension were defined as follows. The leader with "good" tax comprehension has a command of specialized tax vocabulary such as "regressive," "subventions," and "general fund." He has a differentiated and coherent view of taxes; not all taxes are alike. He demonstrates contextual knowledge by his awareness of current state tax-legislation activity or understanding of the relation between assessment and property tax rates or by his ability to explain the complex financing arrangements for the Oakland coliseum. His opinions on taxes are interrelated and might be called a "belief system." [2]

Business association president: Some expenditures were from the general fund before, but now the money . . . comes from the room tax.

Chamber of commerce board member: I think the subventions should flow into the area of pressing need.

Business organization executive: If they were successful [in attracting new industry] they'd increase the assessed valuation within the city, and the tax rate and the tax bill could ultimately be lowered.

2. See Phillip E. Converse, "The Nature of Belief Systems in Mass Publics," in *Ideology and Discontent,* ed. David E. Apter (New York: The Free Press, 1964), pp. 206–214; and Anthony Downs, *An Economic Theory of Democracy* (New York: Harper and Row, 1957), p. 79.

The "average" respondent does not have a systematic set of opinions on taxes. His opinions tend to be fragmented and unrelated to each other. He does not use a specialized vocabulary but has a common sense or visceral reaction to tax questions. He will not be as informed as the "good" respondent, and there may be errors in his tax knowledge. The "average" respondent knows what his friends tell him or what is made salient by the newspapers. For example, this businessman shows concern about the assessment scandals which were then topical: "As far as taxation, we definitely have to come in with something new because of the problem which existed in the past . . . that assessment exposure business . . . I've forgotten the name of the man here . . . and we're not through yet." He may avoid answering the question "Is there any place you think the city is spending too much money?" by pointing to a county function he would like to cut: "Yes, welfare. Of course, that's county, but city people live in the county." That is to say, he does not want to differentiate between governmental jurisdictions and the use of his taxes. This neighborhood respondent indicates the common-sense approach to tax preferences by supporting an increase in the business licenses: "I imagine each business has a different business license. . . . They'd squawk, but they'll write it off on their income tax. It's amazing the things they can write off on their income tax—and by the time they're through writing off, they don't pay any."

The "poor" respondent knows very little about taxes and is often afraid to venture an opinion, replying with "don't knows" or giving short, incomplete answers. For example, a garden club president answers most questions with: "I don't know . . . never thought of that. . . . It might be all right to do that. Why not? . . . Well, yes, they might. . . . Can't really think. . . ." In some cases the "poor" respondent does not understand the question at all, as this neighborhood association leader indicates in his answer to the question, "Should we increase the state income tax with a sharing arrangement to the city?": "Well, what is it? I don't know what it is. Do we pay it? . . . Sort of like on the money that comes into the store?" Or the leader may understand the question but lack the relevant knowledge. This professional association president, in answer to "What do you think about the city relying on state and federal agencies for financial support?"

responds: "Do they? They don't, do they? It seems to me where the cities in California get anything from them it's in cases of disaster. They get federal aid then, don't they? But the state doesn't give the cities any money, does it?"

Obviously a person can learn about taxes and finance in school or from his friends. However, I find that tax knowledge is instrumental knowledge; the citizens who know about taxes require the knowledge for some personal business or professional reason. Although it would be preferable to have most Oakland citizens possess some comprehension of taxes and finances, it is the business respondents who are knowledgeable. Tax policies create costs for business and influence the climate for profit. How significant to business these policies are in fact is not relevant for us. What is relevant is that businessmen pay attention to taxes, as indicated in Table 12.

TABLE 12: Citizen-Leaders from Business Organizations Have Greater Tax Comprehension than Other Organizational Respondents

| | Organizational Type | | | | | |
| | Business | | Social/ Professional | | Other | |
Tax Comprehension	No.	%	No.	%	No.	%
Good	10	53	3	20	9	28
Average	8	42	4	27	15	47
Poor	1	5	8	53	8	25
Total	19	100	15	100	32	100

Oakland citizens learn about taxes as members of organizations which take official positions on city finance. I found that the leaders of organizations which have official views on city finance also exhibit greater tax comprehension than citizens who are not affiliated with such organizations, as shown in Table 13 (a). Tax knowledge can be expanded by contact with people who are concerned about and aware of the city's financial condition. Thus, those leaders who have "a great deal" of contact with city officials also have greater tax comprehension than those leaders who have less contact—such as listening to the mayor's speech at a luncheon—as shown in Table 13 (b).

TABLE 13: Leaders of Organizations which Have Official Views on Finance or Greater Contact with City Officials Have Better Tax Comprehension than Other Leaders

Tax Comprehension	(a) Organizational View on City Finances				(b) Frequency of Contact with City Officials					
	Yes		No		A Great Deal		Some		None/Just Speakers	
	No.	%	No.	%	No.	%	No.	%	No.	%
Good	15	44	6	20	12	52	4	18	6	32
Average	15	44	12	40	10	43	10	45	6	32
Poor	4	12	12	40	1	4	8	36	7	37
Total	34	100	30	100	23	99	22	99	19	101

Public acceptance of a tax and tax comprehension are linked. If a person understands the purpose of a particular tax and why it was levied, he will be more likely to accept it. For example, Oakland's citizen-leaders do not accept the sewer service charge because it has not been adequately explained (see chapter 4). Some twenty-three out of forty-one leaders (56 percent) offer unfavorable comments about the sewer service charge. Only those leaders with better than average tax comprehension accept the charge and offer favorable comments, as is indicated in Table 14.[3] There are no differences between average and poor comprehension in this respect.

TABLE 14: Citizen-Leaders with Good Tax Comprehension Tend to Favor the Sewer Service Charge More than Leaders with Less Tax Comprehension

Comment on Charge	Tax Comprehension Rating					
	Good		Average		Poor	
	No.	%	No.	%	No.	%
Favorable	12	86	3	20	3	25
Unfavorable	2	14	12	80	9	75
Total	14	100	15	100	12	100

3. This relationship held when I controlled for organization; in other words, an alternative explanation that businessmen favored the charge out of self-interest, independent of tax comprehension, was not supported.

Despite the city's efforts to explain the need for the charge, leaders are still confused as to what the charge is for and how it differs from the East Bay Municipal Utility District's sewer charge. The confusion comes about because our respondents cannot be expected to know about sewers. Yet the city in its educational efforts has expected that the public would be able to distinguish not only between sanitary and flood control sewers, but between the city's and the East Bay Municipal Utility District's plant. Even some of the leaders who responded positively did so on the basis of their feelings about flood control, and their response does not have anything to do with sanitary sewers, to which the charge is in fact related. Similarly, citizen-leaders believe that sewers are the East Bay Municipal Utility District's business and not the city's. Finally, they do not understand why their property tax does not pay for such things. Confused distrust seems to be the common thread running through the comments:

Business organization executive: I still have not gotten it through my head, and I don't know what I'm paying for . . . particularly in the area in which I live. There is no sewer service there at all. All of the homes have septic tanks.

Service organization vice-president: Well, I feel that it's a kind of double taxation. I think it's an easy way of getting the money, but it's kind of snide, too. They put it on you, and they claim it isn't a tax, but it is!

Service organization president: They did that [established the charge] without the vote of the people and I thought it was unjust. . . . If your tenant runs up a big bill . . . well, two years later you get an 8 percent penalty, plus you have to pay the bill. . . . It's wrong. Anyway, there already is a sewage bill on the water bill you get. They should have added it to the water bill and not set up a whole new agency. People didn't even know about it; it just came.

Chamber of Commerce board member: I thought it was very unusual when we first got the bill. We assumed it was paid for when we paid our property taxes. The city is looking for new sources of income, so we're getting unusual taxes.

Those who responded favorably usually stressed how small, how nominal the charge is—"Surely no one ever complains about it."

It may be argued, however, that if our middle-class educated sample responds so unfavorably, then surely the potential for complaint and unhappiness with the city is greater for the average citizen of Oakland.

TABLE 15: The Higher the Tax Comprehension of a Citizen-Leader, the More Likely He Will See the Connection between Taxes and Services

| | Tax Comprehension Rating | | | | | |
| | Good | | Average | | Poor | |
Tax-Service Connection	No.	%	No.	%	No.	%
Makes the connection	21	95	21	78	10	59
Does not make the connection	1	5	6	22	7	41
Total	22	100	27	100	17	100

In my estimation the most important feature of tax comprehension is that it is a primary condition for understanding the connection between taxes and services. The long-run support of leaders for changes in the tax structure or increased city services lies with those elites who have some understanding of city finance. Those leaders who have knowledge about taxes also tend to see that the taxes they pay are related to the services they receive (Table 15). In central cities it is often difficult to see the connection between taxes and services.[4] However, Oakland's citizen-leaders are exceptional since 79 percent of our sample do see this nexus. To substantiate this conclusion I also compared the number of city services which leaders wanted to increase with the number of different tax sources they were willing to raise. The average number of taxes which leaders would raise increased with the number of city services they would expand. In other words, citizen-leaders who want to increase spending for a greater number of services also support a greater number of tax sources. Unlike previous work which indicates a preference for increased services without increased taxes or actually a cut in taxes, our

4. Dick Netzer, "Federal, State, and Local Finance in a Metropolitan Context," in *Issues in Urban Economics,* ed. Harvey S. Perloff and Lowdon Wingo, Jr. (Baltimore: Johns Hopkins Press for Resources for the Future, 1968), p. 446.

citizen-leaders see the connection between taxes and services.[5] Tax knowledge is therefore not just a means for enhancing a businessman's profit-and-loss statement; it is an important pre-requisite for an expansion of public services through those *leaders* who desire expansion and make the tax-service nexus. Officials can work with such knowledgeable leaders to increase public support for taxation (see chapter 7).

WHO SHOULD PAY?

The question of equity in the distribution of the tax burden has been of interest to social philosophers for centuries. Citizen-leaders want taxes to be fair and equitable; fairness is the common denominator of all the interviews. The standard of fairness, however, is subjective and shifts with the individual. Furthermore, most leaders have quite simple notions of tax justice.

A constraint on citizen-leader acceptance of complex notions of equity is the lack of tax comprehension which precludes the formation of a coherent belief system on questions of tax policy. To begin to get at the question of what is fair and what is equitable, the total tax structure has to be considered. Yet many citizen-leaders isolate their opinions on each tax; beliefs and opinions on tax policy are fragmented. Perceptions about the sales tax illustrate this fragmentation.

The sales tax is a good way to get revenue from the nonproperty owner. Then "at least the consumers . . . will have to pay their share." No leader points out that the property taxpayer is also a consumer. Only a few respondents explicitly consider the sales tax an offset to the property tax. There is the implicit hope in the interviews that by getting everyone to pay, their personal burden would be reduced.

"Getting everyone to pay" is the way the citizen-leader expresses his desire for equality in taxation. The citizen-leader is

5. For a national cross-sectional sample where the tax-service nexus was not made, see V. O. Key, Jr., *Public Opinion and American Democracy* (New York: Alfred A. Knopf, 1961), pp. 165–168; and Eva Mueller, "Public Attitudes Toward Fiscal Programs," *Quarterly Journal of Economics* 77 (May 1963): 210–235. For the problem of lower-class respondents not making the tax-service nexus, see Morris Janowitz, Deil Wright, and William Delaney, *Public Administration and the Public: Perspectives Toward Government in a Metropolitan Community* (Ann Arbor: Bureau of Government, University of Michigan, 1958), pp. 29–44.

unconcerned about the income distribution features of taxation. Redistributive effects are not explicitly considered, because the citizen-leader does not understand this aspect of a tax system and because the criterion of equality in taxation, of sharing the burden, is of paramount importance.

Both fragmentation of tax opinion and the lack of concern over income redistribution are symptoms of deficiencies in tax comprehension. Respondents who are unaware of tax and financial matters use simple ideas of tax equity. The simple criteria of "somebody else" and "let's all pay equally" are products of the unsophisticated, as Table 16 shows.

TABLE 16: The Lower the Tax Comprehension, the More Likely the Individual Will Hold Simplistic Notions of Who Should Pay

	Tax Comprehension			
	Good		Average to Poor	
Who Should Pay	No.	%	No.	%
Complex	12	55	3	7
Simple ("somebody else," "fair share," "it's fair")	10	45	41	93
Total	22	100	44	100

I classified citizen equity criteria into four categories: (1) a segment of the population, "let somebody else pay"; (2) everyone should, a fair-share concept; (3) a nonspecific concept of "it should be fair"; and (4) a complex, partly tactical concept. From Table 17 it can be seen that 78 percent of citizen-leaders employ simple concepts of equity such as "it should be fair," and the segment and fair-share concepts.

TABLE 17: Citizen-Leaders Tend to Have Simple Notions of Equity

Who Should Pay	No.	%
Simple—A segment of the population ("somebody else")	25	38
Simple—Everyone should ("fair share")	23	35
Simple—Nonspecific ("it should be fair")	3	5
Complex	15	23
Total	66	101

The use of simple concepts of equity should not be mistaken for an irresponsible motivation to shift the tax burden. Of course some leaders do want to get rid of the burden; however, many of the respondents do not invoke criteria which will completely shift the tax burden from themselves. Kaufman is partially correct in his observation that "most people are aroused principally by taxes that fall on them." [6] The "segment" category contains in part those respondents who are quite happy to shift the tax burden to someone else, as Kaufman suggests. For example, this neighborhood leader wants to tax commuters: "I think that Oakland is the hub of the county operation—many county offices are here and thousands of people come to work here from the suburban areas. I think we should actually be putting a tax on these individuals, who are using our streets, our police protection, etc. I think we should make them pay." This neighborhood and poverty program leader would rather tax the rich than the poor: "It [revenue for Oakland] shouldn't certainly come from taxing the poor people's property. . . . All I know is that the rich are pretty well off; they seem to be buying more property than selling. You might try hitting the guy who has a sizable amount of property. That way you're hitting the people who run the government." Then there is the service organization leader, a landlord, who wants the poor—"those people on welfare"—to pay taxes, otherwise they will spend their money for "liquor and other nonessentials."

However, the motivation to shift the tax burden to one's opposite is not as irrational as it appears. Ability and benefit principles are employed implicitly and explicitly in making these judgments:

Business organization manager: [Taxation] has to be related to what is the end result. Who are the beneficiaries . . . the city or just a small group—and then you can see who should pay for it. There should be some relationship between those who benefit and those who pay—if it's at all possible.

Respondents like this border on being classified as part of the fourth category, which is the complex conceptualization of many

6. Herbert Kaufman, *Politics and Policies in State and Local Governments* (Englewood Cliffs, N.J.: Prentice-Hall, Inc., 1963), p. 69.

different payers involving a broadened and differentiated tax structure. However, when the use of the benefit principle leads the respondent to single out only a few groups, then that respondent was classified as part of the "segment" category. This possible overlap actually strengthens the point I am making. The let-somebody-else-pay syndrome is not always a blind striking-out by the unhappy taxpayer seeking to shift the burden.

The "blind" type is more likely to be found in those people who assert a simplistic concept of "fair share." These respondents go beyond statements that a tax should be fair and equitable; they insist that everybody should pay an equal share. They support the sales tax because everybody pays. Behind this notion of fair share is the idea that a tax should not discriminate; there should be equality in taxation.

Neighborhood association leader: I'm for any tax that can be leveled evenly on the people. . . . As long as they are leveled and not aimed at the specific group, we're not too picky. Most people grumble when they pick up a paycheck with all the taxes taken out. We pay it and we have the privilege to grumble if we wish.

Those citizen-leaders who have a complex conceptualization of equity certainly do not blindly seek to shift their own tax burden. They have a complex notion of everybody-should-pay. This complexity comes from their better tax understanding and the introduction of nonequity criteria. Thus, they all see the connection between taxes and services, and most of them have "good" tax comprehension. However, the citizen-leaders with complex concepts of equity are more concerned about the economic and political feasibility of many tax sources. Their criteria are geared to whether a source will have a significant yield and whether the community will support it, and not whether the tax is necessarily fair or that the specific choice will minimize their burden. Everybody-should-pay is their standard because they are seeking a "broadening of the tax base." They do not intend that everybody should pay the same amount, but that everybody should make a contribution. They are concerned about who benefits and who can afford to pay, but these principles are commingled or buried with other considerations such as whether it will pass:

Chamber of Commerce president: It depends on how the city presents it. . . . If I don't misjudge the temper of the time, any proposal
to increase taxes on any level has two strikes against it. . . . It's one
thing as to what the paper [the *Oakland Tribune*] or the Chamber
of Commerce or other civic groups might do, and it's another thing to
say whether the public would go along with it or against it. Take
the school tax that we supported. . . . It still failed. . . . There's a
built-in opposition to any tax proposal you can make at this time. This
doesn't mean that some effort couldn't pass it, but nothing would slide
through with any degree of unanimity.

The person who expects to find some arbitrary standard of tax
justice or equity in these responses of Oakland citizen-leaders
will be sadly disappointed. Most citizen-leaders do not know
enough to be aware of tax principles. For the small minority who
do have the requisite knowledge, equity is only one concern
which may get lost in the pragmatic search for feasible revenue
sources.

WILL CITIZEN-LEADERS PAY MORE
BECAUSE THE CITY NEEDS IMPROVEMENT?

Judging the performance of an organization is fraught with
more difficulties than the average person can realize. Students of
organization theory have succeeded in making a complex subject into something of an unresolved muddle.[7] The problem stems
from the lack of a single overriding criterion. Effectiveness has to
be multidimensional because the organization has multiple goals.
Similarly, those people, such as our citizen-leaders, who in part
constitute the environment for the city as an organization also
have different standards, or criteria, for judging city performance. Simply put, citizen-leaders expect different things from a
good government. For some, a good government is efficient; for
others, a good government provides services such as lighting and
street curbs. Recognizing this multidimensional aspect to evaluations, the interviews were coded using a three-point scale of performance: good, needs improvement, poor. This rating is intended
to provide a crude index of how favorably citizen-leaders perceive the city operation.

7. Warren G. Bennis, *Changing Organizations* (New York: McGraw-Hill
Book Co., 1966), pp. 34–63.

Oakland citizen-leaders see the city in negative terms. Only 16 percent of them indicate that the performance of the city is good; 20 percent of the leaders indicate that the performance is poor. Most of the leaders, 64 percent, characterize the city as needing some improvement. This generally negative view of the city does not mean a complete rejection of the city operation. "Needing improvement" means the identification of some specific area of unhappiness or that the city can make better use of its resources.

There are generally three dimensions which underlie the leaders' reactions to city performance. These are: efficiency of operations, adequacy of services, and a concept of self or identity. Sometimes an interview will involve all three, and other times only one dimension will be expressed. For clarity, I will quote from those interviews which stress one dimension.

Efficiency of operations.—In the "poor," the most negative, category, this leader stresses his belief that the city is inefficient:

Neighborhood association president: I worry about [the money's] use in the sense of efficiency. Twenty years in this office here and I'm in contact with all the government agencies, and I find that there is a tendency to be not on the ball as far as work is concerned. Down there there are more people standing around having coffee breaks than working.

Another respondent thinks that the city could be efficient if it could "be run more like a private business."

On the "good" end of the spectrum, these respondents think the city is efficient:

Noncity governmental official: My observation is that they do a very good job. They operate quite effectively in all their departments. They have good, tight budgeting; they control it and operate in a good manner basically.

Business organization president: They're doing about as well as they can. . . . I think we have an efficient city operation; Keithley [the city manager] is a darn good man.

Adequacy of services.—Most of the respondents can suggest areas in which to spend more money for adequate services. The following respondent, however, feels the output of the Oakland political system is inadequate because, as a taxpayer, he is getting nothing for his money:

Neighborhood organization chairman: The poor pay, but they don't get anything for it. They get the poorest service, the poorest streets, the poorest schools—anyone can tell. It's ridiculous we have to live this way. . . . The tax situation is deplorable as to what we get in return.

Another respondent, however, thinks Oakland is providing adequate services but has not received credit for it:

College official: I rather suspect they are doing all they have to. Things like repair of streets, sidewalks, maintenance. . . . I think Oakland has done a lot of things it hasn't received credit for—for example, the Oakland coliseum complex, the airport, the industrial development that's under way.

Obviously these two respondents do not agree on the adequacy of services. Whether this discrepancy represents an actual difference in this distribution of services is beyond my purview, but it is quite clear that the above neighborhood respondent perceives that there are differences and this colors his evaluation of the city: "You go up to the hills and see the street cleaning and the clean gutters and all the lights working and all those parks and nice schools, and then you look here—and what do you see?"

Concept of self.—Although it is empirical nonsense to conceive of a city as having a negative concept of self or identity or exhibiting symptoms of an inferiority complex, our respondents discuss Oakland as if the city were a neurotic person feeling somewhat inferior to its glamorous sibling, San Francisco. A businesswoman makes the same diagnosis: "all Oakland needs is some pride. This darned inferiority complex!" However, this social club leader does not have much pride:

I do feel that Oakland is very slow in many ways, like in their business. Compared to San Francisco, well, no wonder people go to the city [San Francisco] to shop. . . . I can't understand a city like Oakland. We've always said we're the bedroom of San Francisco. . . . We should be more alert about having things over here. Oakland's a sleepy town. It's dull.

A negative concept of self can also be expressed in more concrete terms which are also linked to inadequate services:

Business organization president: Oakland has let the quality of citizenship go down. . . . There's more crime and undesirable and run-down neighborhoods and streets than there ought to be in a city like this. The nicest areas are around Lake Merritt; people don't want to go down there as they don't feel safe at night.

But things are getting better for some:

Business association president: In the last few years we've done something and are beginning to do more, but before that we took a back seat for years to San Francisco. Now that things are changing, lots has got to be done.

And for a few, Oakland is doing even better than San Francisco:

Service organization past president: They're doing a fine job; they are ahead of San Francisco by a long shot. . . . Like that Oakland coliseum complex. They're making progress, not like that big city, San Francisco [where] there's a lot of yak-yak and they never get anything done.

Eighty-four percent of the citizen-leaders do perceive Oakland in essentially negative terms. I have showed the extremes, the "poor" and the "good" evaluations, to indicate the dimensions of performance which citizen-leaders use. For different reasons, citizen-leaders come together to feel that Oakland needs improvement. The significance of prevailing discontent lies in the expectation of stimulating demands for an expansion of public services. Whether such demands would also result in a correlative tax policy is an open question. Civic discontent is not necessarily a determinant of citizen support for increased taxes even though such discontent is a major condition for increased demands.

WILL CITIZEN-LEADERS PAY MORE
BECAUSE THEY USE CITY SERVICES?

Before talking with the leaders of Oakland, I had felt that a citizen's use of city services and facilities would be quite important in explaining the citizen's tax and expenditure preferences. Obviously the user of a facility or service provides a built-in constituency for stable or increased expenditures. In this section, however, I will show that leaders do use city facilities but that use is not simply related to support for increased expenditures.

Citizen-leaders say that they use city facilities and services. They are quite aware of less visible services, such as sanitation services and the potential value of fire and police protection. They are users of the library, parks, and recreational facilities (Table 18). Only three leaders claim no use of city facilities. Most leaders mention that they use one and two services. Culture and recreation and public safety are the functions most often mentioned. The nonresident leaders mention the use of city facilities with the same frequency as residents. The commuter, in other words, does realize that he is being provided services. The point is that almost all of the leaders are aware of and mention using city services.

TABLE 18: Citizen-Leaders Use City Facilities and Services

Frequency of City Services Mentioned			Specific City Function Mentioned	
No. of Services	No. of Respondents	%	Function	Frequency
0	3	5	None at all	3
1	31	52	Culture and recreation	42
2	20	33	Public safety	21
3	4	7	Streets and sanitation	14
4 or more	2	3	Other	14
Total	60	100		

I would expect that the user of a service might know the service's deficiencies and thus would be willing to spend more on that service. However, as Table 19 indicates, users are not the ones who want to spend more on the service they use, since only about one-third of those who use a service also want to spend more on that service; support for increased expenditures is just as likely to come from nonusers. Thus, if a city official plans to create support for expansion of a particular function, he might consider including nonusers as well as users in his constituency. We need to understand the conditions under which use is related to tax support. It may be that use which generates no discontent is related to keeping expenditures stable. On the other hand, users who are unaware of actual service levels and costs may be a source of support.

TABLE 19: Users Do Not Want to Spend More

Service	Leaders Who Mentioned Use and Want to Spend More	Leaders Who Did Not Mention Use and Want to Spend More
Culture and recreation	33% (N = 42)	17% (N = 18)
Public safety	29% (N = 21)	38% (N = 39)
Streets and sanitation	29% (N = 14)	22% (N = 46)

That ignorance of costs may be functional in supporting a city facility is evidenced by the many positive references to the coliseum complex. Twenty-five out of thirty-one respondents mentioned the coliseum favorably. These respondents think not only that the facility is "just great" but that it is "going to bring a lot of revenue in." Unfortunately, the city pays $750,000 a year for the coliseum with practically no return on its investment. There also seems to be some confusion, evidenced in the interviews, as to how the coliseum was financed. A few respondents seem to reinforce their positive feelings toward the coliseum by believing that they voted for its financing when actually the issue was never on the ballot. In fact, one of the more knowledgeable respondents objects to the method of financing precisely because it was not put to the voters: "It's basically wrong to usurp the taxpayer's basic right to decide on large outlays of capital. It's a great project . . . but the principle of the lease-purchase arrangement is fundamentally wrong." Only a handful of leaders actually understand exactly how the coliseum was built and financed. The majority of leaders do not understand and could care less. The citizen-leader uses the facility, likes it, but does not understand that he is paying more than his admission fee.

Contrary to my own expectations about human behavior, citizen-leaders will not pay more just because they use city services. Use, itself, may or may not be a condition for increased services and taxes. The citizen-leader is just as likely to support a service he does not use as one he does. Nonuse and use based on ignorance, as in the case of the coliseum, are functional equivalents;

both may lead to support for expanded services. Hence, the quality of use must be defined before the relationship between use and tax support will become clear. The problem of support is not with the informed and knowledgeable leader, for if he understands the need he will support increased taxes regardless of personal use. The problem of support is with the uninformed. How does the experience of using city facilities and services affect the uninformed leader's financial policy preferences? If the experience leaves the leader uninformed, he may or may not be willing to support expanded services. A little bit of use may be dangerous. City officials who wish to raise the level of recreational service should not rely solely on leaders, for example, whose recreational preferences are determined by an occasional trip to the zoo.

CITIZEN-LEADERS WILL PAY MORE
BECAUSE THEY WANT TO SPEND MORE

Citizen-leaders want to spend more. The typical leader suggests several specific service areas for increased spending; he either rejects the notion of spending less or cannot make specific recommendations for cutting. He is discontented with city performance, so he wants to spend more. Because he sees the connection between services and taxes, he may even be willing to pay more. Leaders, however, do not agree on where to spend.

A majority of citizen-leaders (54 percent) could suggest at least two areas for increased spending; only six respondents could not suggest any area. In other words, 90 percent of the citizen-leaders suggested at least one area for increased expenditure.

Leaders were asked, "Where should the city spend more to meet the needs of the community?" Practically all of the responses are quite specific: more for police salaries and uniforms, better lighting, more street repair, more on parks, more for schoolbooks and teachers, more to bring business here. But as I have said, there is no consensus with the possible exception of schools, which is each group's second choice. This can be better seen if the respondents' preferences are divided by race and residency, as in Table 20. White residents want to spend more on public safety. Nonresidents want to spend more building up and attracting business and industry. Nonwhite residents want to spend more on the poor and poverty. This latter category is not strictly a city function or service but a specific target for city services. It is, however, mentioned as a specific area for spending. For example, a leader of a professional association thought the city should spend more "in cleaning up some of the slums and in spending more in working with people who are on welfare to help these people find a useful role in life. There's a massive problem with our socio-economically deprived people."

TABLE 20: No Agreement on Where to Spend More

| | Race and Residency | | | |
| | White/ | White/Non- | | |
Spend More on Service Area	Resident	resident	Nonwhite [a]	Total
Education	14	5	6	25
Public safety	16	3	2	21
Business and industrial development	8	7	3	18
Culture and recreation	11	3	3	17
Streets and sanitation	9	2	3	14
Poor and poverty	4	3	7	14

[a] In the sample all nonwhites are residents.

When the question is turned around by asking, "In what areas is the city spending too much money?" and "Are there any services which the city provides which should be cut out?" two important things happen. First, respondents are not likely to identify specific services for cutting. Instead they talk in terms of the city being inefficient, cutting out the fat and waste, and spending less for the poor or those on welfare. Second, over half of the sample either cannot think of a service to cut or rejects completely the notion of spending less (Table 21). It has to be granted that more knowledge of city activities is required to know where to cut than to know where to add, which may in part explain the lack of specificity and the number of "can't think of any" responses. But when these data are considered with the data on spending more plus the overall negative rating of city performance, it seems reasonable to conclude that many (conservatively, at least one-third to one-half) of the citizen-leaders want to increase city services and spend more.

TABLE 21: Should the City Spend Less?

	White		Nonwhite		Total	
	No.	%	No.	%	No.	%
Spending too much on:						
Waste, red tape, and fat	6		4		10	
Poor and poverty	8		0		8	
Waste and the poor	7		0		7	
Specific city activity	6		0		6	
Yes, subtotal	27	48	4	40	31	47
Can't think of any areas	10		2		12	
No	15		1		16	
No, not spending enough	4		3		7	
No, subtotal	29	52	6	60	35	53
Total	56	100	10	100	66	100

However, will citizen-leaders pay more for these increased services? Unfortunately, I did not have the foresight to ask that question. But I believe that many of these leaders would be willing to pay increased taxes. For one reason, leaders who do not want to spend less also support increases in a greater number of tax sources than leaders who definitely believe that expenditure levels should be cut. Secondly, leaders who are unwilling to spend less have better tax comprehension and make the connection between taxes and services more often than leaders who want to cut (see Table 22). Although the differences in the data are not as marked as they should be, they do indicate by direction some support for my conclusion. When leaders who understand the connection between taxes and services do not want to spend less and may want to spend more, they may also be willing to pay more.

To summarize the preceding few sections, citizen-leaders are unhappy with the city as it is; they want change because Oakland needs improvement. Many of them want to spend more and understand that they have to pay taxes for increased expenditures. They want the money spent efficiently and without waste. However, while there seems to be sentiment for raising the level of service, there is not much agreement on priorities for allocation.

TABLE 22: Citizen-Leaders Who Do Not Want to Cut City Expenditures Have Better Tax Comprehension and Make the Tax-Service Connection More Readily than Leaders Who Want to Cut

Position on Spending Less	(a) Makes the Tax-Service Connection				(b) Tax Comprehension					
	Yes		No		Good		Average		Poor	
	No.	%	No.	%	No.	%	No.	%	No.	%
Yes, let's cut	21	40	10	71	8	36	14	52	9	53
No, we can't spend less	31	60	4	29	14	64	13	48	8	47
Total	52	100	14	100	22	100	27	100	17	100

WHO WILL PAY?

The purpose of this and the following section is to identify that part of the Oakland community which is attentive to financial and social issues. These leaders make up the potential support nucleus for increased taxes and spending. In the subsequent section the support nucleus will be identified on the basis of awareness of financial and social problems. This section assesses the significance of several variables for defining the support nucleus. These variables include: civic responsibility, specific response content, race and residency, and the leader's organization.

Civic responsibility.—Oakland citizen-leaders are civic-minded, but it is an open question whether this civic attitude is a reliable index of support. There are some people in every city who place the quality of community life as an argument in their utility function. Supposedly citizens with civic responsibility will provide a built-in core of support for service expansion and tax increases.[8]

8. See James Q. Wilson and Edward C. Banfield, "Public-Regardingness as a Value Premise in Voting Behavior," *American Political Science Review* 58 (December 1964): 876–887.

Most of Oakland citizen-leaders are willing to accept the city's tax burden, as is clear from these statements:

PTA president: Well, if it becomes a necessity, I'll go along. I might fuss and fight and cuss and get mad, but if we need it, we need it! . . . If it has to be done, it has to be done.

Civic affairs group president: I don't mind paying taxes. They're rising year after year . . . but if it's for a good purpose, I don't mind.

Service organization president: We're all aware of the fact the terrific burden taxes are, but you can't have quality service unless you pay for it.

Neighborhood association president: I'm willing to go along with any kind of taxation. . . . No matter where we tax, there will always be people objecting, and what do you consider fair anyway? You say you shouldn't tax property and the other guy will say okay, but then where do you shift it to then? My point is this: if you do a good job with the money collected already, we won't worry about how you get it if it's well spent and for the right objectives.

Leaders will pay more, but the operational question is when and for what. Civic types emphasize need, purpose, the right objectives. How is the city official to distinguish the substance from the rhetoric when he wants to push a certain program or get a new tax accepted? One leader's right objective may not be the same as another leader's purpose. The point is that civic responsibility is not a general hunting license but becomes defined in the context of the pursual of a particular policy. Even if civic responsibility were operational in a general sense, each citizen may still differentially place it in his utility or preference function. The limitations of civic virtue should be considered when officials seek support for tax increases.

Specific response content.—I have pointed out in a previous section the importance of tax comprehension. Leaders who can respond to general financial questions with specific tax recommendations, such as an increase in the sales tax, indicate that they have the requisite knowledge. Leaders who cannot be specific will probably not be in the support nucleus. To give these statements some context, let me define two variables.

First, the dependent variable is willingness to accept tax burdens or, succinctly, *tax support*. In the interview, the leader was asked his position on seven different sources of revenue. Citizen-leaders are quite positive in their responses for a majority of the sources suggested to them. For the total sample a computed average of 3.7 sources elicited positive responses. On a percentage basis there is considerable clustering between two and five sources, as is shown by the frequency distribution in Table 23. I assume that a simple average can be taken as a crude measure of tax support. In other words, for discussion purposes, the *number* of taxes supported by a leader is equivalent to his willingness to accept existing and increased tax burdens. If a leader is not willing to pay more, he will tend to react negatively to the suggestion that a particular revenue source be increased. So the dependent variable, tax support, is defined by a computed average of the number of revenue sources given positive responses by leaders. Considering the crudeness of the methods, the clustering around the mean (see Table 23), and the likely problems of validity of the measure, I will use mean tax support to indicate only direction or the ranking of tax support.

TABLE 23: Distribution of Positive Responses

No. of Revenue Sources	Percentage of Respondents
7	3
6	5
5	20
4	30
3	21
2	18
1	3
	100 (N = 66)

Second, the independent variable is specific response content. A specific response by a leader is simply his suggestion for a particular source of revenue when asked, "If the city needs money, where should the city get it?" Over 76 percent of citizen-leaders make specific suggestions. Table 24 shows that twenty-one leaders suggest the sales tax. To a lesser extent income tax, subventions, the property tax, and bonds are mentioned.

TABLE 24: Citizen-Leaders Tend to Differentiate between Specific Sources of Revenue

Suggestion	No. of Respondents
Sales tax	21
Cigarette, liquor, luxury taxes	16
Income tax (commuter and other)	10
Federal/state subventions	9
Property tax	8
Bonds	5
Other	2

Nonspecific responses fall roughly into two categories. The first includes leaders who see taxation as a general object. Sometimes the respondent uses the answer, "Only one way: taxes," as a shorthand notion for a more complex and differentiated conception of a tax structure that becomes apparent as the interview proceeds. More often, however, the general response, "Taxes," is a clue to financial ignorance. In either case, these statements are usually accompanied by the notion of the people as the taxpayer:

Professional association president: The fact is that they're going to get it from the people, that's where.

Church official: The basic source of money for a government is the people who are governed.

PTA president: Where do they usually get it from?—The poor damn public.

The second nonspecific category often rejects the notion that the city might need more money. What the city has to do is to cut out waste and frills and be efficient or at least spend the money differently:

Home-owner association president: They have too many frills down there somewhere, too many extras, maybe a couple of people they don't need.

Business organization official: We have to be shown that they need more revenue because I personally feel that with proper procedures . . . they won't need more money.

When both variables are put together in Table 25, we see that leaders who make specific suggestions on tax revenue rank high in tax support, and leaders who make nonspecific suggestions do not rank high in tax support. In other words, leaders who know something about taxes will make specific suggestions and in turn will support increased taxes. The capacity to make specific suggestions is an important component of tax comprehension.

TABLE 25: Citizen-Leaders with Specific Ideas on Tax Sources Support a Greater Number of Tax Sources than Other Leaders

Specificity of Response	Percentage	Mean Tax Support Ranking
Specific	56	1
Specific and nonspecific	20	2
Nonspecific	21	3
Made no suggestion	3	4
(N = 66)		

Race and residency.—If city officials promote a support nucleus for increased taxation, that nucleus will probably have to convince many of Oakland's white residents that expenditures and taxes should be raised. Many citizen-leaders who are white and residents believe that city expenditures can be cut. Table 26 shows that it is the nonwhite residents and the white nonresidents (both pay taxes) who believe that the city cannot spend less, which I have interpreted as perhaps being associated with a belief that services should be expanded. White nonresident leaders also rank high on the tax support measure, while nonwhite residents are average in tax support. One reason why nonwhite leaders may not have a correlative tax policy to support their desires for expanded services is that they are quite negative in their evaluation of city performance. The white leader is more positive in his evaluation of the city than is the nonwhite. The latter feels he is not getting anything out of his taxes now and questions why he should pay more. He wants services to increase, but until they do he is not willing to increase his tax burden. The white nonresident leader is relatively sanguine about the prospects of the city; he is willing to pay more. For perhaps different reasons, both nonwhites and nonresident leaders will be in the support nucleus.

TABLE 26: White Resident Citizen-Leaders Want to
Cut City Spending

	Race and Residency					
	White Resident		White Non-Resident		Nonwhite	
Position on Spending Less	No.	%	No.	%	No.	%
Yes, let's cut	23	58	4	25	4	40
No, we can't spend less	17	43	12	75	6	60
Total	40	101	16	100	10	100

The organization.—The type of organization the citizen-leader represents is quite important in explaining his views on spending, his contact with officials, and his tax preferences. The organizational base of the support nucleus is weak; about half of the leaders represent organizations that have views on finance. And only about one-third (twenty-three, to be exact) of the leaders indicate something beyond a casual contact with relevant city officials. This is not to say that other leaders have no opinions on finance, but it does open the question of whose preferences are taken into account in making tax policy. As we will see, it is the business and, to a lesser extent, the neighborhood groups who have views and contact with city officials.

That a person is a leader of an organization is no guarantee he will have opinions on taxes. Nor do all organizations care about city finance. Taxes, expenditures, and finance are subjects for the City Hall specialist and for the person who has some need to learn about such things. For an organization to care about city finance or to care enough to have official views on the subject, city finance has to be relevant to the purpose of the organization. Therefore, business and neighborhood organizations have such views and the other organizations represented in the sample do not (Table 27). In fact, holding views on finance may be too close to politics, an area of potential conflict for some organizations. As one women's club president puts it: "We strive not to take a stand too much on politics and religion, mainly because the club consists of conservatives and liberals and there is nothing in between. Such a stand would tend to be divisive in these matters. . . . However, . . . we do a lot of grumbling on city expenses." Another social club president has similar feelings: "The club has never gotten into politics. In fact, we are very careful in our meetings to be bipartisan. . . . We're very careful, particularly about controversial things."

TABLE 27: Business and Neighborhood Organizations Have Official Views on City Finance

| | Organizational View on City Finances | | | |
| | Yes | | No | |
Organizational Type	No.	%	No.	%
Business	15	44	4	13
Neighborhood	10	29	3	10
Other	9	26	23	77
Total	34	99	30	100

When an organization considers city finance significant, then that organization provides a frame of reference for the leader and his opinions. Citizen-leaders view finance through organizational glasses. PTA and other education-oriented respondents express concern about school finance and the difficulty of and the need for passing bond issues. Or a motel association's leader responds to a general question completely in terms of the transient occupancy tax: "We just got through a big battle over the room tax. This went into effect two years ago. . . . Prior to that it was mentioned for two years before that; we fought it for six months, and the council dropped it; then they brought it up again and we fought it all the way, but it became law. Out of the fight we gained a couple of things." The respondent goes on to explain that the funds are earmarked for convention and tourist promotion and that the motel owners have representation on a mayor's committee to recommend allocation of funds.

Leaders who have some reason to be concerned about city finance exhibit a marked difference in amount of contact with city officials. As we see in Table 28, listening to a department official speak is the usual contact experienced by most of the leaders without financial views. However, leaders who do have something to say about city finance have "a great deal" of contact with officials. As a target area committee chairman puts it: "You've heard the saying, 'As long as you keep quiet, no one knows what's bothering you, but when you holler, everybody knows'—well, we holler."

TABLE 28: Citizen-Leaders with Views on City Finance
Have Contact with City Officials

	Organizational View on City Finances			
	Yes		No	
Contact	No.	%	No.	%
"Some" to "great deal"	32	94	11	39
"None" to "just for speakers"	2	6	17	61
Total	34	100	28	100

Contact is for the few; only about one-third of the leaders have a great deal of contact, and 11 percent of the respondents' only contact with officials was to hear a guest speaker from the city (see Table 29). However, even speaking engagements can have a marked effect on the individual's perception of finance. For example, here is a respondent who missed the speech but got the message:

I should have been able to hear the city manager. I was on the Rotary Program Committee and was responsible for the January program. We had him there to speak and he hit very heavily on finance. But I was out of town or I'd have more to tell you. I know that financial problems are great and I know why: property taxes are diminishing, freeways are taking land, houses are being torn down, people are moving out. Land that would be bringing in city property tax is not. The city manager sees everything in terms of property tax income.

Contact is for the leaders who represent organizations with official views on city finance. Table 29 shows that the business and neighborhood leaders are in the high categories of contact with city officials. The sequence is clear. First, business and neighborhood organizations have official views on finance (Table 27). Second, leaders who represent organizations with official views have high contact with city officials (Table 28). Therefore, business and neighborhood leaders have high contact with officials (Table 29).

TABLE 29: Leaders of Business and Neighborhood Organizations Have Contact with City Officials

	Business		Neighborhood		Other		Total	
Contact	No.	%	No.	%	No.	%	No.	%
"A great deal"	13	68	6	43	4	13	23	36
"Some"	5	26	5	36	12	39	22	34
"Just for speakers"	1	5	0	0	6	19	7	11
No contact	0	0	3	21	9	29	12	19
Total	19	99	14	100	31	100	64	100

Contact with particular officials varies by the leader's organization, as Table 30 indicates. Business leaders have contact with the mayor, council, city manager, and departments. Neighborhood leaders have contact mainly with the mayor, council, and departments. Service and social and professional leaders have contact mainly with departments. The less a leader is concerned about finance, the more likely he will have contact only with departmental officials.

TABLE 30: Leader Contact with Particular Officials Varies by Organization

	Contact with [a]		
Leader's Organization	Department/ Commission	Mayor/ Council	City Manager
Business	15	15	12
Neighborhood	9	8	1
Service	10	5	0
Social/professional	5	3	0
Other	3	2	0
Total contacts	42	33	13

[a] Of the 49 respondents who indicated contact with specific officials, over half made plural responses.

There is no doubt that business leaders care about city finance. However, are business leaders part of the support nucleus for increased levels of service and taxes? Many business leaders will not be part of the support nucleus. They do support a greater number of different taxes because they are anxious to find alternatives to the property tax. Business leaders are two-to-one against the property tax. However, business leaders in the sample want to cut city expenditures (see Table 31). They have more contact with the manager than other leaders and are in agreement with the manager that the city can be more efficient. The city can cut costs and hold the property tax rate stable. Thus business leaders are interested in finance, but their interest does not necessarily lead to expanded services. Efficiency, not taxes, is their motto.

TABLE 31: Business Leaders Want to Spend Less

| | Leader's Organization | | | |
| | Business | | Other | |
Position on Spending Less	No.	%	No.	%
Yes, let's cut	13	68	18	38
No, we can't spend less	6	32	29	62
Total	19	100	47	100

This section explored some aspects of the question, "Who will pay?" Again I stressed the importance of tax comprehension by introducing the concept of specific-response content. I also felt that for Oakland the support nucleus for service and tax expansion probably should include nonresidents. Finally, I warned against relying on civic virtue or responsibility and I also pointed out the circumscribed interests of concerned business leaders. In the next section, I will further specify the support nucleus.

THE IMPORTANCE OF BEING AWARE:
THE POTENTIAL SUPPORT NUCLEUS FOR SOCIAL CHANGE

City officials cannot remedy Oakland's social, economic, and political problems without considerable community support. To give such support, citizen-leaders have to be made aware that there are problems. This section demonstrates that only a minority of Oakland's citizen-leaders are aware of these problems.

By examining the total interview, I coded the sample on two dimensions. The first dimension indicated an awareness of the revenue "crisis" of the city which was called financial awareness. The second dimension indicated an awareness of the problems of the poor, poverty, and business in depressed areas of the city; this dimension was called social-economic awareness. As an example, this teacher, a professional association leader, succinctly indicates an awareness of both dimensions: "there are serious financial problems. . . . The city is in trouble because the tax rate is such that it is not adequate to relieve the city's problems. We have slums to clean up and massive problems of similar sorts." This Chamber of Commerce member has a slightly expanded view:

Oakland is like many center cities and has very severe financial problems. This is partly because you have an increasing number of impoverished people coming into this area where there's housing available that is all falling apart and cheap to rent. And the middle-income people are moving out to the suburbs. . . . Throughout the United States, the downtown city areas are becoming home to the old and the poor segments of our population, to the various ethnic and Negro groups, and this creates problems.

As we can see in Table 32, leaders who perceive both problems constitute only 35 percent of the sample. More often, respondents are aware of neither problem or only aware of one of them. For example, this professional association leader sees only the financial problems: "Property values are way down, and the city doesn't have the gross income it should have. But considering the drawbacks, we're in pretty good shape." Those respondents who see the city's problems only in financial terms complain about the high tax rate and that taxes are outrageous. Those who are aware of the economic and social dimension complain about the lack of business and industrial development, such as the need for a new produce center or a convention complex, and the neighborhood leader perceives the problems in terms of his constituency: "In Oakland there aren't enough jobs for people, especially our Negro and Mexican poor. . . . We do have a critical situation. We'd hate to say we're ready for another Watts, but it's the only thing you do or say to be heard these days." Awareness of both problems is greater among the white nonresidents (nine out of sixteen) than the other respondents. Nonwhites show a greater social-economic problem awareness than resident whites. Moreover, four out of ten nonwhite respondents have awareness of both financial and social-economic problems, while only one out of four white residents are aware of both.

TABLE 32: A Minority of Citizen-Leaders Has
Awareness of Both Financial and Social-
Economic Problems

Problem Awareness	No.	%
Financial and social-economic	23	35
Financial only	11	17
Social-economic only	10	15
Neither	22	33
Total	66	100

As we have seen in the previous analysis of business leaders, financial concern does not necessarily mean social concern. In general, contact with city officials, official organizational view, and tax comprehension are all related to financial awareness but not to social-economic awareness. Respondents who have contact with city officials have a greater awareness of both problem areas than those leaders with minimal or no contact. This relation is particularly pronounced for those with financial awareness, as shown in Table 33 (a). As I expected, the greater the tax comprehension, the greater the financial awareness, shown in Table 33 (b); tax comprehension is not related to social and economic problem awareness. Similarly, respondents from organizations that have an official financial view have more awareness of financial problems, shown in Table 33 (c). There is no relation between organizational view and social-economic problem awareness.

Financial awareness also affects a respondent's views on who should pay. Those respondents who are aware are more likely to express the "complex" or "segment" notion than those who are not aware. Those respondents who are not financially aware tend to employ the "fair share" concept of everybody pays. One interpretation might be that, since the fair share respondent does not perceive that city taxes are high and that the city is operating under severe financial constraints, he is unlikely to feel the tax burden in personal terms; and so he is not motivated to have some other segment pay or to seek a broadening of the tax base as the complex types do. He thinks he pays his fair share and expects others to do the same.

TABLE 33: The Greater the Contact with City Officials, Tax Comprehension, and Membership in an Organization with Views on Finances, the Greater the Awareness of the City's Financial Problems

Financial Problem Awareness	(a) Contact					
	A Great Deal		Some		Speakers None	
	No.	%	No.	%	No.	%
Yes	19	83	9	41	6	32
No	4	17	13	59	13	68
Total	23	100	22	100	19	100

Financial Problem Awareness	(b) Tax Comprehension					
	Good		Average		Poor	
	No.	%	No.	%	No.	%
Yes	17	77	13	48	4	24
No	5	23	14	52	13	76
Total	22	100	27	100	17	100

Financial Problem Awareness	(c) Organizational View on City Finances			
	Yes		No	
	No.	%	No.	%
Yes	22	65	10	33
No	12	35	20	67
Total	34	100	30	100

As I expected, the respondents who have awareness of the social and economic problems of the city do not want to spend less or to cut out services; indeed, it is these respondents who mention more services and increased spending, as is shown in Table 34.

TABLE 34: Citizen-Leaders Who Are Aware of the City's Economic and Social Problems Are More Likely to Want to Increase City Expenditures than Those Leaders Who Are Unaware

| | Social and Economic Problem Awareness | | | |
| | Yes | | No | |
Position on Spending Less	No.	%	No.	%
Yes, let's cut	11	33	20	61
No, we can't spend less	22	67	13	39
Total	33	100	33	100
No. of Services for Which Leaders Are Willing to Spend More:				
0–1	10	30	20	61
2–3+	23	70	13	39
Total	33	100	33	100

The twenty-two respondents who are aware of Oakland's social and economic problems and reject the suggestion of spending less represent the support nucleus for increased spending. This nucleus, however, starts shrinking when we discover that six leaders do not have financial awareness and that of the sixteen left only fourteen see the connection between taxes and services. This 20 percent of the original sample is quite a distinguished group. They come from a variety of organizations (only four from business); half of them are nonresidents; half have "good" tax comprehension; about a third have "a great deal" of contact with city officials; almost all of them evaluate the city as "needing improvement"; and they support a greater number of tax sources than the average respondent.

Another way to estimate the support nucleus is to return to Table 32. Thirty-five percent of the sample of citizen-leaders are aware of both dimensions of Oakland's problems as I have defined them. I believe that an awareness of both dimensions by citizen-leaders is crucial. To have only partial or no awareness could be damaging to any effort by the city to change fiscal and expenditure policies. Considering that the sample is supposedly representative of the upper income, better educated, and higher occupational status element of Oakland, the fact that 65 percent of the sample does not have the requisite awareness is disappointing. From the information in Tables 32 and 34, I estimate that those who belong to the potential community support nucleus for increased spending and yet have some comprehension of current fiscal conditions constitute 20 to 35 percent of the sample.[9]

As the reader can see, it is difficult to know whether leaders would support tax increases. It may be that tax support can only be defined in terms of specific referendums and issues. Nevertheless, the composite picture I draw of Oakland leaders disturbs me. On the one hand, there is a group of business leaders who have the knowledge to understand the complexities of taxation but exhibit little social concern and want the city to spend less. These leaders do not necessarily seek to minimize their own tax burden, but they are not overly concerned about expanding the level of services through increased taxation. On the other hand, another group of leaders have the requisite social concern but do not understand the fiscal facts of life. These leaders want to expand services but do not sufficiently appreciate Oakland's no-money situation. In general, leaders evaluate the city's performance as inefficient, inadequate, and inferior when compared to its neighbors in the Bay Area. But unhappiness with City Hall is not necessarily linked to an awareness of major problems. Although the leaders' tax comprehension and negative performance evaluations are important conditions for tax support, they are not sufficient. Unhappiness with Oakland's major financial, social, and economic problems probably is the central motivation for leader support. To the extent that Oakland's elites are not aware or are not sufficiently concerned with these severe prob-

9. See Mueller, where 30 to 50 percent of her cross-section sample is "willing to pay additional taxes, at least for a program which they view as being important" (Mueller, p. 221).

lems, the expectation for support for increased taxes is considerably reduced.

CITIZEN TAX PREFERENCES

In this second half of the chapter, I will discuss the tax preferences of citizen-leaders. If taxes are going to be increased, the next question will be, What type of tax would the leaders prefer to pay? Seven specific forms of revenue will be considered: (1) sales tax, (2) federal/state assistance, (3) user charges, (4) state income tax with sharing to the city, (5) property tax, (6) business licenses, and (7) payroll or municipal income tax. The discussion will begin with the most favored revenue source, the sales tax, and will proceed in order of the leaders' preferences to the least favored, the municipal income tax.

THE SALES TAX—EVERYBODY'S FAVORITE

Citizen-leaders like the sales tax; 74 percent of them would increase it if taxes had to be raised (Table 35). This support is not surprising because, as a general rule, upper income, better educated, and higher occupational status citizens favor the sales tax.[10] In the opinion of the respondents, the sales tax has all the virtues of the perfect tax. It is painless, hidden, easy to adminis-

TABLE 35: Raise the Sales Tax?

Position	No.	%
Yes, everyone pays, fair and equitable	10	15
Yes, if it excludes necessities	5	8
Yes, other	34	52
No, it's regressive and hurts the poor	4	6
No, other	11	17
Don't know	2	3
Total	66	101

10. This was the case in Wisconsin. See Leon D. Epstein, *Votes and Taxes* (Madison: Institute of Governmental Affairs, University of Wisconsin, 1964). For a comparison with Michigan, see Elizabeth L. David, "A Comparative Study of Tax Preferences," *National Tax Journal* 21 (March 1968): 98–101.

ter; and above all, it is equitable because everyone pays his fair share, even the people on welfare. Leaders express some concern with its regressive aspects, but only a few oppose it on these grounds.

Support for the sales tax is based on a wide range of opinion. Concern about regressiveness, effect on the poor, effect on business, the definition of the tax base, and ease of collection are all expressed by citizen-leaders. After briefly indicating each concern, I will conclude by showing how support for the sales tax extends to excise taxes.

As I explained in chapter 1, the sales tax in California is not regressive. However, some leaders believe it is and consequently reject the sales tax or defensively accept it. This college executive is in the minority who rejects it:

Well, I am basically opposed to the sales-tax approach. In the first place, the sales tax isn't a tax the city can control; the state handles it. There's a redistribution that goes back to the city and the county, and this is of course the most regressive tax there is and really puts an unfair burden on those less able to pay.

A representative of the poor clearly states his objection:

It would be bad. A lot of people here can't eat now for the little money they are getting, and they can't buy all they need now.

The following leaders defensively accept it:

Chamber of Commerce executive: There's always been a heavy feeling against it [by the Chamber]. Personally, I think it's more equitable than the others; the sales tax is alleged to be a regressive tax in its effect, which I deny personally.

Business association president: Well, I think the sales tax hits everyone's pocket fairly equally. It seems that way to me, though they say it hits the poor guy more, but I don't see how. . . . It still seems based on what people will buy. If people will buy luxury items they pay for it.

Social organization president: Everybody has to pay it; it means that everyone is paying rather than the property owner. You read in magazines and newspapers all the time that say this is the tax off the poor and it lets the rich off the hook, but I'm not that much of an economist to say whether that's good, bad, or indifferent.

Businessmen support the sales tax as long as they are not put at a disadvantage. As one business association leader says:

Wearing my merchant's hat, I would be reluctant to support a city sales tax increase if this city was the only one in the area that had the increase. I think we'd be penalized. If done on a county- or state-wide basis, I would personally support it . . . assuming that funds were needed and put to a good use . . . but not to isolate Oakland as being the only one in the area with an additional tax.

However, there is some disagreement over the definition of the tax base:

Social club president: I'm against the sales tax if it's unlimited. They shouldn't put a general sales tax on such necessities as food and medical services. Taxes like this aren't a fair tax; the poor people have to pay more. It should be on luxury items, like automobiles, TVs, radios.

Merchants association executive: I'd say the best source of taxation is something that is equitable, like a sales tax. Eliminate any type of tax that requires a tax consultant to figure them out. You should pay as you go. The sales tax accomplishes this easily. People who spend more, pay more. The city should tax services as well as products. They could put a blanket tax on everything and by doing this could be able to cut the tax rate. Even food should be taxed except for those people who couldn't afford it.

In discussing whether food should be taxed, one club president says:

What's the difference? Whatever they include, they include. Let's say a person is on relief. If sales taxes do go on everything, eventually their income or relief has to go a bit higher to pay for it. The relief people will make up the difference.

One of the virtues which the respondents stress, besides its being fair and equitable, is the ease with which you can increase the sales tax:

Neighborhood association president: People wouldn't holler for a penny or two higher.

Neighborhood association president: It's the most painless way of raising revenue.

Noncity government official: You couldn't increase the property tax, but another penny on the sales tax for something specific, not general budget purposes, the people won't howl.

And as one foe of bureaucracy put it, "It doesn't take another bureaucrat to go ahead and do it."

Because everyone pays and since it's small and does not hurt, citizen-leaders believe the sales tax to be a fair tax and give it their support. These same notions, mixed with a little morality, are extended by the leaders in support of excise and sumptuary taxes. In addition to the present cigarette tax, citizen-leaders would like more people to share the burden by including liquor and horseracing. For example, one businessman who is upset with the welfare burden says:

Yeah, taxes on liquor, cigarettes and horseracing. . . . I'm trying to reach the person who is not paying taxes in Oakland . . . the person who doesn't have any money invested in Oakland—they will have to pay their share.

Other respondents, whether they use them or not, see liquor and cigarettes as nonessentials, as luxuries for which the individual could afford to pay. There is no concern about the possible regressive aspects of these taxes, while there is concern about the social problems associated with alcohol consumption, particularly among the few lower-class respondents. A PTA president puts it nicely:

I'm for the cigarette and liquor tax, especially liquor, not that I'm—well, I like a drink once in a while myself; I'm not agin' it. But liquor creates so many problems—lack of work, problems to the family, that takes funds from the community—that I would be for increasing it a good deal, the tax on liquor.

Support for excise taxation is based on a set of diverse criteria involving morality and restricted consumption, notions of ability to pay and of luxuries, and simply as a revenue-seeking device to "get the consumer." Taxes on consumption, such as sales and excise taxes, are popular among citizen-leaders because these taxes give the illusion of equity. Certain leaders want to spread the burden, but they want to spread it fairly. Support for consumption taxes allows leaders to believe that they are doing both.

SHOULD THE CITY RELY ON STATE AND FEDERAL AGENCIES FOR FINANCIAL SUPPORT?

The respondents' views on intergovernmental fiscal relations give a perfect example of the desire to have one's cake and eat it too. A composite picture runs like this: We cannot *rely* on big government; we have to be independent and maintain our own preferences. On the other hand, everyone's getting money from them and we have as many problems. We have to get our fair share too as long as there are not too many strings. So in principle I'm against it; I believe in a strong local government. But of course in practice we have no choice. The actual breakdown is shown in Table 36. Respondents who reject federal aid are less than one-third of the sample. They exhibit a slight ideological hangover when answering the question, "Should the city rely on state and federal agencies for financial support?":

TABLE 36: Reliance on Federal/State Fiscal Aid

Position	No.	%
Yes, let's get our fair share	8	13
Yes, they have to for some problems	14	22
Yes, but with minimal strings and maintenance of local preferences	5	8
Yes, but in principle they should not	7	11
Yes, other	12	19
No, fear of outside control	11	17
No, other	7	11
Total	64	101

Real estate association president: All of that is more federal control. That's closer to socialism. We got along fine without it, but we are so close to it now it's hard to combat. The same goes for the state; the more power in the central form of government, the closer to socialism.

Neighborhood association president: I would like to destroy the bureaucracy as such. I'd like to put everything back to the level of the common man, to run things with grass-roots groups. I wish the federal government would get completely out of the city and state governments.

Many of the respondents view the federal level as the government; but in so doing, they also express a fear of central government, particularly of central government control:

Social organization president: The state, yes; the federal government, not at all. Don't like to see the government in city business.

Service organization vice-president: Your federal government has grown so large that it's become top-heavy, and now some of these moneys should go back to the cities or to the states if for no other reason than to get away from the political pressure this money always gives the party in power to use. . . . It gives too much power to the federal government, all this money.

Service organization president: Negative, negative, negative, no! Absolutely not. I think that this has become a problem with all city governments—that they're becoming more and more dependent on outside support to take care of their activities, and all that means is that you relinquish more of your own domain. If you take money from the state or federal government, they're going to want to control what you do with the funds.

As we move to those favoring federal and state aid, the responses become more pragmatic, with less worry about control and more concern with problems and fiscal solutions. The following statement is typical of the transitional statement where principle and practice are commingled:

Social organization president: Generally speaking, I'm not in favor of that. Under the existing circumstances you almost have to. The federal government has a giveaway plan and city officials would be criticized if they didn't go after the money. It's a fact of life and you've got to live with it. But in principle, I'm opposed to higher governments returning money. It just results in greater and greater governmental control.

Here is a respondent who has made the transition:

Service organization president: Well, I have no objection to it—and I think that the fears of bureaucratic control of local things are highly overrated. That doesn't happen at all. . . . Fundamentally, if you look at it, you raise the money where you can get it, and you spend it where it's needed.

There is also an acceptance of the intergovernmental fiscal status quo:

Chamber of Commerce official: I think that now that the eggs have been pretty well scrambled, no one will unscramble them.

Some respondents single out problems which they believe to be of national significance, or a local need which is not being satisfied, as a means of rationalizing the acceptance of federal funds:

Chamber of Commerce board member: As distasteful as it is for me— recognizing that the tax load right now is way beyond what the average taxpayer should have to assume—it's perhaps a rightful thing that a larger proportion of taxes collected by the federal government should be returned to California for problems in this area . . . not just for the bricks and mortar but for the rehabilitation of the human element, too.

Another business respondent would use federal funds selectively. He does not like the poverty program but believes that retraining is essential in "depressed areas" like Oakland, and any "city-sponsored function such as the hotel complex, if they can get federal funds to build it, is okay."

Other respondents want to make sure Oakland gets its share:

Civic leader: There are federal funds available and we should take advantage of such offers. If other cities are on the grab, we should get our share. Of course, I mean for anything worthwhile, not to just get.

Neighborhood association president: If other cities are getting it, why shouldn't we? I don't think we're rugged enough to stand on principle.

Although there may be a few holdouts for independent home rule, our mainly Republican middle-class sample believes that to some extent Oakland has to rely on outside funds. It is accepted. As a church official puts it:

Oakland . . . gets millions and millions from the federal government. This gets down to the whole idea of federal spending, whether you believe in it factually or as a matter of principle. We've come to a point where federal money does fill certain gaps; it's accepted.

Another indication that federal and state subventions are accepted is that, of those twenty-eight respondents who were asked whether Oakland should be aggressive in getting outside funds, 90 percent answer yes or feel that Oakland is already aggressive. The feeling is that the mayor and city manager are alert to these opportunities and that Oakland should get all that it can:

Labor official: They're pretty successful at it. They make political speeches against it when they're running, but when they get in office they try to get their fingers in the pie as soon as possible. The last mayor, the one who is now in jail, ran his campaign on "Give the government back to the local people," but before he was even installed in office, and before Congress had enacted those Demonstration Cities bills, he flew to Washington to get some.

A neighborhood association president summarizes this section for us:

I think Oakland has been very aggressive. Without federal funds, Oakland would have sunk right into the bay.

SHOULD YOU PAY FOR WHAT YOU USE?

Citizen-leaders believe that a person who uses city services should pay for them; 71 percent of the leaders favor increasing user charges and fees. The problem with user charges is determining how far the city can go in extending this commercial procedure. As a matter of principle, leaders support the concept of user charges, but leaders circumscribe its application when considering an actual charge. The city is able to use these fees and charges because citizen-leaders are not aware of them; user charges are hidden.

Once user charges are defined to the respondent in the interview, they elicit favorable responses. Intuitively it seems fair to the leader that a person should pay for what he uses. However, after a few moments of reflection, many respondents will start to differentiate between clientele and service. Increasing a particular charge depends on who uses it, and whether he can afford to pay more; it also depends on the type of service—is it a luxury that has a private competitor like a golf course? Sometimes the same person feels that the city should recover its costs but not charge excessively to cut down usage by the poor or children. Roughly about one-third of the leaders unequivocally support raising user charges, while another third qualify their answer by the particular charge, and a final third are definitely against such charges (Table 37).

TABLE 37: Increase User Charges?

Position	No.	%
1. Yes, should pay for what you use	11	17
2. Yes, it should pay for itself	8	12
3. Yes, only if the people can afford to pay	8	12
4. Yes, for some charges and not for others (combination of 2 and 3)	10	15
5. Yes; other	9	14
6. No, it's double taxation	5	8
7. No, discourages use of facility	5	8
8. No; other	9	14
Total	65	100

"To pay for what you use" sometimes involves the benefit principle; for example, a social club president is quite explicit in this respect: "Where it is to the benefit of the individual, I think he should pay the cost." But most respondents employ the principle implicitly:

Business organization president: You'd have the objection that you'd have just a few people paying taxes for the others, but then they're using these things.

Neighborhood association president: If he plays [golf], he should pay. Yes, the user should pay.

Civic leader: It's fair for the people who use things to pay for them. I'm for anything that will improve Oakland, like the coliseum. It seems reasonable that they should pay for what they use. Of course,

I feel sorry for the people who can't afford things. I'd like everyone to have everything they want, but we can't always do that.

There is also concern about the service being self-supporting. It is in this category that cost is somewhat related to pricing policy.

Chamber of Commerce board member: I think wherever possible people should pay for what they use. That includes the park and recreational facilities, and golfing, and the coliseum complex. . . . They should go at the market. Why should the taxpayers subsidize them? Look at the golf course and things like that—you'll find they charge less than they can. . . . The Building Department should figure out what it costs to run an inspection, and they should relate that to the fees.

The price, however, may be more related to what other communities are charging and not to costs at all. The spokesman for the *Oakland Tribune* comes close to actual City Hall practice:

I think it's pretty largely dependent on how our charges in this field compare with those of neighboring communities. If these charges are much lower than next door, you might easily be able to raise them.

The usual comment only stresses that the activity should pay for itself:

Professional association president: I've always been for that. For instance, I get infuriated about our park system here. It's excellent. . . . But they're always screaming for more money. They should charge, and they'd probably even get more people. I don't think it fair to say we're going to put in, say, a new bus system, tell it to pay for itself, when the park system doesn't have to. There's no real reason for this. It should pay for itself; everything else has to. . . . Why shouldn't we pay 25 cents to get in; it wouldn't hurt anybody, probably not even the poor people. They're always saying we've got to take care of the poor people, but these aren't the people who trip through the place anyway, probably.

But to our respondents, paying for itself or being self-supporting does not mean that the charge can be used as a general source of revenue:

Service organization officer: I think it's all right, but only if they use it for improving, say, the golf course; if they used the green fees for keeping up the golf course. Only if it's for improving the facilities— [otherwise] they might be taxing certain people who use these facilities on a regular basis to finance other city things. You'd be putting a hardship on certain individuals for the benefit of the whole.

Not all charges can be self-supporting, particularly when the charge is for something which is viewed as an essential service, such as library access for the young or some service for the poor:

Neighborhood association president: I don't think that anything that's going to broaden a child's imagination should have a charge that the very low income child can't afford, but the golf course—that's an expensive sport, sure. I don't think inspection fees should be increased. Here you are dealing with basic necessities, something the individual has to do to improve their property. Fees should not be prohibitive.

Neighborhood association president: User charges. That's very good. But the wealthy people are most likely to use these things and they can afford to pay it, . . . but that makes it unlikely for the poorer people to use these things. User charges would be hard on poor people. . . . Shouldn't have to pay for anything to do with education—the library should be free. We need access to all those books, and the kids should be able to use it all the time.

Throughout the answers to the user charge question, leaders express the feeling that soon the government will be charging for the air we breathe. Exasperated at the logic of user charges, a union official exclaims:

Then logically it would be fair for them to charge if the Fire Department puts out a fire for you. Or if you ask the police to catch a burglar —can you see a cop asking for five dollars before he goes running after him? What is government for? It's to give service, isn't it?

However, the same person supports raising building permits because they are for the "convenience of the business." But a permit designed to keep a building safe "is not a fair way to raise money." Thus there is a certain amount of ambivalence in the "yes" responses.

This is less the case in the "no" responses:

Business organization official: No, it defeats the purpose originally intended in the idea of city functions; it seems a duplication of charges and seems needless. We make the facility available for use by the public; we provide them and then we charge again. No.

Neighborhood association chairman: They're too high now. The average citizen shouldn't be double-charged. He pays taxes and then he has to pay another fee. . . . It should be absorbed.

Some objections are raised because an increase in fees would cut demand for already underutilized facilities:

Professional association president: I wouldn't be for it. If the city raises this, well, lots of groups who use things now wouldn't use them and the city would lose.

Service club president: Well, our facilities are being used so little now that I think we'd lose more than we'd gain. It would be cheap economy. . . . We could raise Fairyland because it's in such demand, but not facilities where there is no demand.

As one of the more knowledgeable respondents remarks, "You can't pay for a park just by a user fee." If you commercialize it too much, it is no longer a park.

Although there are isolated comments as to the potential public irritation the city might incur if it raised charges, there is little awareness of what the city actually charges. For example, in answer to the question of which charges might be eliminated, most leaders cannot suggest any. A few do suggest parking meters as keeping customers away from the downtown area, while others recognize meters as a means to control parking but feel the city is overemphasizing revenue aspects: "It seems to me we are thinking of meters as a source of revenue, not as a source of public service. I don't think they should be thought of as revenue." This emphasizes another source of citizen ambivalence— that many charges carry dual functions; regardless of the legal niceties, a charge can be both a regulatory and a revenue device.

What can now be said to the question, "Should you pay for what you use?" The answer is "Of course, yes." However, it is a "yes, but . . ." or a "yes, except. . . ." The benefit principle tends to be clouded by people's beliefs about fairness, ability to pay, and expectations concerning the output of the political system. Just how commercial can the city become? It *cannot* be entirely commercial or on a businesslike basis when:

(1) The charge carries a dual revenue and regulatory function
(2) The charge is not levied because of the consensus that the service is a public good which the political system should provide for "free"
(3) The charge is for a service which is not used at capacity
(4) The charge is set so that all segments of the population will be able to afford the service
(5) The charge is set on the basis of what other communities charge and not on the basis of cost calculations

With all these exceptions, the city is able to employ user charges and fees because people are generally unaware of them. It is only if the city makes a specific charge salient that these opinions come into play. For example, suppose the city decides that there should be a nominal entrance charge for the new museum. Support for this charge would then depend on whether the individual thinks museums ought to be free, whether he worries about poor children being excluded, and whether he has just taken a trip to Europe and found out that there museums charge fees.

STATE INCOME TAX WITH SHARING
TO THE CITY—LATENCY IN A TAX PREFERENCE

City officials prefer sharing taxes with the state; for example, California could increase the state income tax and then distribute a share of the revenue to cities. When presented with this arrangement, citizen-leaders are slightly in favor of it. However, leader opinion in this case is not well established and is illustrative of latency in a tax preference.

Fifty-three percent of the sample favor this arrangement, but the positive responses do not exhibit much depth or intensity. These responses are usually clipped and seem to indicate a lack of thought. "It would be fair," or "I guess our income tax is low now," or "might be least painful" are typical responses. Another indication that opinion has not crystallized are the indifferent responses: "We wouldn't be gaining anything—robbing Peter to pay Paul." Of course, there are several respondents who truly do not discriminate and are indifferent to the various tax resources suggested in the questionnaire. However, in general, leaders do have tax preferences. For example, after asserting that the property tax should be lowered and that the sales tax is preferable, this indifferent respondent replies to the state income tax question:

It doesn't interest me one little bit. . . . I have only four pockets— one is labeled city, one says county, and the other two say state and Uncle Sam. The few pennies left over go into a coffee jar, and that's what I get to spend for myself. No matter how they split it or how they claim it, it all comes from me and I know it.

Some of the positive responses hinge on the respondent's positive feelings toward income taxes in general. There are comments like "Well, that would not be regressive" or "I'm comfortable with the income tax, where people do actually pay according to ability." The tax association respondent is more positive than the other leaders:

I would say that would, by all means, be the best way of doing it. In fact, I'll carry it further and say that there should be one tax at the federal level and they should apportion it out to the state and then down to the cities.

Citizen-leaders would rather have state aid than state sharing. Most of the negative comments center around a suspicion that not much money would come back because most of the revenue would be eaten up in administrative costs. In addition, there is the fear that the state will have greater control over local affairs:

Social organization president: I am not in favor of the state taxing and giving it back. . . . I am opposed to this for the same reason I don't like the federal government levying a tax and then returning it. One reason is the great administrative cost in the handling that ensues. Someone in Sacramento would be able to decide what Oakland needed and Oakland might not be able to get funds for what they really needed—like a library, for example.

If ever a state income tax sharing arrangement became a reality, then one would expect that fears of state control or positive feelings toward progressive taxes and a broadening of the tax base might come into play. For the present, it would be more conservative to interpret these responses as an example of latent opinions and not as a sign of confirmation one way or the other.

THE PROPERTY TAX—HOW BAD IS IT?

The main point of this section is to take exception to the prevailing wisdom that the property tax has had it and that it cannot be raised. After setting the pessimistic context for the tax, I will indicate that the tax's attentive public or constituency is fragmented. Then we will consider citizen-leaders' positions on increasing the tax. Slightly less than half of the leaders conceivably *would support* an increase under the proper conditions of justification. In my view, a critical limitation on a property tax increase is that city officials believe the tax cannot be raised. When asked if property taxes should be raised, a few respondents answer:

Social club leader: I think there would be a revolt; the taxpayers would revolt.

Tax association president: I think they'd possibly have a strike—an outright Boston Tea Party rebellion around here.

Chamber of Commerce official: The potential . . . is as high as they can collect. Much higher and you'll get a tax revolt where thousands of people won't pay their taxes. . . . It reaches the point where it becomes confiscatory.

Professional association president: You see, it's impossible to raise the property tax anymore. The politicians won't permit it. The citizens are up in arms *now*.

Is it really this bad? Just how close are we to a taxpayers' rebellion? How accurate is the city manager's perception that the property tax rate cannot be raised? There is no doubt that throughout the interviews there is a general negative feeling toward the property tax. A common opening remark to the question, "If the city needs money, where should city officials get it?" is "not from the property tax." Sometimes half in jest or seriously intended, this remark is a surrogate for unhappiness about the business environment, the fact that a great deal of land has been taken off the tax rolls, and that even though the tax rate may have been stable, assessments have been increasing.

Property taxpayers are by no means a uniform group with a single, clear position. As one respondent puts it, "Well, when they say property owners are unfairly burdened, it is and it isn't true. It depends on what type of property owner you are. Apartment owners get it back by raising their rents." But our respondents who are apartment house owners are quick to point out that it is difficult to pass on increased taxes because of the high vacancy rate in Oakland. Or because business is so bad "the poor little merchant" cannot absorb an increase in his rent due to a tax increase. Similarly, the single residence owner does not have the same point of view as the large industry. Nor do all businesses have equal burdens with respect to the property tax on their inventories.

The constituency for the tax is not defined solely by the payers; it also includes the users. A service organization president expresses the lack of control by the payer:

I feel that it's unfair to the property owner to be constantly given the responsibility of supporting the whole metropolitan area. It's got to be made a little more equitable. . . . I agree that the property owner is the one that benefits from city endeavors like police and fire protection, but at the same time we're getting more areas which are federal and state areas and which are not tax-paying areas. They have a say in the spending but they don't pay. . . . Here, all registered voters can vote on school bonds. The fact is that you are getting too much of this ability to vote levies against the property owners by people who have none of their own or who are actually living on federal or state land.

To confound matters, over one hundred different governmental agencies and districts in Alameda County levy and use the tax. One downtown real estate man, who objects to raising the property tax because it is too high now, says:

Now there are all sorts of districts. . . . There's the county tax, the unified school district tax, the junior college school tax, the school for institutionalized pupils tax, the air pollution tax, the mosquito abatement tax, the Bay Area Rapid Transit tax, the East Bay Regional Parks tax, the East Bay water tax, the East Bay #1 tax, and lots more.

They're all property taxes; so when you're talking about a property tax, there isn't such a thing as a city property tax.

Considering that the city of Oakland has often had the highest property tax rate in the state during the past decade, and in view of the confusion which exists over a multiplicity of governments as well as recent tax assessment scandals, it is surprising to find that the sample does not completely reject the property tax as a possible source of revenue. In fact, the sample splits roughly in half. The 15 percent in the "Raise—unqualified" category who say "It would be all right with me" are not often clear as to why. The group contains a diverse set of respondents: a labor official who prefers the property tax over a sales tax; a small-business owner with the same preference; and PTA members who feel they have no alternative, at least for schools. This group also in part reflects indifference or a neutral intensity toward the property tax. One PTA president who said, "Tell them you found a nut who has no complaints to make," represents this viewpoint: "We have a great hue and cry to relieve the property owners, and I think this is so much—what word shall I use that you can print? —eyewash. You know, . . . I feel that if I am relieved of $1.00 of my tax when I pay the property tax I'll just pay for it another way."

TABLE 38: Raise the Property Tax?

Position	No.	%
Raise—unqualified	10	15
Might raise—support requires justification	21	32
No raise, ever	23	35
Lower now	12	18
Total	66	100

Leaders in the "might raise" category are not at all indifferent. They find it unreasonable to talk about raising any tax without knowing for what purpose. These respondents emphasize need and are usually among the civic minded. They are willing to pay more only if the need is explained and justified to them:

Chamber of Commerce official and industrialist: Well, if this [a property tax raise] is needed to preserve the values that now exist and to help trigger a much better redevelopment and rehabilitation program, then we would have to accept it as a needed cost. I don't believe . . . that we should be sitting on our hands.

Downtown business association executive: We're not anxious to see property taxes increase, and there would have to be a very good reason for it to gain our support. Like everyone else, we'd like to see a reduction, but we know it's not always feasible. . . . I'd like to see taxes lowered. But if a raise is necessary and there are good and valid reasons for an increase, we might go for that.

Social club president: The property owners, now . . . they're taxed over and over, and yet we do need schools, we do need things.

Neighborhood improvement association officer: We had two meetings of the board . . . and we discussed the property tax. I advocate it and several others . . . are in favor of higher property taxes—but not extremely high. We need better schools . . . and we think . . . education and welfare is a necessity. . . . If they're showing us just reason, we might even consider them raising it five cents or even five dollars. But we want to know.

Service club president: My answer would have to be based on the need. For what purpose is it? If it's necessary. If I feel that we get value in return for what we spend and if we have a good administration spending it.

Social club president: I might be a different kind of beast—I hate to pay taxes, but I realize the government has to operate the same as I do. If the tax rate on my home goes up, it goes up.

Sometimes the reputation of the city can be a factor in property tax support. As one college executive puts it: "The property tax rate? Depends entirely on how they handle their money, and I have the feeling that the city actually handles it quite well. . . . We really get a good bargain in the city operation. . . . And I haven't seen any evidence of a spendthrift attitude of the city officials in Oakland either."

Later, when I summarize citizen-leaders' positions on revenue sources (see Table 41, p. 247), the "might raise" category is classified as a positive response. A simple yes-and-no coding would place most of these respondents in the "no" category, but this would be misleading since these respondents may not like the property tax but they do provide a potential source of support for a raise if the city properly justified it.

The "no raise" and "lower now" categories definitely are against the tax. They differ only in the degree that the "lower now" category would actually support a cut in the rate:

Business organization director: I would definitely think there's no need for it. We're highly overtaxed as it is. I lived in San Francisco until two years ago, and the rate is lower than here. This is really high here. It seems as though every time we need additional money, they run to the property tax; it goes up and up. I definitely would be against this.

The respondent goes on to say he would support lowering it, but "I'm not so naive as to believe that if you cut it out in one place you don't need to get it from another." The person who wants to maintain the property tax as it is states:

Merchants association president: The consensus of opinion is that it has been raised up to its peak already. . . . It's high now, but I don't think I'd really cut it. It's already hard for the city to operate with the funds it has, but I sure wouldn't raise it.

Although there is a great deal of complaining about the property tax, there is also a great deal of realism in accepting its burden. No doubt there would be resistance to raising it, but it is probably erroneous to assume that it cannot be raised. Under the proper conditions of justification, where a raise could be tied to specific services, a property tax increase might be politically feasible. A coalition between leaders who are willing to pay more taxes and poor people who are not so willing is not as remote a possibility as it sounds.[11] That property taxes cannot be raised is an old refrain which has been ignored over the years by local governments when they have needed revenue. Indeed, there may be a limit to the property tax, but no one knows beforehand where that limit is. As a knowledgeable tax association executive sees it: "I'm one of the worst prognosticators because I thought fifteen years ago that the property tax had reached its zenith and couldn't go higher, but I've turned out to be quite wrong. The trend in California seems to be that the property taxpayer is pretty well burdened with the cost of government."

11. As an example of such a possibility see Wilson and Banfield.

However, City Hall officials, like the city manager, share with some citizen-leaders the same pessimistic viewpoint on the feasibility of a property tax increase. In Table 39 we see that relatively more leaders who have contact with the manager are against a property tax increase than leaders who have contact with other city officials. As we saw in chapter 2 the manager is trying to stabilize or lower the property tax rate. As long as such agreement exists, the formation of a coalition to raise property taxes is unlikely.

TABLE 39: Citizen-Leaders Who Mention Contact with the City Manager Hold a Negative Property Tax Position

	Contact with		
Property Tax Position	*City Manager*	*Mayor/ Council*	*Department/ Commission*
Positive	3	14	20
Negative	10	19	22

DON'T DO ANYTHING TO HURT BUSINESS

Leaders definitely feel that somehow the welfare of Oakland is linked to the welfare of business. In response to the question, "Should Oakland raise its business licenses?" the typical respondent might say, "I don't know what a business license is" or "I don't know what the charge is now, but I do not want to do anything that might hurt business." Table 40 indicates that 68 percent of the citizen-leaders are against raising business licenses or do not know what a business license is or are equivocal. Only 31 percent of the respondents are in favor of raising business licenses.

TABLE 40: Raise Business Licenses?

Position	*No.*	*%*
Yes	20	31
No, it will hurt business	18	28
No, other	13	20
Don't know what they are	9	14
Depends	4	6
Total	64	99

It is not just businessmen who want to avoid increasing their costs of operation; in fact, there is no relation between organizational affiliation and position on the business license increase. Businessmen are more likely to know what the license is. Some are inclined to view it as a trivial cost of operation; others are against it because they do not see the business license as a significant source of revenue, while still others are in favor of a raise for some businesses and not for others. A Chamber of Commerce or tax association official is more likely to view an increase positively if Oakland's charges are lower than other jurisdictions. Leaders have the notion that Oakland has to be competitive. In any case, nonbusiness organizations are equally concerned that the city do nothing to discourage business:

Professional association executive: No, because you're hitting at one small segment . . . and this segment is having a hard time surviving right now. I'd put it on the bottom of the list if it had to be there at all.

PTA president: No, you make it too tough for business and you discourage them. They move down to the next town.

Union official: I don't think it would be good, but it would be better than an increase in the sales tax.

Neighborhood leader: I think we need to attract more business, and we shouldn't do anything to prohibit the businesses coming in. I wouldn't like to see anything that would tend to make a man want to go to another city to open a business. They should lower it rather than raise it. I'm definitely in favor of even giving concessions to get businesses started in Oakland.

It is doubtful that "Oakland would soon be a ghost town" if business licenses were raised, as one respondent claims. But it is equally clear among our leaders, with or without knowledge of business licenses, that increases would have to be selective and should not put Oakland's businessmen at a disadvantage.

ALL THAT GLITTERS IS NOT GOLD:
THE MUNICIPAL INCOME TAX

The municipal income tax is an attractive revenue source, but city officials are not likely to adopt it for some time because citizen-leaders do not approve of it. There are more advantages to a municipal income tax than disadvantages. It yields very large revenues; it is relatively easy to pay because of withholding; and both residents and nonresidents pay. It does require an organization to administer the tax, but the costs of administration are low, usually 2 to 5 percent of yield.[12] The equity of the tax is subject to question because, to make the administration of the tax feasible, deductions and exemptions are usually not taken into account and the tax only applies to wages and salaries. All in all, though, it is a juicy source of revenue and the city of Oakland would like to have it. No California city has yet adopted it; Oakland is waiting for another city to break the ice.

Only eighteen out of sixty-five leaders (28 percent) were in favor of the municipal income tax; 69 percent were against it. The thought of one more income tax form to fill out is too much for our respondents. A constant refrain is that it would be confusing, too complex, too complicated, and too difficult and costly to administer. I surmise that the individual's frustration at administering his own tax returns is projected to the city running into high administrative costs. Of course, the administration costs are usually quite low.

Similarly, a mass exodus of workers from Oakland is not a likely outcome, but a handful of respondents do feel that workers would move or that they might commute to some other city. Fear of a worker exodus is analogous to the common fear that discouraged businesses will move elsewhere. Indeed, it is a more general problem of local finance, which is not to adopt a tax that may put the city at a competitive disadvantage and possibly erode the tax base. Officials hope that surrounding cities will adopt the new tax first, so that they can do the same. As one of our respondents put it: "It would be a cute trick if they could get away with it. Politically, this would be the quickest way of political suicide in the world."

The main argument in favor of the tax is that it would get the commuters, but position on the tax is not related to residency. Of the sixteen nonresidents 25 percent are for the tax, which is not much lower than the 33 percent of the residents who are for it.

12. Robert A. Sigafoos, *The Municipal Income Tax: Its History and Problems* (Chicago: Public Administration Service, 1955), pp. 59–64.

Business organization—nonresident: I think that it is just and it has great merit. Take New York state, which is comparable. Their state income tax is considerably more than ours. They met great resistance, but they put it in; so that a man living in Connecticut pays the New York tax on what he earns. Now, he earns more because he's working in New York; he couldn't earn that much in Connecticut, and I think it's comparable here. I work in Oakland; my car is on the streets; the police protect me—it's reasonable for me to pay.

Neighborhood association—resident: Why not? Lots of people make their money here, lots. People living in Walnut Creek work here and then drive out every night. They should hire Oakland people to work in Oakland anyway. Let Piedmont people pay an income tax to Oakland; that's where they make their money.

The more typical negative comments are as follows:

Social club president: I think they would have just an absolutely intolerable time trying to administer it. We could find ourselves in a heavy problem; I don't know that the costs of administering it might not eat it up.

Chamber of Commerce official: It would be a mistake unless San Francisco had one, and San Leandro, etc. Many employees would say, "Let's move out of Oakland."

Business organization president: I don't think that is a fair tax . . . because then the people are paying dual taxes; they are paying where they live and where they work. That's unfair and that's not right.

Social club official: No, I have to fill out the forms.

Service club secretary: Very poor! I'm strictly against that. . . . I know a lot of women from out of town who work down in Oakland, and they spend money buying clothes at noontime, right downtown. . . . I don't think the general public would be very responsive to it.

If Oakland officials do not want to commit "political suicide," they not only have to wait until San Francisco passes a payroll tax, but they will also have to do considerable selling among Oakland's opinion makers, of whom we believe our sample to be fairly representative. Otherwise everyone may "move to Australia," which one of our respondents thought would be the consequence of adopting a municipal income tax.

SUMMARY OF CITIZEN-LEADER TAX PREFERENCES

Table 41 shows that citizen-leaders prefer the sales tax as a source of revenue by a slight margin over federal and state aid. The myth of local independence has been submerged in the leaders' recognition that Oakland's problems surpass its resources. Leaders want as much federal and state aid as the city can get. User charges, as an aggregate category, have the leaders' support, but such support might crumble in the context of increasing a particular charge. The 71 percent of leaders in favor of user charges is probably an exaggeration or an upper limit on the support for such charges. Support for state income tax with city sharing is probably understated, because opinion on this revenue source has not crystallized. Once this sharing arrangement becomes a realistic alternative source of revenue, leader support would increase due to the favorable disposition toward federal and state assistance. Generally, leaders are not in favor of increasing the property tax, but support for justified increases is greater than many city officials realize. Many leaders do not want to hurt business, and they do not know about city rates and practice; consequently, leaders are reluctant to support an across-the-board increase in business licenses. The payroll or municipal income tax is the leaders' least preferred source of revenue. Leader support for the municipal income tax will develop as other California cities start to use it.

TABLE 41: Citizen-Leader Positions on Revenue Sources
(in percent) [a]

Specific Revenue Sources	Would You Increase or Rely on this Source?			
	Positive Response	Negative Response	Don't Know or Depends	Total
Sales tax	74	23	3	100 (N = 66)
Federal/state assistance	72	28	—	100 (N = 64)
User charges	71	29	—	100 (N = 65)
State income tax with city sharing	53	39	8	100 (N = 66)
Property tax	47	53	—	100 (N = 66)
Business licenses	31	48	20	99 (N = 64)
City payroll/income tax	28	69	3	100 (N = 65)

[a] Figures may differ slightly from previous tables due to rounding.

7

Politics, Policy,
and City Revenue

In this concluding chapter I would like to go beyond Oakland to consider some general policy implications for our money-hungry cities. No doubt my Oakland experience provides a certain orientation to my opinions; however, in discussing Oakland with officials and observers of other cities, I find that Oakland is not particularly unique in its fiscal behavior. Its officials, like many throughout the nation, believe that there are insufficient available resources to meet their problems, that the public is hostile to increased levels of governmental taxation and spending, and that they have few choices left except to appeal, with futile expectations, to the federal government. In short, local officials perceive a fiscal crisis. As a working assumption, I accept the reality of this perception of crisis, but I maintain that local officials, despite the difficulties, must accept the responsibility of obtaining more money as their primary objective. The officials' hard choice is either get more or do less, and our cities cannot afford to do less.

A POLITICAL PROBLEM

The current fiscal crisis of our cities is a political problem, not just an economic one. Although there may be some poor states,

Note: An earlier version of this chapter was published in *Financing the Metropolis: Public Policy in Urban Economies*, vol. 4, *Urban Affairs Annual Review*, ed. John P. Crecine (Beverly Hills: Sage Publications, Inc., 1970).

some poor cities, and some undernourished rural areas, there is no long-run scarcity of resources. Viewed in the aggregate, in fact, some observers can make our cities' fiscal problems disappear. The Tax Foundation, in making fiscal projections for state and local government to 1975, concluded that revenues would grow sufficiently to create a surplus and that only a minority of jurisdictions would have difficulty meeting future revenue requirements.[1] We all agree that such projections have to be taken with caution and skepticism: tax yields may not rise automatically with rising incomes and assessments may never catch up with market values. On the bright side, however, wars, both domestic and foreign, have certainly raised and "displaced" the level of national public spending.[2] And if foreign wars end, cities may be able to dig deeper into the federal fiscal barrel through some ingenious method of spreading the country's wealth. Once the federal government's largesse is distributed, city managers and mayors can stop thinking about a tipplers' tax where barroom habitués get penalized because they do not like to drink at home. In the aggregate and in the long run, there is no major fiscal problem that rising incomes and economic growth cannot take care of. In the short run, however, the fiscal crisis is very real to local elected and appointed officials. Distant goals such as the implementation of tax sharing may be worthwhile pursuing, but they do not help to balance this year's budget. How to get more revenue now is an important political problem for local officials. What can social scientists tell these frustrated public servants?

Public finance theorists tell us what is desirable: taxes should be equitable, neutral, contribute to fiscal stabilization, encourage productivity and growth, and be simple and easy to administer. Economic, income, and administrative effects should all be con-

1. Tax Foundation, Inc., *Fiscal Outlook for State and Local Government to 1975*, Research Publication no. 6 (New York: Tax Foundation, Inc., 1966), pp. 11–12.

2. See Alan T. Peacock and Jack Wiseman, *The Growth of Public Expenditure in the United Kingdom* (Princeton: Princeton University Press, 1961), pp. 24–28, for the concept of displacement and the relationship of social disturbances to revenue. Ira Sharkansky, in *The Politics of Taxing and Spending* (Indianapolis: The Bobbs-Merrill Co., 1969), points out that the displacement concept does not exactly fit the public expenditure experience of the United States; see his chapter 5, pp. 146–175.

sidered. If a contemplated tax does not meet our diverse set of criteria or if it is no better than existing taxes, then we would prefer increasing the rates of the old tax rather than adopting the new. Suppose the property tax was the ideal tax and the income tax the worst fiscal option. The local official, in a condition of fiscal extremis, would be told to raise the property tax rate rather than adopt that inelastic, regressive, and far from neutral local income tax. The official would respond that he cannot raise the rate because there would be a taxpayers' revolt. Instead he would insist that the tax base must be broadened to include the awful income tax, by which he means that he wants some way to get the same taxpayer to pay more for the same public goods and services. Should this local official be castigated because he ignores what is theoretically desirable in doing what is politically possible? Would you like to be designated "fiscally perverse"?

Local officials live with some psychological guilt because they have to manipulate the environment and at the same time ignore some of the standards which they have been taught. For example, equity, tax justice, and similar notions are not realistic guides to action, but just sources of bureaucratic anxiety. Myrdal, after examining the principles of public finance, concludes that "it is vain to attempt to isolate a purely economic problem from its political setting." [3] And Myrdal's description of the behavior of officials is consistent with my own observations:

I do not blame the politicians and tax experts who legislate and administer as best as they can. They look abroad to see how similar matters are ordered there, they quote the literature whenever convenient; they form opinions on the nature and on the practical aspects of their problems and then come to some sort of conclusions. The reasons which they advance bear the unmistakable doctrinal imprint of the high principles. Occasionally a problem of tax incidence is touched upon but hardly ever fully discussed.[4]

Too often when we say the problems of local finance are political, we mean that public decision making is inadequate, that local governments are balkanized so that they provide miniscule services and have minimum support, and that local officials are

3. Gunnar Myrdal, *The Political Element in the Development of Economic Theory* (Cambridge: Harvard University Press, 1954), p. 185.
4. *Ibid.*, p. 187.

inept and stupid in their fiscal behavior. "Political" becomes a garbage-pail word to explain what seems to be irrational behavior. Political, however, can be used in a positive sense to convey the "how" of doing things. How many political scientists in the country can a priori determine the political limits of a proposed tax? How many could develop a strategy to get a new tax accepted by the public?

If we are going to develop policies which can help solve the financial dilemmas of our cities, we need a multiple approach. We need federal policies which will share the wealth in the long run, and at the same time we need realistic policies and tactics for our state and local officials to pursue in the short run. But it is not enough to urge officials to take a multiple approach, to get money from a variety of sources. What is also required is a new orientation toward the reality of taxation. While social scientists worry about economic elasticity and local officials ignore it, no one is very much concerned about political elasticity.[5] How does public tax support or resistance change when tax rates are changed? Would it be possible to develop a sensitive measure that could determine the political feasibility of new taxes? Can the range of local options be extended by a better understanding of the political conditions of fiscal reality? In the following pages, I want to adopt the viewpoint of the local official. At the same time I want to argue with his definition of fiscal reality. How real is the fiscal crisis? How hostile is the public to increased levels of taxation and spending? Without committing political suicide, the local official can act. Indeed, he must take action to ensure that his resources are equal to his problems. Otherwise our cities will continue to drift into decay and our citizens into disillusionment.

PANACEAS

The problems and solutions of local finance are old hat. The refrain that we need money is well known, and I imagine that people are tired of hearing about the famine of money.[6]

5. The need for developing political elasticity coefficients was pointed out to me by Robert Biller.
6. The term "famine," which I find so descriptive, was used by a member of a tax symposium; see Tax Institute, Inc., *Financing Metropolitan Government* (Princeton: Tax Institute, Inc., 1955), pp. 3–10.

Strengthen the property tax; find new sources of nonproperty tax revenue; states should not fiscally constrain and choke local governments; be efficient with expenditures. These nostrums have been repeated so much that they are not likely to be effective.

Instead, the local official calls in a tax consultant who, after reviewing the situation, suggests that city officials adopt a new tax. If the particular city does not have a sales tax, then the sales tax will be recommended. If the city has a sales tax, then the income tax will be recommended. The rule for this game is: always recommend a new tax. However, it is unlikely that a novel operational suggestion will come out of this procedure. Either the revenue source has already been tapped or the suggestion has previously been considered and rejected as politically infeasible. The list of available and practical revenue sources is quite short, and a quick, comprehensive solution to the local finance problem just does not exist. Yet the advice mill goes on: cities continue to have experts review their fiscal situations; [7] professional finance organizations conduct conferences and issue policy guides; [8] tax associations and business organizations state their tax preferences and hope for efficiencies; [9] and governmental interest groups testify before legislatures and state principles of tax reform.[10] The payoff, however, for the frustrated local official is difficult to discern.

Nor is the federal government much help. The local official is at the extremities of a Rube Goldberg system known as fiscal federalism, which is a euphemism that masks local poverty and discretion, and at the same time holds out a fiscal carrot for a better world to come. Local officials who wait for the federal and

7. For example, see Research Advisory Committee (Francis Boddy, Chairman), *Twin Cities Metropolitan Tax Study: Recommendations of the Research Advisory Committee* (Minneapolis, December 1966).

8. See Municipal Finance Officers Association, "National Conference on Local Government Fiscal Policy," *Municipal Finance* 39 (February 1967): 93–96.

9. See Committee for Economic Development, *Modernizing Local Government: To Secure a Balanced Federalism* (New York, July 1966); and Southern California Research Council, *Taxation by Local Government: Los Angeles County, A Case Study*, Report no. 13 (Los Angeles, ca. 1966).

10. See League of California Cities, *Statement of Principles and Alternatives Regarding Tax Reform* (Berkeley, October 1966).

state governments to pick up the tab are bound to be disappointed. Some local officials, however, expect the federal government, like the Canadian Mountie and his fearless dog, to rescue their cities from fiscal ruin. No doubt in the long run some form of fiscal first aid such as tax credits, categorical grants, or revenue sharing will balance problems and resources.[11]

Local officials, however, should not hold their breath waiting.[12] A large part of such aid will still be for "extras," for national problems on local sites, and not for minor street repairs and new hoses for the fire department. Moreover, someone is bound to tie some strings to make conditional so-called unconditional grants: somebody else's money is never quite as free as one would like. Of course some version of the Heller-Pechman plan would provide state and local officials with some discretion, but revenue sharing is probably intended as a not-too-large supplement for local efforts. Using Heller's figures, which would distribute $6 billion or about $30 per capita, California would get about $560 million.[13] Assuming that the cities would get at least half of the grant and that the money would be distributed by population, Oakland, for example, might get roughly $6 million, and the city would share some of the grant with the school district and the county. If the city received one-third of the $6 million, then this $2 million would be welcomed by city officials, but it would not even cover one year's wage increases for municipal employees.

As Heller views it, tax sharing would provide "financial elbowroom" and would slow down state and local tax increases.[14] Pechman, however, believes that the "amount of assistance should

11. For an excellent review of these fiscal remedies, see George F. Break, *Intergovernmental Fiscal Relations in the United States* (Washington: Brookings Institution, 1967). See also Harvey E. Brazer, "The Federal Government and State-Local Finances," *National Tax Journal* 20 (June 1967): 155–164.

12. In 1960, Berle suggested that the credit needs of local government be financed by federal guaranteed bonds, but local governments still must rely on their own credit; see Adolph A. Berle, Jr., "Reflections on Financing Governmental Functions of the Metropolis," *Proceedings of the Academy of Political Science* 27 (May 1960): 66–79.

13. Walter W. Heller, "A Sympathetic Reappraisal of Revenue Sharing," in *Revenue Sharing and the City*, ed. Harvey S. Perloff and Richard P. Nathan (Baltimore: Johns Hopkins Press for Resources for the Future, Inc., 1968), pp. 8–9.

14. *Ibid.*, pp. 18–27.

be large enough to make possible a significant increase in the level of state-local services." [15] But in any case, given other demands on the federal cookie jar, the assistance, if it comes at all, will not be large enough for service expansion and probably will nourish only a few hungry cities (no small chore). Even if the grants were large enough for city officials to rely on the funds for expanded and usual services, what happens when the level of national income goes down and there is less to share? The services provided out of federal funds would not be easy to cut. Is it so out of the question that our economy can have a few bad years in which income goes down, or am I suffering from depression hangover? Income elastic revenue sources are fine as long as income increases.

The message is clear: local officials will still have to increase tax rates and search for new revenue sources. They will not find the tax that everybody is happy to pay. But there are ways to cut down the pain of taxation and perhaps enhance the official's revenue efforts.

WHAT TO DO

ASSESSING THE ENVIRONMENT

Local officials do not relish going to the public on money matters because in their view it is a risky business; the officials might not get what they want. Instead of looking for revenue, they could end up looking for jobs. There is always the risk of an unfavorable outcome, but this risk can be reduced if officials will invest some of their resources to find out about their own communities before putting a proposed bond issue on the ballot. It is easy for a councilman, for example, to assume that he knows his community. After all he got elected. Elections, however, provide only muddy clues to public preferences. Besides, there may be a lag between the time of getting elected and the time of getting money, so that preferences can always shift. When bond and tax issues fail to pass, the officials blame it on a hostile public and keep their sanity by not reflecting on their own performances.

15. Joseph A. Pechman, *Financing State and Local Government,* Reprint 103 (Washington: Brookings Institution, 1965), p. 78.

In talking with local officials, I have urged that they get out of their offices and find out about the environment in which their organization operates. The usual response is that there is no time for excursions; they are too busy fire fighting the details of internal administration. But if mayors, councilmen, and managers will not gather the basic intelligence to ensure an adequate resource base, then who will? Finding out what people want, what they will pay for, and what the traffic will bear may possibly provide clues to building a winning tax coalition; and at the very least such intelligence can dispel some of the fiscal fictions which local officials cherish.

Officials are sometimes reluctant to raise taxes because they believe that taxes have reached a political limit. "How do you know, Mr. Mayor, that the property tax has reached a political limit?" Answer: "I do not know; I just feel it." A political limit is a fuzzy constraint, perhaps fictitious, which local officials worry about but have difficulty predicting. Even social scientists cannot tell when a political limit is about to be reached. Unlike budget constraints, political limits are not finite. One problem in identifying political limits is that they keep changing over time. Since the 1930s, the property tax has continued to be on the brink of reaching the limit of taxpayer rebellion. Nevertheless, the tax limit tends to be raised when people want more, when operating costs go up, and when local officials are in fiscal extremis and feel there is no other way to go except to raise the rate. It would be a mistake for officials to assume that there is a political limit on any revenue source without first doing some checking. If local officials know their community and keep their intelligence current, then it is unlikely that they will be trapped into thinking that they are more constrained than they really are. A political limit is a question of political feasibility, something which the local official should assess for himself.

Some officials will react to such "know your community" advice by saying that they are well informed. After all, they talk to a head of the Chamber of Commerce, a real estate board president, a tax association official, and perhaps a League of Women Voters' representative. But can a local official know his community when he restricts his contacts to those who seek him out? The local official should worry about how representative his conversations are of community sentiment. My impression is that local officials generally talk to one another. At professional meetings where the like-minded gather, there are splendid opportunities to reinforce each other's distortions about the public. When everyone around the official is saying that the property tax cannot be raised, it is likely that the official will also believe the same thing.

Local officials, however, should not fall into the generalization trap, when social scientists find it difficult to generalize about our diverse cities. For example, Harvey Brazer found wide differences in city expenditure patterns which varied by the state and type of city; a core city of a metropolitan area is different from an industrial suburban city, which in turn is different from a resort city.[16] Because citizens have different wants and needs and because state and local officials have come to different agreements on who will do what, cities do have different responsibilities and resources. Cities are not all the same. Although such a situation is a nightmare for the academic social scientist or the national policy maker, it is an opportunity for the local official. He has a chance to tailor local resources and support to match local desires and demands. This is not to say that local officials, on occasion, should not look at the big picture, but that global generalizations, particularly on money matters, should not stultify local action and initiative. The world of local finance is filled with enough Chicken Littles who expect that any day our cities will collapse in fiscal ruin.

THE HOSTILE ENVIRONMENT: REALITY OR FICTION

Local officials tend to perceive the environment as hostile. It is not that they are paranoid, but there is a fear of private citizens and other public officials. At the local level special districts and the county can encroach on their tax base. The no-money situation at the local level also tends to discourage cooperation between local governments: what is mine is mine and if I do anything for you, you have to pay. Reimbursement rather than cooperation describes local intergovernmental relations. At the state level the legislature may preempt new revenue sources or

16. Harvey E. Brazer, *City Expenditures in the United States*, Occasional Paper no. 66 (New York: National Bureau of Economic Research, 1959).

take away existing ones. Whatever fiscal meaning is left to notions of independent home rule, the local official feels he is competing with other jurisdictions not to provide service but to get money. Home rule does not preserve local resources for local problems. Instead, city officials like other officials, have a restricted hunting license to scramble for revenue.

Thus, the city official views other officials with some suspicion and with some sympathy; all of them are very much in the same fiscal rowboat. But the public is another matter. Whether correct or not, the official sees the public more in terms of tax resistance than in terms of expenditure support. When the local school district has trouble raising its tax ceiling and passing bonds, the city official often feels that the public is hostile to tax increases. He reasons that the public has always supported the schools, and if there is little support for schools there certainly will not be much support for sewers.

No doubt there are cities where the public is so frustrated and alienated from the local government that direct appeals for tax increases are not feasible. However, there are probably many cities where taxpayers' attitudes are not as hostile as officials think. There is not much empirical evidence that the public is more benign than hostile, but there are some indications that an assumption of public hostility should be questioned. Bollens and his colleagues found that 37 percent of St. Louis city residents agreed that taxes were too high when service levels were considered. The poor and less educated citizens had the greatest resentment of local taxes.[17] In a Detroit area study, Janowitz, Wright, and Delaney found a similar dissatisfaction with tax burdens in the lower class. In their total sample "forty-one percent thought taxes were too high, 'considering what they got from the government.'"[18] For federal fiscal policies, Mueller found from a national survey that "half of the people interviewed said that they were prepared to pay additional taxes in order to make possible larger outlays on two or more government pro-

17. John C. Bollens et al., *Exploring the Metropolitan Community* (Berkeley and Los Angeles: University of California Press, 1961), p. 277.
18. Morris Janowitz, Deil Wright, and William Delaney, *Public Administration and the Public: Perspectives Toward Government in a Metropolitan Community* (Ann Arbor: Bureau of Government, University of Michigan, 1958), pp. 36–44.

grams." [19] However, she also found that people's fiscal attitudes are incongruent; they favor increased spending, while disliking increased taxes.[20]

Of course, we would like to find that everyone wants and is willing to pay for more public services. Local officials, however, can be encouraged because these numbers are not more negative than they are. Suppose Bollens had found 80 percent of the people of St. Louis fed up with taxes instead of his 37 percent figure; then the situation would be as dark as officials describe it. However, roughly 56 to 60 percent of the public may not feel that taxes are too high, so that there may be some maneuvering room for increased local taxation.

The cited studies are a little dated, and since public fiscal attitudes vacillate, it would be desirable to have additional evidence before local officials modify the hostility assumption. One positive finding of a recent Advisory Commission on Intergovernmental Relations study was that over the 1950–1967 period over 50 percent of the growth in the state tax revenue was a result of the political process.[21] In other words, increases in state revenue are not just a matter of economic growth but also reflect that state legislatures can and do raise rates and increase taxes. In California, Governor Reagan was able to increase taxes and his popularity at the same time, and Governor Rockefeller has certainly expanded the revenue base of the state of New York. In Cleveland political leaders were able to double the city income tax, and voters passed a $100 million bond issue to handle water pollution problems.[22] In Michigan, despite growing discontent over increased assessment, "85% of the school districts that asked voters to approve higher millages eventually won the increases." [23]

One can also find many examples of city voters rejecting bonds and tax referendums. Rejection, however, should not be taken as conclusive evidence of the hostility of the environment. Voter

19. Eva Mueller, "Public Attitudes Toward Fiscal Programs," *Quarterly Journal of Economics* 77 (May 1963): 221.

20. *Ibid.*, pp. 222–228.

21. Advisory Commission on Intergovernmental Relations, *Sources of Increased State Tax Collections: Economic Growth vs. Political Choice*, M-41 (Washington, D.C., October 1968), p. 4.

22. *Newsweek*, May 26, 1969, p. 68.

23. *Wall Street Journal*, May 21, 1969, p. 1.

rejection may just reflect the inadequacies of the tactics and assumptions of the local official's tax campaign. Consider the local official who bases his campaign on the assumption that elections reveal preferences, or that citizens vote only on the merits of the issue, or specifically that they want a museum or they don't want a museum. This official may have lost the election before the vote. Why some issues pass and others are rejected is not a simple question to be explained away by assuming that voters are hostile to better schools, sewers, or a zoo.

Why people vote the way they do in local elections is a complex business. Perhaps in more pastoral times at the turn of the century, local voting was related to local issues. Prior to the depression of the thirties, for example, local governments were our chief tax collectors.[24] Today there are many hands in the taxpayer's pocket, and local tax voting may be just a convenient means to get back at the federal government's Internal Revenue Service.

There is some evidence that local elections are used as psychological punching bags by some voters. Various authors have interpreted negative voting on local bond and tax issues as expressing the political alienation of the voter in which the vote becomes a means of protest not only against the local political system but also against the citizen's general deprived condition.[25] Usually, local elections do not attract much of a turnout, but when the turnout is high, there is a greater chance for defeat of tax and bond issues.[26] One explanation for this phenomenon is that the citizen who is deprived or disinterested in the community

24. James A. Maxwell, *Financing State and Local Governments* (Washington, D.C.: Brookings Institution, 1965), pp. 15–22 and Chart 1–2, p. 17.

25. For example, see John E. Horton and Wayne E. Thompson, "Powerlessness and Political Negativism: A Study of Defeated Local Referendums," *American Journal of Sociology* 67 (March 1962): 485–493; and Fredric Templeton, "Alienation and Political Participation," *Public Opinion Quarterly* 30 (1966): 249–261.

26. Alvin Boskoff and Harmon Zeigler, *Voting Patterns in a Local Election* (Philadelphia: J. B. Lippincott Co., 1964), pp. 16–17. See also Richard F. Carter and William G. Savard, *Influence of Voter Turnout on School Bond and Tax Elections*, U.S. Department of Health, Education, and Welfare, Cooperative Research Monograph, no. 5 (Washington: Government Printing Office, 1961). For a contrary view, see Clarence N. Stone, "Local Referendums: An Alternative to the Alienated-Voter Model," *Public Opinion Quarterly* 29 (1965): 213–222.

usually stays home, while the citizen who is satisfied or interested in the community usually votes in favor of the issue. In a high turnout election more unhappy citizens are drawn into the electorate and thus increase the chances of defeat.

Nor is short-term economic interest, where the voter seems to maximize his income, a reliable indicator of the outcomes of local referendums. Short-term economic interest, such as the property owner without children who opposes school tax issues, for example, does not always prevail because some people may support tax issues out of a sense of civic responsibility or pride. Banfield and Wilson present some evidence which suggests that winning coalitions can be built out of the poor who have nothing to lose and those upper income citizens who have civic responsibility.[27] In a study of bond elections near Atlanta, the authors found a positive relation between income level and approval of bond issues. Both low and high income voters supported the bond issues, but support was greater among the upper income groups.[28]

Certainly many citizens consider issues, such as the particular service which the bonds will finance, but local officials should not assume that the merits of an issue will automatically sell it. Voting decisions may involve concepts of self-interest, or civic responsibility, or feelings of the worth and performance of the local government, or outlets of protest against national taxes. Since there are many reasons for voting against something, I find it encouraging to find examples of taxpayer support. Evidently, the taxpayer revolt virus has not infected us all. Finding evidence one way or the other, however, will not disclose the hostility of a particular community. Local elected and appointed leaders should not assume but ascertain the reality of community hostility.

TAX PUBLICS: MAKING LITTLE ONES
OUT OF A BIG ONE

Part of the hostility assumption is probably due to the local official's tendency to perceive taxpayers as an undifferentiated

27. James Q. Wilson and Edward C. Banfield, "Public-Regardingness as a Value Premise in Voting Behavior," *American Political Science Review* 63 (December 1964): 876–887.
28. Boskoff and Zeigler, pp. 45–47.

group. The term "taxpayer revolt" is a clue to this perception. How often does the local councilman get a nasty letter complaining about high taxes? How often is the assessor's office filled with pickets, signs and all, complaining about increases in assessment? Of course these events do occur, but not often; in fact, most people pay their taxes most of the time, and a low delinquency rate is one indicator that taxpayer resistance is not particularly intense.

Moreover, it is my impression that most taxpayers are indifferent to taxation. One reason for this indifference is that taxation, whether by design or not, is complex and difficult to comprehend. Taxation is a policy area where one must be an expert to understand the arithmetic of rates, assessments, the secured roll, and equalization. Most citizens are not motivated to master the rudiments of tax knowledge. They do not have to understand the whys and wherefores of tax paying nor do they probably know how much they pay or when they pay. The ordinary citizen knows simply that he is a taxpayer.

To care about taxes, they have to be high enough so that the citizen is conscious of them. The citizen has to know he is paying, and what he is paying has to be significant relative to his income or the profit position of his business. With withholding at the federal level, property taxes prorated as part of a monthly mortgage payment, and the use of indirect taxation by state and local authorities, our tax system has been designed to reduce the public's tax consciousness. One study, for example, found that 31 percent of high-income taxpayers were unaware of their marginal income tax rates.[29] Now their tax bite is high enough so that these citizens should be aware, but a large minority were not. Therefore, it is reasonable to expect that, as the tax bite gets smaller, the proportion of tax-conscious citizens would be considerably reduced.

To say that most taxpayers do not care about taxes does not exclude that some taxpayers do care, which brings us once again to the subject of tax publics (see chapter 3). Clustered around each proposed or existing local tax is a tax public composed of

29. Bruce L. Gensemer, Jane A. Lean, and William B. Neenan, "Awareness of Marginal Income Tax Rates Among High-Income Taxpayers," *National Tax Journal* 18 (September 1965): 258–267.

attentive citizens who have some reason to care. One reason for their concern is that these citizens pay much more in relation to most citizens; for example, a charge for city sewer services may only involve $1 or $2 for a residence, while a large cannery may pay $2,000 a month. For industry, business and real estate operators, taxes are a cost element which has to be watched. Being a large payer, however, is not the only reason for concern. Some citizens become members of a tax public because the government has involved them in the administration of a tax. The wholesaler or distributor of tobacco products may get involved depending on who is tapped to collect a cigarette tax. Sometimes the involvement is strictly to settle administrative matters such as billing procedures to be used by the telephone company for a utilities consumption tax. Sometimes the involvement is of more direct concern because the proposed tax may affect the demand for the goods or services which are going to be taxed. Sales and excise taxes, such as a transient occupancy tax, can generate concern especially when rates are not uniform at the local level. Sometimes concern turns into stiff resistance which local officials would find hard to anticipate. For example, the city manager of a small community in the San Francisco Bay Area recently proposed a gross receipts basis for a business license. His proposal was defeated by the small businesses in his community; there was no resistance from the large businesses. As he explains the outcome, the small businessman was afraid to let the competition know too much about his business. The license fee was trivial; it was the intelligence opportunity which generated concern.

In addition to the citizens who pay attention to specific taxes, there are the professional tax watchers who by definition are members of all the tax publics. The full-time employee of a tax association has a difficult job since his own resources are quite limited in trying to follow the activities of the many agencies within his jurisdiction; he is generally ineffective in terms of support or resistance to tax measures. Nevertheless, as the apostle of efficiency in government, he will show up at city budget and tax meetings. To round out the picture of a tax public, I would also include the representative of the local Chamber of Commerce and similar organizations.

To summarize, a tax public is that small group of citizens who care enough about a specific tax to bargain with local officials over rates or perhaps work to influence the broader, usually indifferent, public to defeat a tax referendum. Therefore, the tax public is the primary target for official persuasion and action and, perhaps, cooptation into the supportive coalition for a tax increase.

TAX COALITIONS: MAKING A BIG ONE
OUT OF LITTLE ONES

Because most people do not care about taxes, the local official, by default, must provide political leadership in building a winning tax coalition. With the exception of the few friends of the museum or zoo, most cities do not have groups of people who advocate increased taxes. At the same time, there are groups that would like lower taxes but only sporadically agitate for them. The political arena of taxation is relatively quiet, and it is the local official who must stir things up if he wants adequate resources to work with. In my mind, the question is not whether to stir, but how to stir and how much.

The tactics that the local official can use depend on his assessment of the hostility of the environment. Tactics are bracketed by the official's willingness to confront the community. At one end of the spectrum of his options, he can avoid the public when he believes the environment is hostile. At the other end, he can contact the public and negotiate and work with its attentive segments when he believes the environment is relatively benign. If he does not need money next fiscal year, he can wait for the federal or state donation. If he needs a little money to meet increased operating costs, he can use public avoidance tactics. If he needs a great deal of money, he will have to go to the public whether he likes it or not.

Depending on how much money the official needs, the tax coalition that he will build and work with will vary. If a proposed tax is small and will not be felt by a large number of people, the official need not form a large coalition but only accommodate the small tax public that cares. But if a proposed tax or bond issue will have a widespread effect requiring at least a majority vote or a large payment by a large number of voters, then coalition formation becomes difficult and complex. It is this latter community coalition that will test the political leadership of the local official.

Although much of American politics is coalition politics, I find it embarrassing to admit, as a political scientist, that I have not learned a secret blueprint for building a winning coalition. However, there are some clues I can suggest. The local official first should develop a support nucleus composed of citizen-leaders who will work and donate resources for developing community-wide support. The composition of the nucleus should reflect the diversity in the community; it should not be just a group of the official's friends. It should contain nonresidents and residents, Democrats and Republicans, the poor and the rich, selfish and civic types, and taxpayers as well as beneficiaries. Even if the proposal is to finance a zoo, a Friends of the Zoo is not enough, and there usually is not a Friends of the Sewer System to rely on.

As we saw in chapter 6, Oakland's leaders would have to be coached in order to build an effective support nucleus. The local official, therefore, should not assume that the citizens in the support nucleus are aware of particular financial and service problems. Most of these leaders will make the tax-service nexus in a general way; they will understand that costs of government are going up and they will appreciate that taxes have to keep pace. It is important, however, that the local official make a *specific* connection between the proposed revenue source and community benefit. The connection must not be just that the restrooms in the park need remodeling and so a bond issue is required. The official who uses a capital improvement program which contains only a shopping list of buildings, land, and improvements is bound to have trouble. Rather, making the tax-service nexus for the support nucleus involves stressing output: less crime, less flooding, fewer accidents, more business, better health, higher incomes and employment skills. In most domestic policy areas, the production function (the relationship of inputs to outputs) is a mystery. At best we know that there is a tenuous relationship between spending and output.[30] The local official, however, should not let this lack of knowledge interfere with making the best appeal he can to muster support. He does not have the promise to eradicate crime tomorrow, only that a few

30. See, for example, Ira Sharkansky, "Government Expenditures and Public Services in the American States," *American Political Science Review* 61 (December 1967): 1066–1077.

additional policemen will improve the situation. The appeal should be tailored to each individual of the support nucleus. For example, the same museum bond issue can attract tourist business for the merchant, provide greater educational opportunities for kids and cultural activities for parents, improve a specific neighborhood and enhance the tax base. Once this group of leaders sees some personal payoff to the official's proposal rather than relying on a vague sense of civic do-good, the official can turn his attention to campaign tactics (for example, timing the election) to win broad community support.

Although the local official should try to make the tax-service nexus for each leader, the official and his support nucleus have less reason for doing this when designing tactics to win public voting support. Social scientists are still seeing the top of the iceberg when it comes to understanding and predicting the public's preferences for taxes and services.[31] The local official, for example, can fall into the trap of activating a segment of the public that has latent opinions which are hostile to tax increases. The problem is that it is difficult to predict who will support or who will resist when the salience of a particular issue is low.[32] However, there are some premises which the local official should take into account in his decisions. First, he should not assume that voters are aware of existing taxes (their cost burden) or existing services (their benefits). Second, he should not assume that, even if voters are aware of taxes or services or both, they will make the tax-service nexus.

Perhaps democratic theorists would prefer a fully informed voter who, after calculating his costs and benefits, would reveal his preferences in an expenditure or revenue referendum.[33] Also

31. For an excellent review of what we do know, see James M. Buchanan, *Public Finance in Democratic Process: Fiscal Institutions and Individual Choice* (Chapel Hill: University of North Carolina Press, 1967), pp. 181–210.

32. For the problems of gauging latent public opinion, see V. O. Key, Jr., *Public Opinion and American Democracy* (New York: Alfred A. Knopf, 1961), pp. 263–287; and Raymond A. Bauer, Ithiel de Sola Pool, and Lewis Anthony Dexter, *American Business and Public Policy* (New York: Atherton Press, 1968), pp. 94–96.

33. See William C. Birdsall's analysis of the realism of an ideal referendum in "A Study of the Demand for Public Goods," in *Essays in Fiscal Federalism*, ed. Richard A. Musgrave (Washington: Brookings Institution, 1965), pp. 280 ff.

local officials who would like to know where they stand would probably like to have referendums which are mandates. But this is not the case and short of doing away with referendums, officials should take advantage of what others see as disadvantages in the system.

The citizen's separation of taxing decisions from spending decisions provides the official and his support nucleus with an opportunity to stress the benefits of a proposal rather than its costs. In most situations when a resource constraint is introduced, expenditure suggestions will diminish. This is true in planning activities and capital improvement programming, and it is likely to be true in voting on referendums: there is a higher probability of voter approval when a spending measure is *not* connected to its means of financing.[34] Awareness of one's tax burden is not necessarily conducive to increased expenditure support. Consider property owners, for example. They are more likely to know their property tax burden than renters, and from statistical studies we know that the greater the proportion of homeowners in a jurisdiction, the lower the level of taxes and expenditure.[35] The voter who is motivated by an economic calculus cannot be solely relied on to increase the public budget. While he may support bonds for fire stations because of ultimately lower costs to him, he may not support bonds for lighting some other part of the city. If the choices are made clear, he can vote down those proposals where his costs outstrip his benefits. The mix of public services is such that he can always find something to express a negative preference.

Ironically, the local official has to rely on voters who do not make individual cost-benefit calculations or, perhaps, are just inconsistent. In our cities, the poor want more services and do not vote; and if they did, it might be a vote of protest. But if the local official encourages their turnout, on the basis of benefit, he may receive a favorable vote although implicit in the vote may be the expectation that somebody else will pay. Furthermore, the

34. Buchanan, pp. 202–204.

35. See Robert L. Lineberry and Edmund P. Fowler, "Reformism and Public Policies in American Cities," *American Political Science Review* 61 (September 1967): 712; and Otto A. Davis and George H. Haines, Jr., "A Political Approach to a Theory of Public Expenditure: The Case of Municipalities," *National Tax Journal* 19 (September 1966): 259–275.

knowledgeable homeowner is not necessarily consistent in his attitudes toward the financing of public goods. He can also be a source of support for some things which are not in his apparent self-interest. For example, one might think that homeowners without children would tend to dislike the property tax because of its use for schools. However, in one study of tax preferences, homeowners with or without children in the public schools expressed much the same attitudes toward the property tax.[36] In a statistical analysis of educational taxes and expenditures, the negative relation to the proportion of homeowners also disappears.[37]

Stressing benefits by the local official and the support nucleus is a sensible counterweight to the public's tendency for small, "incorrect" budgets, because as Downs states, "rational ignorance among the citizenry leads governments to omit certain specific types of expenditures from their budgets which would be there if citizens were not ignorant."[38] We probably do tend to underestimate and be ignorant of the possible benefits of city programs. At the same time citizens are inclined to believe that there is waste and bureaucratic nonsense at city hall so that budgets could be cut. Frequently, opposition to tax rate increases will be stated by prescribing efficiency: "They don't really need more money if they would wisely use the money they have." Stressing benefits is a way of making visible the hidden benefits of usually invisible city programs. If Downs is correct in his observation

36. Elizabeth Likert David, "Public Preferences and State-Local Taxes," in *Essays in State and Local Finance*, ed. Harvey E. Brazer (Ann Arbor: Institute of Public Administration, University of Michigan, 1967), pp. 89–90.

37. Alan K. Campbell and Seymour Sacks, *Metropolitan America: Fiscal Patterns and Governmental Systems* (New York: The Free Press, 1967), pp. 150–154.

38. Anthony Downs, "Why the Government Budget Is Too Small in a Democracy," *World Politics* 12 (July 1960): p. 544. I agree with Downs, and in this chapter I have assumed an undersupply of goods and services by local governments. However, there are some writers who believe that this assumption may not be correct and that there may be, in fact, an oversupply of services by public organizations. See William A. Niskanen, "The Peculiar Economics of Bureaucracy," *American Economic Review* 58 (May 1968): 293–305; and Alan Williams, "The Optimal Provision of Public Goods in a System of Local Government," *Journal of Political Economy* 74 (February 1966): 18–33.

that "every citizen believes that the actual government budget is too large in relation to the benefits he himself is deriving from it," [39] then local officials should not be squeamish in consciously manipulating the benefit side of a proposal.

Thus stressing benefits and not costs and leaving the tax-service nexus obscure are tactics which local officials might consider for generating voter support from the general public. Those voters who do not know their individual burden and want the particular public good will support the referendum. Those who do not want the benefit but have nothing to lose may stay home, but if they turn out there is less reason for negative voting. Those few citizens who ferret out the cost implications and make their own calculations will vote their preferences. While an economic calculus approach may be suitable for gaining the cooperation of a small tax public, such an appeal is probably not suitable for building voter support. Although a city's financial imperative motivates the official, there is no reason for him to assume that segments of the public will have similar feelings. Community coalitions are not likely to be built where the payoff appears only as increased taxes. Benefits are the cement of the community coalition.

There are cases where stressing benefits may not work, particularly when the immediate beneficiaries are a minority and may not vote. Consider the local official who requires more revenue to meet increasing welfare case loads. If the Oakland leaders of chapter 6 are representative, is it possible to even assemble a support nucleus? What kind of an appeal to elites and the general public can be made in such cases? Perhaps it would be possible to demonstrate that welfare programs are good for business and somehow make a contribution to the community. Suppose it is impossible to demonstrate this, then what? Here the local official may be forced to argue for an interim strategy: raise tax rates while pushing for state and federal action. Thus a support nucleus could be assembled to pressure the state or the federal government to take over completely the financing of welfare and at the same time encourage the public to accept an interim tax increase. The local official could make this strategy palatable by pointing out that the increase is not so large because a large share of it

39. *Ibid.*, p. 550 (author's original italics omitted).

is deductible from state and federal income tax.[40] He can also show that alternative sources of financing are more expensive than his suggested tax increase. The official would try to shift the issue from *whether* welfare should be financed to *how* it should be financed. There is no guarantee that the local official would be successful. Building tax coalitions is neither simple nor easy; however, the attempt to do so is worthwhile.

SELLING PUBLIC SERVICES AND GOODS

One way to avoid the public and still get revenue is to allow citizens to buy the public goods and services they desire. The public usually buys some portion of city output through devices such as permits, licenses, fees, and service charges. These revenue sources have different names but have much the same characteristics: (1) the citizen has some discretion in his purchases; (2) he gets some benefit which others who do not pay do not get; (3) he pays part of the city's cost of production; and (4) the amount he pays is nominal and painless. For convenience, I will call these revenue sources user charges. The point I want to make is that if the local official manages his user charges with some finesse, these charges can become a lucrative source of hidden taxation. But there are limitations, as will be explored.

For many economists user charges are an attractive source of financing because of the obvious parallel to the private market. Some economists, such as Brownlee, see limited opportunity for user charges; [41] but others, such as Netzer, believe that there is a "significant potential for greater and more sophisticated application of user-charge-type financing." [42] Along with economists' support for user charges come their concerns about allocating resources efficiently, income distribution effects, and the benefit principle. All of these concerns converge in the choice of the gov-

40. I am indebted to Jesse Burkhead for pointing out to me the relationship between deductibility and taxpayer resistance.
41. O. H. Brownlee, "User Prices *vs.* Taxes," in *Public Finances: Needs, Sources, and Utilization* (Princeton: Princeton University Press and National Bureau of Economic Research, 1961), pp. 421–432.
42. Dick Netzer, "Federal, State and Local Finance in a Metropolitan Context," in *Issues in Urban Economics*, ed. Harvey S. Perloff and Lowdon Wingo, Jr. (Baltimore: Johns Hopkins Press for Resources for the Future, Inc., 1968), p. 457.

ernment good for user-charge financing and in the determination of its price.

At first glance the choice of which "good" to sell is easy. At the local level practically all services and goods could be financed from user charges, because much of the local government's output satisfies "merit wants." [43] Public education is a good example of a merit want where the individual benefits and could pay for that benefit. Once, however, a community decides that education is important, not just to the individual but to the community as well, then it becomes legitimate that the property tax pay for the individual's education. Public education is the outcome of perceived social benefits. (Some might argue that with the current campus unrest the social costs outweigh the benefits.) We often create these social benefits by our own change of attitudes. There is nothing inherent in the nature of the good, education, which prevents a simple identification of benefits and charges with the individual.

There are, of course, some goods which technically involve collective benefits and costs, but these are not as prevalent as one might think. Many of the services which local governments provide, such as recreation, police protection, and free books, have their analogous counterparts in the private sector. Parks can be fenced off, and fire protection can revert to an earlier system of individual payment. Theoretically, most of the goods and services which local governments produce could be sold to the public. I suppose if a survey were taken of the provision of ambulance services in our cities, the investigators would find a wide variety of financing and a mix of public, business, and charitable or voluntary operators. The point is that the service is similar but the means of payment is very much a function of community attitudes.

The citizens of a community define what is public and what is private, and within the public sector they also define what may be sold and what is free. Regardless of theorizing on the nature of public goods or devising methods to allocate costs, it is what people expect of their local political system that limits the official's choice of a good for user-charge financing. The official can

43. Richard A. Musgrave, *The Theory of Public Finance: A Study in Public Economy* (New York: McGraw-Hill Book Co., 1959), p. 13.

influence these expectations; he does not have to supinely accept them, but he must recognize that they exist. In any event the case for user charges is too often viewed as a problem of connecting burdens and benefits, as a technical question of allocating costs and dividing benefits. The "perfect" local user charge is not one where the payer gets the benefit, or where resources are properly rationed, or where service levels are determined, or where there are no income distribution effects. For the local official the perfect user charge may have these features but of overriding importance to him is whether the public will resist paying for the service. If we can assume that the city will provide the service anyway, then perfect user charges are those which are paid and bring in additional revenue.

After the official decides on the good or service, he must also decide what price to charge. Many of the problems and opportunities of user charges converge when price is determined. Although it is tempting to suggest that local officials should study price elasticity of demand and marginal costs of contemplated user charges, it is unlikely that they will or can.[44] Most officials are indeed cost conscious (they like to cut costs), but they do not know what their output costs. They believe the city should be reimbursed for its costs, but in practice they can estimate only a fraction of them. It is not unusual to find local charges which have not been revised for thirty years and the charge no longer covers the cost of administering it. This lag is a result of the thrust of local public accounting which is directed toward corruption control and not cost information. But I would not suggest completely changing this accounting orientation. If a city is in the utility business, then it will probably pay to install cost information systems because the revenue potential is considerable.[45] On the other hand, I do not see the value of an elaborate cost accounting system to determine that the entrance

44. See Wilbur R. Thompson, *A Preface to Urban Economics* (Baltimore: Johns Hopkins Press for Resources for the Future, Inc., 1965), pp. 280–283, for a discussion of the "managerial finesse" which would be required.

45. For underpricing by municipal utilities, see J. A. Stockfisch, "The Outlook for Fees and Service Charges as a Source of Revenue for State and Local Governments," in *1967 Proceedings of the Sixtieth Annual Conference on Taxation* (Columbus: National Tax Association, 1968), p. 89. In Oklahoma, for example, utility charges are sustaining the cities, see Walter F.

fee to a museum should be twenty-five cents. For most of the minor fees, price can be determined by a slight extension of the prevailing local practice.

Officials set prices by checking with other cities and professional organizations. Such practices are useful shortcuts to price determination, but there is some danger that the price will become a fixed standard unresponsive to changing cost conditions. Rather than just checking to find out what the neighboring city charges, perhaps it would be advantageous for local officials to cooperate on an exchange of cost information. Prices could then be set by an agreement which would provide, at a minimum, for full cost reimbursement to the various cities. I do not know about the legality of price fixing by governmental units, but certainly such an approach would reduce the official's fear of losing customers to the competition.

Furthermore, the current set of practices contributes to an illusion of full payment. When he pays, the user assumes he is paying for the total costs of the services; he has no way of taking into account the subsidy from other tax sources. If the public golf course green fees are only a fraction of those of the private course, the user is more likely to interpret the difference as a matter of lesser quality of service for the public course and not as subsidization by the public for the same quality. As long as local officials are going to incur some political and economic costs because they institute a user charge, it would be preferable from a revenue perspective to get full payment rather than just the illusion of it.

Full cost reimbursement, however, is not enough. In some cases, local officials should attempt to set the price to make a profit. I agree with Vickrey's statement: "If any specific charges are to be made, they should in nearly all cases be designed in part to contribute to the public treasury over and above the amount that would flow in on the basis of charges strictly reflecting marginal costs." [46] It is seldom that one will find a charge that makes a profit, and when a city makes a profit it is more a

Scheffer, "Problems in Municipal Finance," *Western Political Quarterly* 15 (September 1962): 528.
46. William W. Vickrey, "General and Specific Financing of Urban Services," in *Public Expenditure Decisions in the Urban Community*, ed. Howard G. Schaller (Washington: Resources for the Future, Inc., 1963), p. 64.

matter of accident than design. Users generally do not like the idea of paying more just to enhance the city's bank account. They would prefer that their cost be commensurate with the benefit they receive because such a profit would only be a hidden tax. True enough; so if taxes are hard to come by, why not have charges which are taxes?

Furthermore, user charges provide an opportunity to get the rich to pay for services which the public subsidizes. Generally it is considered desirable if local governments concern themselves with providing goods and services and allow the federal government to worry about income distribution and stabilization. For local governments we should, as Brazer says, "regard effects on income distribution and stabilization as being incidental and unsought, to be avoided as much as possible." [47] At the local level, we do not want our taxes to have unintended consequences; we want them to be neutral. When this criterion of neutrality with respect to income distribution obstructs the local official in his gathering of revenue, however, he should ignore neutrality and let the federal government compensate for his actions. Usually officials are not neutral anyway, as they affect income distribution, in the name of equity, without knowing who is subsidizing whom.[48] In recreational activities, for example, they set prices low enough (below costs) to accommodate children and low-income families, but this practice often favors middle and upper income users. Officials could correct this practice by having price discrimination by income grouping which may be administratively difficult but is worth trying. At the very least, officials could discriminate by the type of service or good. Marinas, golf courses, and sailing lessons could bear a higher charge because their users are mainly from the middle and upper income groups.[49] To be sure, this is not an argument for economic equality.[50] The poor as well as the rich can increase their fiscal

47. Harvey E. Brazer, "Some Fiscal Implications of Metropolitanism," in *City and Suburb: The Economics of Metropolitan Growth,* ed. Benjamin Chinitz (Englewood Cliffs, N.J.: Prentice-Hall, 1964), pp. 128–129.

48. See Maxwell, pp. 168–178.

49. See Wilbur Thompson, "The City as a Distorted Price System," *Psychology Today* 2 (August 1968): 31.

50. For the most part, I agree with John Kenneth Galbraith that "inequality has ceased to preoccupy men's minds"; see *The Affluent Society* (New York: New American Library, 1958), p. 72.

support for local services. What I am also saying is that the rich can and probably are willing to pay more than the poor and that local officials should in this situation increase fee schedules at least until the subsidy from general taxation is removed. The problem with the criteria of neutrality is that local officials cannot be neutral when setting prices for the poor and it certainly does not pay to be neutral when setting prices for the rich.

My attitude toward revenue maximization is not constrained by principles, but I offer the following principle: charge the highest amount possible so long as the original purpose of the public activity is not compromised or destroyed. This is more than saying "charge what the traffic will bear," because it implies that there are limitations related to prices which the official has to consider. Price has to be compromised when it conflicts with the purpose of the public activity. If the city wants to perform its recreational objective for kids (regardless of the distribution effects) and have a cool summer for the community, the price for swimming should be low enough to keep the kids in the pools and off the streets. Similarly, I do not agree with those who recommend that charges should cover the full cost of regulation.[51] For example, Stockfisch suggests that in Los Angeles fees be increased to cover the deficit in animal regulation and control.[52] He does not suggest just how he would make sure the dogs would be controlled, given the higher fees. Since many people in our cities are poor, the high license fee plus the cost of a rabies shot will discourage poor citizens from licensing their dogs. If animal control has some known relation to public health, then perhaps such charges should be lowered or eliminated. There are times when regulation takes precedence over revenue maximization.

Some goods have to have a nominal or zero price. In the short run, too visible charges may reduce citizen support for increased taxes. In the long run, such charges could shake the citizen's allegiance to the local political system. When contemplating revisions to local fee structures, the official usually restricts his

51. See Break, p. 219.
52. J. A. Stockfisch, "Fees and Service Charges as a Source of City Revenue: A Case Study of Los Angeles," *National Tax Journal* 13 (June 1960): 100–101.

attention to a particular charge and service. The problems of running a local government are complex enough and it is understandable why officials may ignore possible second-order effects, such as citizen support. But the cumulative effects on the citizen of small charges may be serious. After being nickled and dimed to death, citizens may get the notion that their taxes pay for nothing, and their ties to the local political system may be shaken. Thus officials should avoid nuisance charges not just because of administrative convenience but because such action will avoid undermining citizen support. Charges have to be hidden and not cause lasting irritation. Nor is it particularly easy to start charging for something which has been free. If there is a tradition of free summer band concerts in the park, then it is probably not worthwhile to think of ingenious ticket-selling devices. On the other hand if the particular activity is attended mainly by nonresidents, then even an ongoing activity can be charged. Suppose the park department sponsors an elaborate garden show which attracts flower fanciers from all over the state; then an admissions charge is feasible (once the fears of local merchants are assuaged) because the nonresidents will be paying the freight.

In order not to make a lot of people unhappy at the same time, a gradual, selective approach to price increases is a useful tactic. One major advantage of user charges would be lost if the local official did something to increase their salience. They should be paid without pain—once paid, then forgotten—and the payment for a service should not linger in the citizen's memory. However, after an assessment by the official that a particular charge can no longer be raised, then charging for something new is a good way to proceed. I do not completely agree with Vandermeulen when she says, "new fees can easily be devised, but they should be justified on the ground that they are either a more equitable or more efficient way of raising revenue than increasing the rates of present levies." [53] The option of increasing existing rates is not always available, and new fees may have to be adopted even if

53. Alice John Vandermeulen, "Reform of a State Fee Structure: Principles, Pitfalls, and Proposals for Increasing Revenue," *National Tax Journal* 17 (December 1964): 402. Vandermeulen's article should be read by local officials, as it contains several good suggestions for raising revenue.

they are less efficient and equitable. Local officials do not have available a large number of alternative revenue sources. Sometimes the desperate drive for money overrides important criteria such as efficiency and equity, and local officials should not feel guilty just because they have to cope with an imperfect world.

Thus, user charges can be a painless way to increase revenue if the local official knows his costs, tries to make a profit with small, hidden prices, avoids conflict with the basic purposes of his organization, and also appreciates the interdependence between charges and general support by the citizens in a community.

GIVING THE JOB TO SOMEONE ELSE

City officials can give up part of their public business to meet revenue exigencies. For the local official, one of the opportunities of our federal system and fragmented local government is the existence of other public and private organizations which can assume municipal functions. Another opportunity is that we change our expectations about what these organizations should do. The recipe for the governmental marble cake keeps changing. For years school districts have been consolidating to provide more specialized services and perhaps save a few dollars. Now there are pressures for school decentralization as people express demands for neighborhood control. At the same time, there are those who would like the federal government to take over responsibility for such programs as education. Why share taxes when the federal government can pay directly for the services? [54] Yesterday's local problem becomes today's national problem. Who performs which service is not static, and certainly what citizens expect and what officials do can determine what a public organization does. There is no absolute and unchanging definition of local responsibility.

Local officials can shift the locus of financial responsibility by encouraging the adoption of different boundaries for the performance of local functions: public health is a county problem;

54. For this suggestion, see Richard Ruggles, "The Federal Government and Federalism," in *Revenue Sharing and the City*, ed. Harvey S. Perloff and Richard P. Nathan (Baltimore: Johns Hopkins Press for Resources for the Future, Inc., 1968), pp. 62–72.

and with the mobility of criminals, why not consider police protection a national problem. Oakland, for example, did not always have a public library, and it may be that as the revenue straitjacket gets tighter, its officials will see some virtue in having the county or perhaps a private organization provide library service. In a neighboring city, officials decided that they could be more effective in a coordinating role than in the provision of services, so they turned over their sewerage and fire protection problems to other governments and are currently studying how to get rid of a major part of their police department. With the fluidity of who is responsible for what, local officials have an opportunity to give away a few jobs and build some budgetary slack.

There are basically two ways to give away public services: (1) create a new governmental unit to do the job, or (2) transfer the job to an existing governmental unit. Among those who are concerned about local government, I do not think there is much agreement on the wisdom of creating many new units. The Committee for Economic Development, for example, recommended that "The number of local governments in the United States, now about 80,000, should be reduced by at least 80 percent." [55] No doubt there are inefficiencies in so many small governments. No doubt the existing balkanization and overlapping of local government is beyond the citizen's comprehension. Indeed, it is with some temerity that I recommend more governments rather than fewer. Yet the same financial imperatives which, in part, created the present maze are still with us. In 1955 one proponent thought authority financing was the answer, and his remarks are applicable today: "The municipal authority can step into the breach in the walls of municipal finance where constitutional and statutory debt and tax levy limitations and difficult-to-raise property assessments make it impossible to carry on expanded and new functions through regular municipal financing. . . . The municipal authority . . . is a perfectly legal attempt to get out of the present financial straitjacket which states have fashioned for municipalities." [56]

55. Committee for Economic Development, *Modernizing Local Government: To Secure a Balanced Federalism* (New York, July 1966), p. 17.
56. H. F. Alderfer, "Is Authority Financing the Answer?" in *Financing Metropolitan Government*, Tax Institute, Inc. (Princeton: Tax Institute, Inc., 1955), pp. 225–226.

In 1961, Robert Wood suggested the creation of new governments as one political option for financing local government.[57] Wood also suggested adjusting assessments and finding new sources of revenue, but the creation of new governments had a special appeal to him because the same revenue base can be tapped without political repercussions. The special district can, in effect, raise the property tax rate, something which local officials are afraid to do. Wood also quite correctly pointed out that "The creation of special districts cannot be extended indefinitely, tapping and retapping the same revenue sources to the point of confiscation." [58]

Another problem with creating new governments is not that taxpayers will be unhappy because they are paying too much, but that taxpayers will become indifferent and not pay enough. There is a danger of fiscal undernourishment for all the public organizations in an area when there are too many governments. When mosquito abatement, transit, schools, flood control, air pollution, parks, the county, and municipalities all feed off the same revenue source, citizens can easily get confused as to who is doing what and withhold their support and interest. Municipalities, in this fragmented situation, may have to face an indifferent and confused public for tax support. Some special districts may be better off; they will be in a position to run themselves by keeping general taxes down, by not alerting the taxpayers, and by resorting to public-avoidance tactics such as employing user charges and revenue bonds. Other districts, such as schools, where public awareness is keen, may have trouble. Margolis, for example, suggests that a single-purpose government will have more trouble gathering voter support than a government which can present to the voters a multipurpose package. As he says, "the single-purpose special districts may not find themselves with sufficient fiscal strength to fulfill their goals." [59]

57. Robert C. Wood, *1400 Governments: The Political Economy of the New York Metropolitan Region* (Cambridge: Harvard University Press, 1961), pp. 72–73.

58. *Ibid.*, p. 75.

59. Julius Margolis, "Metropolitan Finance Problems: Territories, Functions, and Growth," in *Public Finances: Needs, Sources, and Utilization* (Princeton: Princeton University Press and National Bureau of Economic Research, 1961), p. 262.

Moreover, in a metropolitan area where there are many municipalities and special districts, citizen preferences are clouded,
benefits and costs spill over, and experts conclude that resources
are underallocated to the local public sector.[60] There is also
statistical evidence that for some local functions, the larger the
number of jurisdictions (not including special districts) in a
county area, the lower the per capita expenditures.[61]

Creating new governmental units does have its problems. The
municipality may free resources for the short-term by an arrangement that may come back to haunt it in the future. Therefore, in
situations where there is already a multiplicity of governments
in an area, it would be preferable for local officials to adopt the
second tactic and try transferring the job to one of the existing
units. Such transfers may involve piecemeal consolidation with
other local units, or a surrender to the private sector, or an emphasis on contractual and franchise devices, or perhaps an assumption of responsibility by neighborhood groups.

Opportunism is important in effecting transfers. Suppose a
large regional or state park wants some land to expand its service
area, and the city has been maintaining an expensive recreational
and park area in the proximity of the state park. What better
time is there to get out of the park business, get some cash from
the real estate sale, and get rid of an operating headache? Suppose the county is in the health business, but the city is still
inspecting kitchens for permit purposes. Why not pay the county
to do the inspections and get the city out of the health business?
Perhaps the school district would want to run the city's swimming
pools. The civic auditorium could also become a private theater.
Garbage collection, rather than incurring city costs, could become
a revenue device when a franchise is sold to a private contractor.
A neighborhood group may prefer to undertake the sponsorship
of a branch library rather than see its doors shut to local children.
In all these cases, the recipient feels he is benefiting from the

60. See Brazer, "Some Fiscal Implications of Metropolitanism," pp. 142–
146.

61. Robert F. Adams, "On the Variation in the Consumption of Public
Services," in *Essays in State and Local Finance*, ed. Harvey E. Brazer
(Ann Arbor: Institute of Public Administration, University of Michigan,
1967), pp. 9–45. Of course, this data does not tell us whether the lower
expenditures are due to greater efficiency or less public service.

transfer. One man's white elephant is another man's transportation.

I am not suggesting that the city give away all its jobs and go out of business. On the contrary, I would prefer that cities had sufficient resources to do more, not less. But since they are fiscally constrained, local officials could get rid of those jobs which they do out of habit and which do not reflect any citizen demand for *city* provision of the particular service. Why should a city maintain a large park system for regional use when it does not have the money for tot lots which its citizens want? In any event, it would be a good exercise for local officials to go through: How relevant are the city's activities to its citizens? Perhaps another organizational unit is in a better position to meet citizen demands than is the city. Revenue needs, however, should not be the only consideration. When contemplating piecemeal consolidation, officials should consider political and economic scale questions as well. They should consider the effect of giving away a job on citizen political participation, on the responsiveness of local institutions, on their own capacity to act as political leaders, and also on the efficient use of resources. A little bit of caution in giving up jobs is wise, as it may be easier to give a job away than to get it back.

THE MULTIPLE APPROACH

In addition to selling and giving away services, the local official can use indirect taxes to avoid the public (see chapter 3). Particularly once a sales tax is in the existing structure, then excise taxes for other commodities and services are relatively easy to establish. Consumption of utilities, entertainment, hotel rooms, drinking, and smoking can all be taxed. The link to the sales tax can determine the rate, which can also be raised, almost automatically, as the sales tax increases. Such taxes may hit the poor harder than the rich. Whether or not they are regressive is relatively unimportant as long as the taxes are nominal and do not hurt. In Oakland, for example, a family with $6,000 annual gross income would pay less than one-half of one percent of its income for both the city's sewer service charge and utilities consumption tax. When properly designed, such small excises are not felt, the tax public remains small, and regardless of the original justification of the tax it can be used for general expenditure purposes.

Devices such as user charges and indirect taxes keep the tax structure complex and fragmented, which in turn contributes to the illusion of painless taxation. One problem with the public-avoidance or painless approach is that the taxpayer may soon begin to feel a cumulative pain. Lyle Fitch's description of the local scene indicates that we may be approaching that pain threshold: "Local governments, within the generally narrow confines of state-imposed restrictions, have shown considerable ingenuity in tapping pools of potential revenue, however small; few things on land, sea, or in the air, from pleasures and palaces to loaves and fishes, escape taxation somewhere." [62]

Another problem with the painless approach is that it encourages small tax publics. The few citizens who pay attention to taxes may gain favorable rate schedules or measures of tax liability. They pay, but relative to the rest of the public, they may pay less. The public of course does not realize that there is tax discrimination and keeps paying without complaint. Considering the imperatives of the revenue situation, it may be that such minor discrimination is a small cost to pay for overcoming resistance.

Probably more critical is that the approach does not provide enough resources. It maintains; it does not provide the resources to expand or cope with today's significant social and economic problems. In other words, public officials can use the approach to meet the next round of salary demands; yet many of the public's demands will not be met, as there will be nothing left for lighting, curbs, library service, and recreational facilities. Therefore, for many of our cities, officials will have to take a multiple approach. The official will try to get outside funds; he will avoid the public and work with the small tax publics for small tax increases; and he will seek the support of the community for large revenue increases.

The multiple approach means that officials would have enough money to start the piecemeal rebuilding of our cities. For example, in Oakland, $20 million a year in extra funds could significantly improve conditions. Such a sum is about one-third of Oakland's 1970 budget and would provide the resources to im-

62. Lyle C. Fitch, "Metropolitan Financial Problems," in *City and Suburb: The Economics of Metropolitan Growth*, ed. Benjamin Chinitz (Englewood Cliffs, N.J.: Prentice-Hall, 1964), p. 117.

prove traditional services, to innovate in the methods of delivering services, and to expand into new service areas. Of course, officials and citizens would have to be willing to increase their taxes, but $20 million could be obtained by adopting a municipal income tax ($12 million), raising the property tax ($5 million), and adding new, but painless, excises ($3 million). Moreover, if tax sharing became a reality and officials received enough money to cover the usual annual increases in operating costs, then Oakland would be in fiscal shape to start its face-lifting.

What the multiple approach means operationally is that public officials will have to become risk takers. They may have to gamble on a local income tax, or bonds, or even raising the property tax rate. Unfortunately, high tax rates are often taken as an indicator of an inefficient administration and officials are embarrassed when their rates are the highest in the state. I am certainly sympathetic with the psychological hurdle which officials must surmount if rates are to be raised. But there is also a defeatism in waiting for things to get worse before they get better.

The property tax rate can be raised without a crisis; and if local officials doubt this, they have only to look back thirty years in their own record books to see. For example, in Oakland, from the early 1930s to the present, over 70 percent of incumbent councilmen were reelected regardless of whether the property tax rate, in the previous few years before the election, had been increased, decreased, or not changed. First, local officials should look at their experience over the past several decades to see when the property tax was significantly raised. Second, take each occasion of a large raise and see if in the subsequent election officials were not reelected. Then, if the local officials ascertain that there is no relationship between property tax rate raises and electoral defeat (and that the past is a reliable indicator of the future), they can go ahead and raise the rate. Officials should also recall that there is a time lag between their tax actions and elections which can reinforce the voters' usual confused identification of issues with candidates.[63] Of course, the official's opponent in a contested election can try to make the charge that "he raised the

63. For evidence that electorates may not associate an issue with the appropriate candidate, see Howard D. Hamilton, "Direct Legislation: Some Implications of Open Housing Referenda," *American Political Science Review* 64 (March 1970): 132–133.

property tax." However, there are many cities where local elections are not salient to the voters, where elections are not contested, and where incumbents are usually elected. In such cases it will be difficult for the electorate to associate the tax increase issue with the local official who is seeking reelection. In my view, the political limit on the property tax is mostly a psychological limit that can be overcome if local officials are willing to take action.

Similarly, bonds can be passed. Citizens who remember the depression and urge pay-as-you-go financing do not appreciate its limitations. Certainly pay-as-you-go financing can reduce the risk of reckless spending, save interest, and perhaps attract industry.[64] But at the same time, the postponement of capital improvements beyond the point of preferred replacement can pressure the tax rate by incurring increased maintenance and operating costs. Poor cities may find themselves in a vicious circle in which there is not enough slack in the budget to finance capital improvements, so they are deferred, maintenance rises, and budgetary slack is further reduced. And even if maintenance costs do not reduce slack, then certainly employee demands for salary increases will. In such a situation, officials of cities with excellent bond ratings should surely make the attempt to build coalitions to pass bonds.

CONCLUSION

In this chapter I have argued from two premises: revenue maximization is a criterion of primary importance; and revenue maximization is accomplished by local action. Obviously, other criteria such as efficiency and equity should also be considered, and certainly there may be viable alternatives to local action. It seems hardly any advice at all to suggest that what appears as a fiscal crisis is in reality a crisis of political leadership. Some officials would probably prefer a suggestion for a new tax resource which could easily gain public acceptance and bring in a great deal of revenue.

Based on the successful practice of local revenue gatherers,

64. See Elizabeth Y. Deran, *Financing Capital Improvements: The "Pay-As-You-Go" Approach* (Berkeley: Bureau of Public Administration, University of California, 1961), pp. 30–33.

my shopping list of suggestions is not particularly novel. What is new is the political interpretation of financial options that have already been discussed and justified by others for many years. Throughout this chapter I have tried to counter the prevailing fiscal pessimism that exists at the local level. Without committing political suicide, local officials can do something about the fiscal condition of their cities. What appears to be a political constraint can often be converted into a political opportunity. As long as we continue to define fiscal reality solely in economic and resource terms, innovative suggestions will not appear. Much can be done by adding a political perspective.

I have tried to interest political scientists in the world of local finance; one of the main reasons for doing so is that I believe that political scientists can help local officials by conducting tax policy research. There is a great deal of work to be done; specifically, we need to understand the conditions for citizen support of taxes. How can we tell which cities and neighborhoods will be hostile to tax increases? When will elites and the general public support revenue issues? If the conditions for tax support are haphazard and subject to the vagaries of the citizen's upset stomach, should referendums be eliminated? Do some citizens have a general propensity for supporting tax increases or is such support grounded in specific policy issues? To answer these questions, quantitative measures of tax support which scale the scope and depth of citizen support are necessary. Understanding is also needed of how the structure of the political system affects the kinds of taxes levied on its citizens. Do cities without much political muscle rely more on indirect rather than direct forms of financing? Cities lacking strong political structures may not be able to use the income tax, while strong mayor cities may be able to install a local income tax or use other direct means of financing. Or is the choice of tax tactics a function of political leadership rather than political structure? Aggressive leaders may prefer direct ways of coping with the public, while passive leaders may prefer indirect ways. At least, it might be investigated whether officials are turned out of office after they have increased the tax burden. If the results were negative, then officials would not be so afraid of raising the property tax.

Politics must become a more significant part of the picture of fiscal reality. Right now the politics of city revenue is mostly a nonpolitics which requires the replacement of acquiescence with concern and political skill by both leaders and citizens. As Harlan Cleveland so aptly put it: "Local governments are not broke; they just think they are. Our metropolitan cities and suburbs are bankrupt, all right, but not in resources. They are bankrupt, most of them, in imagination, organization, leadership and will." [65]

65. Harlan Cleveland, "Are the Cities Broke?" *National Civic Review* 50 (March 1961): 126.

Appendix

1. Could you tell me something about the makeup of your organization, who belongs, etc., and your role in it?
2. Does the organization have any views about city expenses and revenue?
3. Does the organization ever present these views to city officials?
4. What about your own views on city expenses and revenue?
5. In what categories do you believe the city is spending too much?
6. Where should the city spend more to meet the needs of the community?
7. If the city should have to spend more, where should the city officials get it (in general)?
8. Should they get it by raising the property tax rate?
9. [If No. 8 is "No"] Would you work for cutting the property tax rate?
10. Should they get it by raising the sales tax?
11. Should they get it by raising the state income tax, with a sharing arrangement to the city?
12. Should they get it by raising the cost of business licenses?
13. Should they get it by increasing user charges?

14. Should they get it from a municipal income tax?
15. What city services or facilities do you (or your organization) use? Do you pay for the use of these facilities?
16. What other services or facilities might be charged for?
17. For what types of services should the users not pay?
18. What services (like fire and police) should the city provide out of general tax revenues?
19. Should the city rely on state and federal agencies for financial support? Should the city be more aggressive in going after these funds?
20. Should the city cut out any services?
21. Do you have any further suggestions for improving the city's financial picture?

Bibliography

BOOKS

Barker, Ernest. *The Development of Public Services in Western Europe, 1660–1930*. London: Oxford University Press, 1944.

Bennis, Warren G. *Changing Organizations*. New York: McGraw-Hill Book Co., 1966.

Bollens, John C., and Schmandt, Henry J. *The Metropolis: Its People, Politics, and Economic Life*. New York: Harper & Row, 1965.

Bollens, John C., et al. *Exploring the Metropolitan Community*. Berkeley and Los Angeles: University of California Press, 1961.

Boskoff, Alvin, and Zeigler, Harmon. *Voting Patterns in a Local Election*. Philadelphia: J. B. Lippincott Co., 1964.

Braybrooke, David, and Lindblom, Charles E. *A Strategy of Decision*. New York: Free Press of Glencoe, 1963.

Brazer, Harvey E. *City Expenditures in the United States*. Occasional Paper no. 66. New York: National Bureau of Economic Research, 1959.

Break, George F. *Intergovernmental Fiscal Relations in the United States*. Washington, D.C.: Brookings Institution, 1967.

Brown, W. H., Jr., and Gilbert, C. E. *Planning Municipal Investment: A Case Study of Philadelphia*. Philadelphia: University of Pennsylvania Press, 1961.

Buchanan, James M. *Public Finance in Democratic Process: Fiscal Institutions and Individual Choice*. Chapel Hill: University of North Carolina Press, 1967.

Burkhead, Jesse. *State and Local Taxes for Public Education*. Syracuse: Syracuse University Press, 1963.

———. *Governmental Budgeting*. New York: John Wiley & Sons, Inc., 1956.

Campbell, Alan K., and Sacks, Seymour. *Metropolitan America: Fiscal Patterns and Governmental Systems*. New York: Free Press, 1967.

Committee for Economic Development. *Modernizing Local Government: To Secure a Balanced Federalism*. New York, July 1966.

Crecine, John P. *Governmental Problem-Solving: A Computer Simulation of Municipal Budgeting.* Chicago: Rand McNally and Co., 1969.

Cyert, Richard M., and March, James G. *A Behavioral Theory of the Firm.* Englewood Cliffs, N.J.: Prentice-Hall, Inc., 1963.

Davisson, Malcom M. *Financing Local Governments in the San Francisco Bay Area.* Berkeley: Institute of Governmental Studies, University of California, 1963.

Deran, Elizabeth Y. *Financing Capital Improvements: The "Pay-As-You-Go" Approach.* Berkeley: Bureau of Public Administration, University of California, 1961.

Downs, Anthony. *Inside Bureaucracy.* Boston: Little, Brown and Company, 1967.

――――. *An Economic Theory of Democracy.* New York: Harper & Row, 1957.

Dror, Yehezkel. *Public Policymaking Reexamined.* San Francisco: Chandler Publishing Co., 1968.

Due, John F. *Government Finance: An Economic Analysis.* 3rd ed. Homewood, Ill.: Richard D. Irwin, Inc., 1963.

Dye, Thomas R. *Politics, Economics, and the Public: Policy Outcomes in the American States.* Chicago: Rand McNally and Co., 1966.

Elison, Larry M. *The Finances of Metropolitan Areas.* Ann Arbor: Michigan Legal Publications, 1964.

Epstein, Leon D. *Votes and Taxes.* Madison: Institute of Governmental Affairs, University of Wisconsin, 1964.

Fabricant, Solomon. *The Trend of Government Activity in the United States Since 1900.* New York: National Bureau of Economic Research, Inc., 1952.

Fenno, Richard F., Jr. *The Power of the Purse: Appropriations Politics in Congress.* Boston: Little, Brown and Co., 1966.

Fisher, Glenn W., and Fairbanks, Robert P. *Illinois Municipal Finance: A Political and Economic Analysis.* Urbana: University of Illinois Press, 1968.

Galbraith, John Kenneth. *The Affluent Society.* New York: New American Library, 1958.

Gerwin, Donald. *Budgeting Public Funds: The Decision Process in an Urban School District.* Madison: University of Wisconsin Press, 1969.

Gordon, Mitchell. *Sick Cities.* New York: Macmillan Company, 1963.

Heller, Walter W. *New Dimensions of Political Economy.* Cambridge, Massachusetts: Harvard University Press, 1966.

Heller, Walter W., et al. *Revenue Sharing and the City.* Baltimore: Johns Hopkins Press for Resources for the Future, Inc., 1968.

Hillhouse, A. M., and Howard, S. Kenneth. *Revenue Estimating by Cities.* Chicago: Municipal Finance Officers Association of the U.S. and Canada, 1965.

Hirsch, Werner Z., ed. *Urban Life and Form.* New York: Holt, Rinehart, and Winston, 1963.

International City Managers Association. *Municipal Finance Administration.* 6th ed. Chicago: International City Managers Association, 1962.

Janowitz, Morris; Wright, Deil; and Delaney, William. *Public Administration and the Public: Perspectives Toward Government in a Metropolitan*

Community. Ann Arbor: Bureau of Government, University of Michigan, 1958.

Katz, Daniel, and Kahn, Robert L. *The Social Psychology of Organizations*. New York: John Wiley & Sons, Inc., 1966.

Kaufman, Herbert. *Politics and Policies in State and Local Governments*. Englewood Cliffs, N. J.: Prentice-Hall, 1963.

Key, V. O., Jr. *Public Opinion and American Democracy*. New York: Alfred A. Knopf, 1961.

League of California Cities. *Statement of Principles and Alternatives Regarding Tax Reform*. Berkeley, October 1966.

————. *Limited Expenditure Funds of Cities*. Berkeley, March 1963.

Lynn, Arthur D., Jr., ed. *The Property Tax and Its Administration*. Madison: University of Wisconsin Press, 1969.

McKinley, John R. *Local Revenue Problems and Trends*. Berkeley: Bureau of Public Administration, University of California, April 11, 1949.

March, James G., and Simon, Herbert A. *Organizations*. New York: John Wiley & Sons, Inc., 1958.

Margolis, Julius, ed. *The Public Economy of Urban Communities*. Baltimore: Johns Hopkins Press for Resources for the Future, Inc., 1965.

Maxwell, James A. *Financing State and Local Governments*. Washington, D.C.: Brookings Institution, 1965.

Mitau, G. Theodore. *State and Local Government: Politics and Processes*. New York: Charles Scribner's Sons, 1966.

Musgrave, Richard A. *The Theory of Public Finance: A Study in Public Economy*. New York: McGraw-Hill Book Co., 1959.

Musgrave, Richard A., and Peacock, Alan T., eds. *Classics in the Theory of Public Finance*. London: Macmillan, 1967.

Myrdal, Gunnar. *The Political Element in the Development of Economic Theory*. Cambridge, Massachusetts: Harvard University Press, 1954.

National Committee on Governmental Accounting. *A Standard Classification of Municipal Accounts*. Chicago: National Committee on Governmental Accounting, 1953.

————. *Municipal Accounting and Auditing*. Chicago: National Committee on Governmental Accounting, 1951.

Netzer, Dick. *Economics of the Property Tax*. Washington, D.C.: Brookings Institution, 1966.

Peacock, Alan T., and Wiseman, Jack. *The Growth of Public Expenditure in the United Kingdom*. Princeton: Princeton University Press, 1961.

Pechman, Joseph A. *Financing State and Local Government*. Reprint 103. Washington, D. C.: Brookings Institution, 1965.

Sacks, Seymour, and Hellmuth, William, Jr. *Financing Government in a Metropolitan Area: The Cleveland Experience*. New York: Free Press of Glencoe, 1961.

Scott, Stanley, and Feder, Edward L. *Factors Associated with Variations in Municipal Levels: A Statistical Study of California Cities*. Berkeley: Bureau of Public Administration, University of California, 1957.

Sigafoos, Robert A. *The Municipal Income Tax: Its History and Problems*. Chicago: Public Administration Service, 1955.

Simon, Herbert A. *The New Science of Management Decision*. New York: Harper and Brothers, 1960.

————. *Administrative Behavior.* 2nd ed. New York: Free Press, 1957.
————. *Models of Man: Social and Rational.* New York: John Wiley & Sons, Inc., 1957.
Southern California Research Council. *Taxation by Local Government: Los Angeles County, a Case Study.* Report no. 13. Los Angeles [*ca.* 1966].
Stone, Harold A.; Price, Don K.; and Stone, Kathryn H. *City Manager Government in the United States: A Review After Twenty-five Years.* Chicago: Public Administration Service, 1940.
Tax Foundation, Inc. *Fiscal Outlook for State and Local Government to 1975.* Research Publication no. 6. New York: Tax Foundation, Inc., 1966.
Tax Institute, Inc. *Financing Metropolitan Government.* Princeton: Tax Institute, Inc., 1955.
Thompson, James D. *Organizations in Action.* New York: McGraw-Hill Book Co., 1967.
Thompson, Wilbur R. *A Preface to Urban Economics.* Baltimore: Johns Hopkins Press for Resources for the Future, Inc., 1965.
Vieg, John A., et al. *California Local Finance.* Stanford, California: Stanford University Press, 1960.
Wildavsky, Aaron. *The Politics of the Budgetary Process.* Boston: Little, Brown and Co., 1964.
Williams, Oliver P.; Herman, Harold; Liebman, Charles S.; and Dye, Thomas R. *Suburban Differences and Metropolitan Policies: A Philadelphia Story.* Philadelphia: University of Pennsylvania Press, 1965.
Wood, Robert C. *1400 Governments: The Political Economy of the New York Metropolitan Region.* Cambridge: Harvard University Press, 1961.

ARTICLES IN BOOKS AND JOURNALS

Adams, Robert F. "On the Variation in the Consumption of Public Services." In *Essays in State and Local Finance,* edited by Harvey E. Brazer, pp. 9–45. Ann Arbor: Institute of Public Administration, University of Michigan, 1967.
Berle, Adolph A., Jr. "Reflections on Financing Governmental Functions of the Metropolis." In *Proceedings of the Academy of Political Science* 27 (May 1960): 66–79.
Birdsall, William C. "A Study of the Demand for Public Goods." In *Essays in Fiscal Federalism,* edited by Richard A. Musgrave, pp. 235–294. Washington, D.C.: Brookings Institution, 1965.
Booms, Bernard H. "City Governmental Form and Public Expenditure Levels." *National Tax Journal* 19 (June 1966): 187–199.
Brainin, David, and Germanis, John J. "Comments on 'Distribution of Property, Retail Sales and Personal Income Tax Burdens in California: An Empirical Analysis of Inequity in Taxation' by Gerhard N. Rostvold." *National Tax Journal* 20 (March 1967): 106–111.
Brazer, Harvey E. "The Federal Government and State-Local Finances." *National Tax Journal* 20 (June 1967): 155–164.
————. "Some Fiscal Implications of Metropolitanism." In *City and Suburb: The Economics of Metropolitan Growth,* edited by Benjamin Chinitz, pp. 127–150. Englewood Cliffs, N.J.: Prentice-Hall, 1964.

Brownless, O. H. "User Prices *vs.* Taxes." In *Public Finances: Needs, Sources, and Utilization,* pp. 421–432. Princeton: Princeton University Press and National Bureau of Economic Research, 1961.

Cleveland, Harlan. "Are the Cities Broke?" *National Civic Review* 50 (March 1961): 126–130.

Connery, Robert H., ed. "Municipal Income Taxes." *Proceedings of the Academy of Political Science* 28 (1968).

Converse, Phillip E. "The Nature of Belief Systems in Mass Publics." In *Ideology and Discontent,* edited by David E. Apter, pp. 206–261. New York: Free Press, 1964.

Curran, Donald J. "The Metropolitan Problem: Solution from Within." *National Tax Journal* 16 (September 1963): 213–223.

David, Elizabeth Likert. "A Comparative Study of Tax Preferences." *National Tax Journal* 21 (March 1968): 98–101.

———. "Public Preferences and State-Local Taxes." In *Essays in State and Local Finance,* edited by Harvey E. Brazer, pp. 74–106. Ann Arbor: Institute of Public Administration, University of Michigan, 1967.

David, Elizabeth Likert, and Skurski, Roger B. "Property Tax Assessment and Absentee Owners." *National Tax Journal* 19 (December 1966): 421–426.

Davies, David. "Financing Urban Functions and Services." *Law and Contemporary Problems* 30 (winter 1965): 127–161.

Davis, Otto A., and Haines, George H., Jr. "A Political Approach to a Theory of Public Expenditure: The Case of Municipalities." *National Tax Journal* 19 (September 1966): 259–275.

Downs, Anthony. "Why the Government Budget Is Too Small in a Democracy." *World Politics* 12 (July 1960): 541–563.

Eckstein, Otto. "Indirect Versus Direct Taxes: Implications for Stability Investment." In *Public Finance and Fiscal Policy,* edited by Joseph Scherer and James A. Papke, pp. 153–166. Boston: Houghton Mifflin Company, 1966.

Fisher, Glenn W. "Interstate Variation in State and Local Government Expenditure." *National Tax Journal* 17 (March 1964): 57–74.

———. "Determinants of State and Local Government Expenditures: A Preliminary Analysis." *National Tax Journal* 14 (December 1961): 349–355.

Fisher, Glenn W., and Fairbanks, Robert P. "The Politics of Property Taxation." *Administrative Science Quarterly* 12 (June 1967): 48–71.

Fitch, Lyle C. "Metropolitan Fiscal Problems." In *City and Suburb: The Economics of Metropolitan Growth,* edited by Benjamin Chinitz, pp. 113–126. Englewood Cliffs, N.J.: Prentice-Hall, 1964.

Gensemer, Bruce L.; Lean, Jane A.; and Neenan, William B. "Awareness of Marginal Income Tax Rates Among High-Income Taxpayers." *National Tax Journal* 18 (September 1965): 258–267.

Hamovitch, William. "Sales Taxation: An Analysis of the Effects of Rate Increases in Two Contrasting Cases." *National Tax Journal* 19 (December 1966): 411–420.

Hawley, Amos H. "Metropolitan Population and Municipal Governmental Expenditures in Central Cities." *Journal of Social Issues* 7 (1951): 100–108.

Herring, E. Pendleton. "The Politics of Fiscal Policy." *Yale Law Journal* 40 (March 1938): 724–745.

Horton, John E., and Thompson, Wayne E. "Powerlessness and Political Negativism: A Study of Defeated Local Referendums." *American Journal of Sociology* 67 (March 1962): 485–493.

Kammerer, Gladys M. "Role Diversity of City Managers." *Administrative Science Quarterly* 8 (March 1964): 421–442.

Kurnow, Ernest. "Determinants of State and Local Government Expenditures Reexamined." *National Tax Journal* 16 (September 1963): 252–255.

Lindahl, Erik. "Tax Principles and Tax Policy." In *International Economic Papers*, no. 10, pp. 7–23. London: Macmillan and Co., Ltd., 1960.

Lindblom, Charles E. "The Science of 'Muddling Through.'" *Public Administration Review* 19 (spring 1959): 79–88.

Lineberry, Robert L., and Fowler, Edmund P. "Reformism and Public Policies in American Cities." *American Political Science Review* 61 (September 1967): 701–716.

Long, Norton E. "The Local Community as an Ecology of Games." *American Journal of Sociology* 64 (November 1958): 251–261.

Mangum, Garth L. "The Benefit Principle." *Municipal Finance* 24 (February 1962): 125–136.

Margolis, Julius. "Metropolitan Finance Problems: Territories, Functions and Growth." In *Public Finances: Needs, Sources, and Utilization*, pp. 229–270. Princeton: Princeton University Press and National Bureau of Economic Research, 1961.

———. "Municipal Fiscal Structure in a Metropolitan Region." *Journal of Political Economy* 65 (June 1957): 225–236.

Morss, Elliott R. "Some Thoughts on the Determinants of State and Local Expenditures." *National Tax Journal* 19 (March 1966): 95–103.

Mueller, Eva. "Public Attitudes Toward Fiscal Programs." *Quarterly Journal of Economics* 77 (May 1963): 210–235.

Municipal Finance Officers Association. "National Conference on Local Government Fiscal Policy." *Municipal Finance* 39 (February 1967): 91–148.

Mushkin, Selma J., and Adams, Robert F. "Emerging Patterns of Federalism." *National Tax Journal* 19 (September 1966): 225–247.

Netzer, Dick. "Federal, State, and Local Finance in a Metropolitan Context." In *Issues in Urban Economics*, edited by Harvey S. Perloff and Lowdon Wingo, Jr., pp. 435–476. Baltimore: Johns Hopkins Press for Resources for the Future, Inc., 1968.

———. "Paying for Services." *National Civic Review* 51 (April 1962): 195–199.

Peabody, Robert L. "Seattle Seeks a Tax." In *State and Local Government: A Case Book*, edited by Edwin A. Bock, pp. 495–514. Birmingham: University of Alabama Press, 1963.

Penniman, Clara. "The Politics of Taxation." In *Politics in the American States*, edited by Herbert Jacob and Kenneth N. Vines, pp. 291–329. Boston: Little, Brown and Company, 1965.

Rostvold, Gerhard N. "Distribution of Property, Retail Sales, and Personal Income Tax Burdens in California: An Empirical Analysis of Inequity in Taxation." *National Tax Journal* 19 (March 1966): 38–47.

Sacks, Seymour, and Harris, Robert. "The Determinants of State and Local Government Expenditures and Intergovernmental Flows of Funds." *National Tax Journal* 17 (March 1964): 75–85.

Scheffer, Walter F. "Problems in Municipal Finance." *Western Political Quarterly* 15 (September 1962): 522–535.

Schmölders, G. "Fiscal Psychology: A New Branch of Public Finance." *National Tax Journal* 12 (December 1959): 340–345.

Shapiro, Harvey. "Economies of Scale and Local Government Finance." *Land Economics* 39 (May 1963): 175–186.

Stephens, G. Ross, and Schmandt, Henry J.. "Revenue Patterns of Local Governments." *National Tax Journal* 15 (December 1962): 432–437.

Stockfisch, J. A. "The Outlook for Fees and Service Charges as a Source of Revenue for State and Local Governments." In *1967 Proceedings of the Sixtieth Annual Conference on Taxation*, pp. 86–100. Columbus: National Tax Association, 1968.

————. "Fees and Service Charges as a Source of City Revenues: A Case Study of Los Angeles." *National Tax Journal* 13 (June 1960): 97–121.

Stone, Clarence N. "Local Referendums: An Alternative to the Alienated-Voter Model." *Public Opinion Quarterly* 29 (1965): 213–222.

Templeton, Fredric. "Alienation and Political Participation." *Public Opinion Quarterly* 30 (1966): 249–261.

Thompson, Wilbur. "The City as a Distorted Price System." *Psychology Today* 2 (August 1968): 28–33.

Tiebout, Charles M. "A Pure Theory of Local Expenditures." *Journal of Political Economy* 64 (October 1956): 416–424.

Vandermeulen, Alice John. "Reform of a State Fee Structure: Principles, Pitfalls, and Proposals for Increasing Revenue." *National Tax Journal* 17 (December 1964): 394–402.

Vickrey, William W. "General and Specific Financing of Urban Services." In *Public Expenditure Decisions in the Urban Community*, edited by Howard G. Schaller, pp. 62–90. Washington, D.C.: Resources for the Future, Inc., 1963.

Wildavsky, Aaron. "The Political Economy of Efficiency: Cost-Benefit Analysis, Systems Analysis, and Program Budgeting." *Public Administration Review* 26 (December 1966): 292–310.

Wilson, James Q., and Banfield, Edward C. "Public-Regardingness as a Value Premise in Voting Behavior." *American Political Science Review* 58 (December 1964): 876–887.

Woo Sik Kee. "Central City Expenditures and Metropolitan Areas." *National Tax Journal* 18 (December 1965): 337–353.

PUBLIC DOCUMENTS

Advisory Commission on Intergovernmental Relations. *Sources of Increased State Tax Collections: Economic Growth vs. Political Choice.* Washington, D.C., 1968.

————. *State and Local Finances: Significant Features 1966 to 1969.* Washington, D.C., 1968.

————. *Metropolitan Social and Economic Disparities: Implications for*

Intergovernmental Relations in Central Cities and Suburbs. Washington, D.C., 1965.

———. The Role of the States in Strengthening the Property Tax. Washington, D.C., 1963.

———. Tax Overlapping in the United States. Washington, D.C., 1961.

California. Board of Equalization. Annual Reports.

———. Controller. Annual Report of Financial Transactions Concerning Cities of California Fiscal Year 1966–1967.

———. ———. Annual Report of Financial Transactions Concerning Cities of California Fiscal Year 1958–1959.

———. Legislature. Assembly, Interim Committee on Revenue and Taxation. Problems of Property Tax Administration in California. Vol. 4, no. 20, Final Report, Part 1, December 1966.

———. ———. ———. Financing Local Government in California. Vol. 4, no. 13, A Major Tax Study, Part 6, prepared by Wilma Mayers, December 1964.

———. ———. ———. The Sales Tax Vol. 4, no. 11, A Major Tax Study, Part 4, prepared by Harold M. Somers, December 1964.

———. ———. ———. Fees and Licenses. Vol. 4, no. 9, A Major Tax Study, Part 2, prepared by Alice J. Vandermeulen, July 1964.

———. ———. Senate, Fact Finding Committee on Revenue and Taxation. Property Taxes and Other Local Revenue Sources. Part 9, March 1965.

———. ———. ———. General Fund Consumption Taxes. Part 2, January 1965.

Carter, Richard F., and Savard, William G. Influence of Voter Turnout on School and Tax Elections. U.S. Department of Health, Education, and Welfare, Cooperative Research Monograph, no. 5, Washington, D.C.: Government Printing Office, 1961.

Oakland. Digest of Current Federal Programs in the City of Oakland. Prepared by Jeffrey L. Pressmen with the assistance of the Redevelopment Agency of the City of Oakland. October 1968.

———. Budget Summary, 1968/69. Prepared by Jerome Keithley, Robert M. Odell, Jr., and Thomas E. Huebner [1968].

———. Tentative Budget Fiscal Year 1968/69. Prepared by Jerome Keithley, Robert M. Odell, Jr., and Thomas E. Huebner. May 1968.

———. "Analysis of the Fiscal Potential of the City of Oakland." Attachment to 1967/68 Budget, May 1967, pp. 1–4.

———. Application for Planning Grant Model Cities Program. April 1967.

———. Seventy-eighth Auditor-Controller's Annual Report. Fiscal year 1966/67.

———. Budget and Finance. Financial Capability Study. Part 1 (no date).

———. ———. "Financial Capability Study." Part 2 (no date).

———. City Clerk. Proposed New Charter of the City of Oakland and Alternative Propositions to be Voted on at the Special Municipal Election Consolidated with the General Election to Be Held November 5, 1968.

———. ———. Council Minutes, 1966–1968.

Research Advisory Committee (Francis Boddy, Chairman). Twin Cities Metropolitan Tax Study: Recommendations of the Research Advisory Committee. Minneapolis, December 1966.

Index

Acceptance stage, 108-113; sequential proposal of taxes, 109; administrative arrangements, 109-110; negotiation, 110-111; use of rhetoric, 111-113; in sewer service charge case, 135, 151-152; and tax comprehension, 193

Administration stage, 91; anticipatory tactics, 113-124; negotiatory tactics, 124-126; consensual tactics, 126-128; in sewer service charge case, 152-159

Administrative belief system, 50, 60

Administrative convenience, 127, 156

Advisory Commission on Intergovernmental Relations, 258

Aircraft, private: in lieu taxes on, 39-40

Alameda County, 16, 35, 38-39. See also Fiscal relations, city-county

Alameda County Industries Incorporated: and sewer service rates, 146, 149, 152, 157

Alameda County Street Aid Fund, 43, 44

Alameda County Taxpayers Association: and sewer service rates, 146, 152, 158

Animal control and regulation, 34

Apartment House Owners Association of Alameda County: and sewer service rates, 149, 152

Assessment, property. See Tax base

Association of Bay Area Governments (ABAG), 65

Auditorium and manager, 72, 73, 74 (table), 77-78

Bay Area Rapid Transit District (BARTD), 65, 66, 70

Benefits, and community coalitions, 266-268. See also Equity: benefit principle

Board of Education, 38, 66

Bradley-Burns Act, 24

Breuner, L. J., 142

Budget(s), 18, 179; uses of, 162, 163, 170; balancing, 176-184; base, 176 and n. See also Budgetary guidance; Budgetary process; Budget cutting

Budget and Finance Department, 36-37, 177. See also Budget Office

Budgetary guidance, 164-176; themes of city manager's letter, 165-167; and revenue-expenditure gap, 166-167; ambiguity in, 167-168, 173; department responses to "hold the line," 168-176, tables, 168, 174

Budgetary process: overview, 9-10; and city manager's use of, 53; city manager's guidance in, 164-168; city manager's review of, 179-184; influence of revenue on, 161-185; disjunctions in, 163-164, 176; and manager-council relationship, 183-184; and administrative efficiency, 184

Budget cutting: as revenue behavior, 176-179; outline of rules for, 178; and personnel requests, 179

Budget Office, 177, 178, 182; role of analysts, 177-179

Budget Subcommittee of City Council, 183-184